ANTI-
AIRCRAFT
A HISTORY OF AIR DEFENCE

ANTI-AIRCRAFT

A HISTORY OF AIR DEFENCE

IAN V HOGG

MACDONALD AND JANE'S LONDON

Design: Janet James and Martin Streetly

First published in 1978 by
Macdonald and Jane's Publishers Limited
Paulton House
8 Shepherdess Walk
London N1 7LW

ISBN 0 354 01163 4

Printed in Great Britain by
REDWOOD BURN LIMITED
Trowbridge & Esher

CONTENTS

List of illustrations

ACKNOWLEDGEMENTS

I should like to thank the staff of the Library of the Royal Artillery Institution, Woolwich, for their assistance in making available documents, books and photographs for research. Without their unstinting help his book would have been impossible to achieve.

I would also like to thank Harry Waller, Jim Humphreys, Dick Barton and many other anti-aircraft gunners of my acquaintance for their conversation and reminiscences, and particularly Major Julian Pearce for his recollections of the 1938 mobilisation and for the photographs he kindly provided.

ABBREVIATIONS

AA	Anti-Aircraft
AAES	Anti-Aircraft Experimental Section, Ministry of Munitions
ABM	Anti-Ballistic Missile
ADGB	Air Defence of Great Britain
AEF	American Expeditionary Force
BEF	British Expeditionary Force
BMEWS	Ballistic Missile Early Warning System
CH	Chain Home
CHL	Chain Home, Low-flying
CSSAD	Committee for the Scientific Study of Air Defence
DEW	Distant Early Warning
ECM	Electronic Counter-measures
GL	Gun-Laying (Radar)
LADA	London Air Defence Area
MID	Munitions Inventions Department
NADGE	NATO Air Defense Ground Environment
NATO	North Atlantic Treaty Organisation
NORAD	North American Air Defense
OHFS	Over-the-Horizon Forward Scatter (Radar)
PDE	Projectile Development Establishment
PF	Position Finder
RAC	Royal Artillery Committee
RDF	Radio Direction Finding (early cover-name for radar)
RHA	Royal Horse Artillery
RNVR	Royal Naval Volunteer Reserve
SAGE	Semi-Automatic Ground Environment
SALT	Strategic Arms Limitation Treaty
SCR	Signal Corps Radio
UP	Unrotated Projectile (Rocket)
USAAF	United States Army Air Force

1 THE BALLOON ON THE HORIZON

On 5 June 1783 the Montgolfier brothers, Stephen and Joseph, gave their first public demonstration of their hot-air balloon. It was a paper sphere, 112 feet in diameter, the hot air provided by an open fire under the staging upon which the basket rested. It ascended to 1,000 feet and descended, in good order, some ten minutes later, and this successful flight generated an enormous enthusiasm for the science of ballooning. The Montgolfiers moved to Paris and there gave a series of demonstration flights, and in one of these an otherwise unremarked gentleman named Giroud de Villette made an ascent some time in the late summer of 1783. After coming down he enthused about the view to be had from such an elevation, and opined that such a basket would be of great value in warfare, allowing a commander to see far and wide and assess the enemy's strength and dispositions. So that within six months of the invention of the man-carrying balloon, it was being evaluated as a weapon of war.

In Dijon lived Guyton de Morveau, Advocat-General to the Parlement de Dijon and amateur scientist. In addition to his legal practice, he taught chemistry at the Academie de Dijon for fifteen years, and in 1782 he relinquished his legal practice and, in company with Lavoisier and others, began working on the *Dictionnaire de Chemie*. In 1792, in the throes of the Revolution, he became a member of the Committee of Public Safety and there, in a discussion on defensive measures, he urged the adoption of balloons. Morveau had already experimented with balloons, after reading of the exploits of the Montgolfier brothers, and he suggested that captive balloons might be a useful adjunct to field armies. The Committee agreed, and he was told to look into the matter.

Hot-air balloons hardly appeared practical, and de Morveau contemplated the use of hydrogen; unfortunately the accepted method of producing hydrogen was by means of sulphuric acid and zinc, a slow business but, more important, a method extremely expensive in sulphuric acid. And at that time sulphuric acid was almost unobtainable, since all the sulphur in France was needed for the production of gunpowder. He approached Lavoisier and a physicist named Coutelle, and between them they developed a method of passing steam over red-hot iron to produce hydrogen in the quantities required. An apparatus was built in the Tuileries, a 30-foot diameter balloon successfully inflated and flown on a tether, and Coutelle was sent to report to General Jourdan, then commanding the French armies advancing to the Rhine against the opposition of the Austrians. Jourdan expressed enthusiasm for the idea and a balloon factory was set up in the Meudon artillery barracks. Coutelle was commissioned as a captain, commanding the Balloon Corps, and was also appointed Director of the Aerostatic Experimental Station, and under his direction the first military balloon, *L'Entreprenant,* was constructed. The Balloon Company was formed on 2 April 1794, consisting of a captain, a lieutenant, a sub-lieutenant, a serjeant-major, 4 NCOs, 25 men and a drummer-boy, and the force went into its first action at Maubeuge.

The balloons were flown tethered, with men of the company hanging on to ropes attached to the observation basket, and messages reporting the movements of the Austrian Army were dropped to the ground below for despatch to General Jourdan. It all worked quite well, and Jourdan was receiving useful information, but the Austrians felt somewhat aggrieved at this new element in warfare, and on 13 June 1794 they wheeled up two 17-pounder howitzers and began shooting at the balloons. And in this casual manner the science and art of anti-aircraft gunnery was born.

The shooting of the Austrian howitzers so alarmed the balloonists that they withdrew, though it seems likely that the shots were of more danger to the ground handling crew than they were to the occupants of the observation basket. The Austrians, however, saw no material results and gave up after a few shots had been fired. The balloon was later moved to Charleroi, and again the Austrians brought up howitzers, this time shooting so well that one shot actually passed between the basket and the envelope of the balloon, much to the dismay of the intrepid balloonists. But the Balloon Corps, now expanded to two companies, continued their activities, receiving considerable praise for the information they acquired, and it was not until 18 January 1799 that the corps was disbanded, bringing to an end the first chapter in the history of air defence.

The next noteworthy step in aerial warfare was taken by the Austrians at the siege of Venice in 1849, when they fixed small bombs to free balloons, with a time-fuzed release device, and flew them in the hope of passing the balloons over the heads of the Venetians, whereupon the fuze would release the bomb to fall within the besieged city. Unfortunately, the wind changed unexpectedly and the balloons dropped their bombs on to the ranks of the Austrians, so that experiment was closed down very rapidly indeed.

Balloons were next put to use during the American Civil War, but there seems to be no record of any form of anti-balloon artillery being deployed to deal with them; from what records there are it would appear that the balloons were raised fairly well behind the lines, out of range of enemy fire but sufficiently far forward to give the field of view required.

In the Franco-Prussian War the German troops had a small observation balloon section, but there was difficulty in providing the necessary hydrogen gas, and the two balloons accomplished very little. It was not until Paris was besieged that the balloons achieved any useful purpose; with the city cut off, the Parisian postal authorities decided to use balloons for carrying mail and, in all, some 66 balloons made their escape from the city, carrying between them 66 'aeronauts' – pilots – 102 passengers and 9 tons of mail, as well as 409 carrier pigeons and 6 dogs. The object of these latter was to set up a return service by virtue of their homing instincts, and some 57 of the pigeons actually made the return trip; the dogs were either less sagacious or (more likely) fell prey to people whose hunger was greater than their civic conscience. At any rate, none of them ever returned.

On 7 October 1870 Leon Gambetta, Minister of the Interior, escaped by balloon and joined the French Government at Tours, where he at once set about whipping up resistance to the Germans. This escape, and the possibility of other national figures leaping over the siegeworks to freedom, upset the German Army who immediately applied to Krupp's armament factory for a weapon with which to shoot at the balloons. Krupp responded very quickly with a 25mm rifle mounted on a pedestal on a light cart.A staging around the pedestal allowed the gunner to climb up and down so that he could keep the rifle's stock to his shoulder at any angle of elevation, and the weapon could be fired at elevations up to about 85 degrees, while it was free to turn through 360 degrees so as to give the fullest possible field of fire.

On the face of it, the idea seemed quite reasonable; the French balloons were 50 feet in diameter, presenting quite a good target, but in practice the difficulties began to appear at once. In the first place, the rifle had no more than the simple V-backsight and barleycorn-foresight as used on the contemporary needle-gun rifle of the infantry, so that there was no accurate way of adjusting the aim to allow for the movement or varying range of the balloon. Secondly, the projectile was a solid lead bullet which left no sign of its passage through the air, and where it went in relation to the balloon was not known to the gunner. Thirdly, there was the problem of producing the gun in the right place to shoot at a balloon, a problem which was attacked by having several guns, dispersing them around the city harnessed up, and having them gallop like a fire brigade when a balloon was seen to be rising. In spite of all these difficulties there was a small degree of success; some of the aeronauts were dismayed to have half-pounds of lead whistling past them, while others were unfortunate enough to have the balloons punctured by shots, one being so badly perforated that it was forced to descend in the Prussian lines. But, on the whole the success rate was low, and the French soon neutralised the guns by launching their balloons at night, so that after a few months the guns were withdrawn and returned to the Berlin Arsenal, and were never seen again in service. One remains, tucked away in an obscure corner of a museum in East Berlin.

From this time onwards balloons became more or less standard items in most armies, though in many cases they were more in the nature of experimental devices than practical service equipment. Such matters as the best shape and size, the method of hanging the observer's basket, the method of generating gas in the field, problems of mooring and sheltering balloons – these were the fundamental problems of the period and they occupied the time of the embryo aviators to the exclusion of anything very valuable in the tactical sense.

Towards the turn of the century the dirigible balloon began to supplant the earlier free balloons; it should be pointed out that 'dirigible' indicates the ability to steer and direct the balloon, and implies its provision with an engine and rudder, and not, as is often supposed, the existence of a rigid framework to carry the gas-bags. Dirigibles could thus be propelled in specific directions and were no longer at the wind's mercy, and this facility immediately led military men to think about propelling them in the direction of the enemy for the purpose of gathering information; some thinkers went even further and proposed using them to drop bombs, though this was felt to be scarcely practical in the early days; the dirigibles had enough to worry about in lifting themselves off the ground, without adding to their troubles with loads of bombs.

Scarcely had the dirigible established itself than the Wright brothers made their historic flight in the USA, and the age of the heavier-than-air craft had dawned. This, in its early days, was considered to be an even less likely threat than the dirigible, and it was almost entirely ignored by military experimenters who felt that the greater potential lifting power of the dirigible would prove to have more practical value in the military role. Within a very few years though, the boot was on the other foot and the aeroplane was being heralded as the most likely form of military craft, due to its greater agility and, what promised to be important, the smaller size it presented as a target.

For with all this activity in the air, questions began to be asked about the possibilities of military use of aircraft and, as a corollary, what the land and sea services could do to counter them. It was generally agreed that aviation's principal – if not only – function in war would be the acquisition of information; just as Napoleon's balloons had extended his commanders' field of view, so the dirigible and the aeroplane would extend the view of the modern commander, but even deeper into enemy territory, and, pertinent to England, the sea was no barrier. German or French aircraft could fly across the Channel and peer down into dockyards and naval bases, selecting targets for naval bombardment or remarking the presence or absence of ships. Obviously, this was something which had to be prevented, and in the middle 1900s the armies of the major nations began to take an interest, if only an academic one, in the matter of air defence. In 1908 the British War Office issued a circular which gave rise to the following headlines in the newspapers: WAR AIRSHIPS: 'NOTHING TO BE FEARED FOR A LONG TIME' OFFICIAL VIEW. The story which followed began: 'In the highest military circles in Great Britain it is accepted that so far airships are a failure.' Indeed, as late as 1913 a senior officer gave as his considered opinion:

> 'I think we are making altogether too much of a bogey, a bogey made in Germany, over this air business. One thing I am fairly certain of, and that is, that at the end of the first week [of war] there will not be many airships or aeroplanes left, and if there are, the pilots, unless the nature of pilots is changed, will be incapable of further action – their nerves will have gone.'

As is very commonly the case, private enterprise made the first overt moves. In 1909, at the Frankfurt International Exhibition, two German gunmakers of high repute exhibited a number of 'balloon guns', and the evidence that such respected names as Krupp and Erhardt were sufficiently impressed by the aerial threat to design and build guns was enough to stimulate military interest to the point of actually doing something.

At Frankfurt the centre of the Great Hall was given over to a large display mounted by Fried, Krupp of Essen and the Rheinische Metallwaren-und Maschinenfabrik of Düsseldorf, makers of the Erhardt designs of ordnance. Krupp showed three weapons: a 65mm gun on a field carriage, a 75mm gun on a motorised carriage, and a 105mm gun suitable for shipboard mounting. Erhardt displayed a 50mm gun on two different motorised mountings, one fully armoured and the other partially armoured. These designs were of considerable interest insofar as they revealed their designers' views on anti-aircraft tactics as much as their views on ordnance construction.

Krupp's 65mm gun resembled a conventional field piece of the day, on a two-wheeled carriage with a solid trail and no shield, but it was capable of elevating to 70 degrees and could pitch its 8.8lb shell to 18,500 feet altitude. The most unusual feature was the mounting of the wheels on hinged axle extensions so that when the gun was positioned ready to fire the wheels could be swung round to the front of the mounting, to lie parallel with the axle. The trail end was then pinned to the ground by a stake, so that by man-handling the wheels the whole weapon could be pivoted in a circle around the trail end, giving an all-round field of fire, considered to be vital in shooting at a rapidly-moving target.

Krupp's second weapon, the 75mm 'motor gun', demonstrated another approach to the moving target problem, the solution in this case being the ability to move the mounting and position it rapidly so as to intercept the flight path of the aircraft or, in another view, to take to the road and chase the target. The gun was installed on the bed of a 50hp motor truck, capable of a speed of 28mph. With 75 degrees of elevation the 12lb shell had a maximum ceiling of 21,000 feet and the gun could be traversed through 360 degrees on the truck so as to cover the entire horizon. Krupp's greatest technical problem was that of absorbing the recoil blow of the gun when it fired, so that the truck was not hammered to pieces; a rough calculation shows that the recoil force would be in the order of 13 tons, and this was dealt with by adopting a system which had recently been proposed, that of differential recoil or dynamic recoil. The gun, prior to opening fire, was winched back in its recoil cradle against the pressure of a compressed air piston and then held in this fully recoiled position, where it was loaded. On pressing the firing lever the gun was released and allowed to run forward under the propulsive force of the compressed air. As it approached the fully-forward position a trip device actuated the firing pin and discharged the cartridge. Thus the explosion and its reaction on the gun had first of all to arrest the forward movement of the 1,000lb weight of the gun, then reverse the motion and begin the conventional recoil stroke, at the end of which the gun was again held ready for loading. The result of this system was to reduce the recoil blow to about a quarter of the normal figure, so that the motor mounting now only had to sustain a force of about 3 tons.

The Rheinische Metallwaren-und Maschinenfabrik (who later adopted the shorter form 'Rheinmetall', by which they are still known) exhibited another approach to the mobility and recoil problems. Their 50mm gun, which was conventional enough, was mounted in a turret in an armoured car: to quote from a contemporary report:

> 'To protect the car, its equipment and gun detachment from hostile fire it is armoured throughout, including the wheels, with 3mm of nickel steel. The entrance, the peep-hole for the driver, and the embrasures in the sides can all be closed and the forward part of the car shut down. The gun with its armoured turret can be revolved on a turntable and the embrasures are provided with shutters.'

While all this seemed quite reasonable, there were a few doubters who objected that they failed to see much point in armouring a balloon gun; the chances of a balloon or aircraft mounting any armament to duel with the ground gun were remote, and there seemed little likelihood of the weapon operating so far forward as to come under fire from enemy ground troops. An alternative reason for the armour was advanced by Colonel Bethell, a well-known contemporary writer on ordnance design, namely that the addition of armour made the vehicle heavier and more robust, allowing it to absorb the recoil of the 5cm gun without having to resort to the complications of the differential recoil system.

Whether or not Bethell's theory is correct – and it has some validity – the fact remains that Rheinmetall demonstrated a second model of 'half-armoured car' which used the same basic chassis but carried an open body of armour plate with the gun on a pedestal at the rear. This must have reduced the weight by a considerable amount but there was still no move to adopt the differential recoil.

If the design of guns allowed scope for differing points of view, this was nothing when compared with the divergency of opinion over the projectiles to be fired from anti-balloon guns. The dirigible was a peculiar target; although it was of a fair size and presented a fine aiming mark, its thin fabric was so unresistant that there promised to be great difficulty in designing an impact fuze sufficiently sensitive to detonate the shell upon striking the balloon but safe enough to survive being fired from the gun. The amount of damage done to a balloon had to be considerable in order to have any useful effect. In May 1909 the German Army had staged a fairly conclusive trial at the Jüterbog Infantry School, near Berlin. Two detachments of infantry were deployed, one armed with service Mauser rifles and the other with Maxim machine guns, their target being a captive balloon 50 feet long at a range of 1,250 metres. The riflemen opened fire first and discharged 4,800 rounds in five minutes, producing no visible result. The Maxim gunners then took their turn, firing 2,700 rounds in two and a half minutes, still without any apparent result. The balloon was then hauled down and was found to have been pierced in 76 places, the fabric having tended to close itself after the passage of the bullet by a combination of its elasticity and the internal gas pressure.

The conclusions drawn from this test reinforced the previously-held opinion that a balloon could not be brought down by infantry fire alone, and that the only time infantry should be allowed to attempt engaging an aerial target was when they were close enough to be able to hit the pilot or observers. The task of actually destroying the balloon was one which should be left to the artillery. And having said that, the German Army more or less sat back and waited for the gunmakers to come up with some suitable answer.

The 'standard' artillery shell of the period was the shrapnel shell, a hollow casing filled with lead bullets and a small charge of gunpowder; actuated by a time fuze, the charge ejected the bullets forward in a cone, moving slightly faster than the remaining velocity of the shell. It was the ideal projectile for the attack of troops in the open; for 'protected' targets, such as buildings or defensive works, the high explosive shell was produced, though in 1909 this was at a relatively primitive stage of development. The high explosive shell was provided with an impact fuze so that it functioned upon striking the target, and the technical problems connected with this were formidable. The fuze had to be sufficiently sensitive to detonate the shell when it struck the ground and before momentum carried the shell too deep into the earth; it also had to be safe, so that the sudden shock of being fired out of the gun would not function it prematurely. Premature fuze functioning in a shrapnel shell was unfortunate, and might damage the gun; premature functioning in a high explosive shell was disastrous, would certainly destroy the gun and would probably kill most of the gunners around it.

Shrapnel shell, in the last analysis, was little more than a method of discharging rifle bullets at long range, so that the eventual effect on a balloon would be little more than that achieved on the Jüterbog trial – lots of small holes with little visible result on the balloon. High explosive was likely to be more effective in that it would blow the balloon apart and probably ignite the hydrogen gas inside, leading to a swift and spectacular end to the target, but making a sensitive fuze was even more difficult when a balloon was the target than when the target was a house, which at least offered solid resistance to the fuze.

The second projectile problem was that of being able to say, with some accuracy, where the shell had gone in relation to the target if it failed to hit, in order that corrections could be made to the pointing of the gun. It might be possible to come to some conclusions from the relative positions of the target and the bursting shells (provided they used time fuzes) but to obtain accurate information meant placing observers out to the flank of the target, which in turn introduced a communication problem.

Krupp, along with their guns, demonstrated their shell solution at Frankfurt, a projectile carrying an incendiary composition in its forward half and a smoke-producing composition in the rear. On firing, the shock of discharge lit a delay device which, in turn, ignited the smoke composition to allow a trail of smoke to stream out behind the shell and thus delineate its trajectory as it passed the target. If the shell was fortunate enough to strike the target, then a sensitive fuze ignited the incendiary material, bursting the shell and scattering the burning substance, igniting the gas and destroying the balloon.

Rheinmetall offered an explosive shell fitted with a 'winged' fuze in which three flanges sprang out in flight and tore a large hole in the balloon as they spun their way through the fabric; at the same time, the force of the impact upon these arms released a trigger to fire the fuze and detonate the shell. Another design carried a 'rocket' fuze which emitted a stream of flame and smoke to allow the flight of the shell to be traced and which was sufficient to ignite the balloon gas if a hit was achieved.

The Frankfurt display stimulated designers and manufacturers in other countries. In Britain, Vickers, Son & Maxim produced a 3-pounder on a pedestal mount. In France the usual solution to any artillery problem was to point one of their famous 75mm guns at it, and so a 75mm motor carriage was designed. In the USA there was little official recognition, since gun design was in the hands of the Ordnance Department, not the Artillery, and they were more concerned with the development of a new field gun at that time; so that the first American anti-aircraft weapon design was another instance of private enterprise.

Colonel R. P. Davidson, commandant of the Northwestern Military and Naval Academy of Lake Geneva, Wisconsin, had since 1899 been experimenting with automobiles for military purposes, and in 1909, possibly fired by reports from Frankfurt, he bought a Cadillac chassis and mounted a Colt machine gun on a pedestal in the tonneau. This seemed to be the answer, so in 1910 he bought two more Cadillacs and fitted them with Colt machine guns. These cars were then entered in the 1910 Glidden Tour, a long-distance endurance test for automobiles which extended from Cleveland, Ohio, via Tennessee and Mississippi, to Dallas, Texas, then to Omaha and finally to Chicago. The two 'Cadillac Balloon Destroyers' were among the nine survivors to finish the course from an entry of thirty-eight which had started. It was a notable demonstration of automobile reliability, but it did little to advance the cause of anti-aircraft gunnery.

The year 1909 was a significant one; in addition to the developments already mentioned, it was the year in which the Esher Committee, set up by the British Government in 1908, delivered its report. This Committee had been charged with examining 'the dangers to which the country might be exposed by the development of aerial navigation', and in its report it stressed that 'the full potentialities of airships and the dangers to which we might be exposed can only be ascertained definitely by building them ourselves'. It was as a result of this conclusion that the British Army and Royal Navy began to construct airships and aircraft and also began conferring between themselves on the subject of defence against foreign aviation. The Admiralty, early in 1910, stated that there appeared to be two forms of defence:

> '(1) Mobile, and (2) Fixed. The mobile defences might be (a) Airships or Aeroplanes, (b) Balloon Guns mounted on motor cars. The Fixed defences might be (c) earth or armour protection above the magazines and cordite factories, (d) high angle fire guns capable of all-round training in the vicinity of vulnerable points.'

These views were communicated to the Army Council, who concurred and passed the whole matter on for the consideration of a body known as the 'Home Ports Defence Committee', since it was thought that only naval bases, dockyards and magazines and similar installations of value to the fleet would be likely targets.

The current views on military aviation were well summed up by Colonel J. E. Capper, CB, RE, then Commandant and Superintendent of the Army Balloon School at Aldershot, in a lecture he delivered at the Royal Artillery Institution, Woolwich, in November 1909. After a resumé of current developments in dirigibles and aircraft, he went on to discuss the question of defence:

> 'At heights of 5000 or 6000 feet the effect of infantry fire is very small on a balloon; the effect of shrapnel bullets is also very small . . . a lucky burst, however, right on, or in, the balloon would prove at once disastrous. At such great heights only howitzers or specially constructed guns with high angles of elevation could reach a balloon.'

Colonel Capper discounted the possibility of an enemy attempting to bombard from the air and considered that the sole function of aircraft in war would be reconnaissance, which he divided into three types, naval, strategic and tactical. He then assessed the chances of injuring any of these forms of mission:

> 'For reconnaissance at sea the balloon is never required to come within range of the enemy's ships . . . and it need run no risk of destruction from an enemy's guns. On land it seems to me that the dirigible used for strategic reconnaissance runs but little danger. It is impossible to keep batteries of artillery or even single guns scattered all over the country with gun crews ready and prepared for instant action for perhaps weeks together, waiting for the possible advent of an airship which will only present a target for a very short period of time.
>
> Moreover in all but very clear skies an airship can take advantage of low-lying clouds to hide itself from view, descending below them for short periods to observe; under such conditions it is very probably that it may not be seen at all . . .
>
> Even the special automobile guns, unless present in great numbers, will probably have very few opportunities of firing; roads will not always run in the proper direction to enable them to get within range of an airship, whilst we know little of the probably accuracy of fire of such guns at targets moving at a great pace high up in the air.
>
> With tactical airships the situation is somewhat different. Tactical reconnaissance requires to be more detailed than strategic. Moreover with a field position large numbers of guns and howitzers will be distributed over a comparatively small area, and many of them will be available for instant action, whilst numbers of men will be on the lookout. The risk to an airship remaining for any length of time over the enemy's position will probably be very great.'

The general tenor of this advice, it can be seen, was that artillery fire would probably scare the enemy off to a distance from which he could not conduct an efficient reconnaissance. But artillerymen thought otherwise. A Captain Sargeaunt of the Royal Garrison Artillery proposed, in a paper published in the *Proceedings of the RA Institute,* attacking the aircraft with shrapnel, 'in order to hit the pilot or mechanism', or with high explosive, 'in order to upset the stability of the aircraft', and, prophetically, concluded his proposals by saying:

> 'It will not be sufficient to rely on our own air fleet, even if numerically stronger than the enemy fleet, at the commencement of hostilities. It might, through a series of misfortunes, be made impotent, or one or two of the hostile airships

might evade it and do incalculable damage, and at present it appears that our air fleet is inferior to that of several foreign powers.'

By this time the Ordnance Board had taken to debating the gun question and had concluded that there were two possible lines of approach: a fast-firing small calibre gun to put a large number of impact-fuzed shells into the air very quickly, in the hope that at least one of them would strike the target; and a larger and more powerful gun to fire shrapnel or high explosive shells which, with a time fuze to burst them at the right height, would have a larger area of effect in the sky so that even a 'near miss' might so some damage. Designs were called for and experiments ordered. At that time the Royal Artillery was sub-divided into three branches, the Horse, Field and Garrison, and the interesting question now arose of who should man such new equipments if they appeared? On the grounds that they were more used to shooting at moving targets, since they manned the coastal defence guns, it seemed that the Garrison Artillery should furnish the anti-balloon force, but another viewpoint was that since these weapons would have to accompany the field armies, and since everybody knew the Garrison gunners were rooted in concrete and *never* went outside their forts, it was obviously the task of the Field branch.

Whatever the arguments, it was the Garrison artillery who made the first move, at their Western District School of Gunnery at Golden Hill Fort on the Isle of Wight. In 1913 they took a one-pounder Maxim 'pom-pom' automatic gun and grafted it on to a pedestal mount from a 6-pounder anti-torpedo-boat gun, increasing the amount of elevation possible. This gun was then installed at New Needles Battery, on the western tip of the island, and a destroyer of the Royal Navy steamed back and forth at high speed off the shore, towing a kite. With a maximum speed across the front of about 30mph and a range of about 2,000 yards the angular movement was well within the capabilities of the gun mounting and the gunlayer, and the practice scored a reasonable number of hits.

While this test showed that the pom-pom was a suitable weapon, it also underlined a problem to which one or two far-sighted men had already called attention – the question of what happened to the shells which missed the target and continued on their way, to fall to earth fuzed and primed to detonate as soon as they struck something. In 1910 Colonel Bethell, in his book *Modern Guns and Gunnery*, dismissed the problem fairly slightingly:

'It has been objected to balloon guns in general that our own troops would be endangered by the shells falling on their heads. This objection is, however, unsound; even if the balloon is attacked by a rival dirigible or aeroplane, it has to be destroyed by projectiles of some sort. And it matters little to the soldier below whether a shell which falls on his head from a height of 5000 feet weighs one pound or twelve. Moreover the Krupp 12-pounder, for instance, ranges some 8 miles at 45 degrees elevation, so that at any rate the troops in the vicinity of the gun would not suffer. Finally, since the object in view is to bring down some tons of balloon or some hundredweights of aeroplane from the sky, the incidental fall of a few 12-pounder shells would appear to be a minor matter.'

But a Major Hawkins, writing in the *Proceedings of the RA Institute* in 1912, was more concerned:

'A great disadvantage of shrapnel is the unavoidable return to earth of its bullets and pieces, a serious matter when we consider the number of shells that will certainly be necessary to get a hit, so that except in great emergency it will not be permissible to fire in directions that will damage our own troops. Moreover, officers and NCOs must have an instinctive acquaintance with the vertical trajectories of their guns so as to decide promptly whereabouts the debris will return to earth.'

In the following year, he advanced a prophetic suggestion:

'One realises, of course, the result to the population of using guns at all, but a plain man can see no other possibility at present: had we kept our proper place in the van of scientific progress by judicious expenditure in the last few years, we might well have mobile aerial torpedos worked by wireless currents which would make the approaches to our dockyards as dangerous to dirigibles at night as the three-mile limit is to hostile ships of war. The civil population, of course, must be warned in time of war that they leave their houses after dark at their own risk.'

Although the consensus of opinion was that some form of specialised weapon was the ideal, the economics of manufacturing, issuing, supplying with ammunition and manning yet another weapon was an obstacle which few armies were prepared to surmount. It seemed possible that some modifications to standard field guns or howitzers, such as giving them a greater range of elevation, might produce a dual-purpose weapon. This was a goal which was to tempt designers for another twenty-odd years before they finally admitted that such a device carried all the defects and none of the advantages of either of its parents, but in those pre-war days it did look possible. Various tests were carried out using ordinary field guns against static balloons or against kits towed by galloping horse teams, and some encouraging results were reported. Encouraging, that is, until the conditions are closely examined, when the deficiencies become obvious. The field gun of the day was rarely capable of more than about 16 degrees of elevation, which meant that the target had to be at a low altitude and some distance away. The US Army Ordnance Department, at that time, were in the throes of developing a new 3in field gun with a split trail of the 'Deport' type, then the newest idea in carriage design. This allowed the gun to elevate to 53 degrees and traverse an arc of 45 degrees without the carriage having to be moved, and this offered the promise of a useful anti-balloon capability. Accordingly, trials were carried out against a towed kite, and since these showed some success it was decided that there was no call for any sort of specialised gun; the new 3in would do all that was needed. Unfortunately, the 3in M1916, as it became, was one of the greatest technical disasters in the recorded history of ordnance, never living up to any of its promise, and in course of time the Americans, like everyone else, had to think about 'special guns'.

Guns, though, were relatively simple; by 1910 most countries knew a lot about firing projectiles out of rifled barrels, and for those who didn't there were plenty of professional gunmakers anxious to demonstrate their prowess. The technique of making guns which would point up into the sky and shoot was no great difficulty. The question of what shells to shoot was amenable to experiment and would doubtless be resolved in due course. But the great problem was that of directing the gun so that the shell would hit the target. The problem was, in fact, threefold: firstly, to point the gun so that the shell would arrive somewhere near the target; secondly, to determine the range to the target; and thirdly, to make accurate assessments of the errors involved when the shell burst and then to correct the fire until the target was hit. These three functions were the basics of all gunnery, and it seemed that the only logical answer must be to apply them to aircraft targets just as they were applied to land and sea targets. But there were some doubters; Lieutenant C. V. S. Skrimshire, RGA was one:

> 'At present [1913] no satisfactory anti-aircraft gun has been designed and, until an automatic sight is produced, the efforts of artillery to inflict damage . . . are unlikely to give adequate results. The impossibility of observing fire, even when the projectile is provided with a 'tracer' or device for following its flight, as well as the great difficulty of finding the range, make the problem one of unequalled difficulty. Many writers have advocated the use of specially constructed high angle guns firing special ammunition . . . but nowhere has any real success been achieved. The rapidly varying height of the target, the quickly changing course as well as the high speed at which the aeroplane travels make it almost impossible to be anything but extremely doubtful of the utility of artillery fire.'

The automatic sight, which Skrimshire was not the only person to demand, was a rangefinding sight used with coastal artillery guns. Each gun had a telescope sight mounting which contained a cam, carefully designed and shaped according to the height of the gun above the sea. Since this height was constant (except for tidal variations, for which a compensating device allowed) it formed the base of a right-angled triangle, the side of which was the surface of the sea and the hypotenuse the telescope's line of sight. Thus, for every range along the sea level there was a corresponding angle of depression of the telescope, and the shaped cam interacted with the gun's elevating gears so that when the cross-wires of the telescope were laid on the waterline of a ship the gun was automatically given the correct elevation to hit the ship.

It can be appreciated from this brief description that adapting an autosight to an anti-aircraft gun was almost impossible since one of the constants in the equation – the fact that the ship must be on the surface of the sea – was missing; the aircraft could be at any height. On the other hand, it shows the preoccupation with putting the sighting system on the gun – which, after all, was the traditional way of doing things – which bedevilled designers for a long time. Only the percipient Major Hawkins had discerned the correct solution, but nobody took him seriously.

> 'the crux is the invention of an autosight . . . If the apparatus were found to be too cumbersome to install on the mounting, it might be used separately, the gun being trained and elevated by electricity. The extra expense would be well repaid by increased accuracy over any other system.'

Generally speaking the preferred solution seemed to be to lay down some simple rules which could be followed in the majority of cases, for as one critic put it:

> 'The use of delicate instruments entailing complicated calculations in the battlefield are quite out of place at present, and a few rough and ready rules which can easily be assimilated . . . could be far more effective in time of war than the use of any special instrument except perhaps a very rapidly acting one-man range-finder.'

In this spirit the German Army instructed its infantry to fire from two to ten lengths ahead of an aircraft according to the estimated range; apparently the speed was considered to be more or less constant. The French School of Musketry produced a formidable set of rules which began: 'As soon as a flying machine is observed, judge its distance rapidly by eye or by telemeter [range-finder] and if the machine is not more than 25 degrees (the breadth of one hand) above the horizon, sight for the estimated distance less 200 metres and fire for thirty seconds', and then got more and more involved as it attempted to cater for approaching, crossing or receding targets.

These rules were as good as could be hoped for with rifle fire, but artillery fire had to be rather more complex. In the absence of an accurate form of sighting system, most people fell back on approximations in the hope that if a great enough diversity of metal was flung into the sky, then by the law of averages some of it ought to intercept the aircraft:

> 'Get a group of fuzed shells ready with the same length of fuze and fire them quickly . . . Suppose the machine is sighted at 6000 yards, travelling more or less towards the guns; the section commander orders ten rounds with 4000 yards fuze, ten with 3000, ten with 2000. He opens fire when the range is 5000 yards. As soon as a burst is observed close up, he comes down to the next group of fuzes.'

Another suggestion was based on the French system of 'collective ranging' in which the range was estimated and each gun opened fire at a different fuze length and range so that the target would be straddled. Having observed the distribution of these first shots and assessed which combination was most close to the target, the battery commander would then order a fuze and range at which all guns would open fire.

Having now looked at the state of the art, such as it was, it will now be appropriate to see exactly what the problems were and to dissect the various factors confronting the would-be anti-aircraft gunner, some of which were not yet apparent in those early days.

First, and so basic as to have been largely overlooked, is the matter of detecting the aircraft at all. Perhaps we should realise that in those days any flying machine was unlikely to be dismissed as lightly as it would be today, but for all that it should be borne in mind that the flying machines of the time were, by modern standards, small, under-powered and relatively quiet. The Vickers Fighting Biplane exhibited at Olympia in 1914 and a fore-runner of the wartime 'Gun-Bus' had a wingspan of 38 feet, while the contemporary Bleriot monoplane had a span of 30 feet, and aircraft engines were commonly of the order of 80 to 100hp. Such a machine would have been able to approach quite close to a battery before being seen or heard, and in no contemporary documents can mention of special 'air sentries' be found.

Secondly came the problem of accurate determination of the range from the gun to the target. The current rangefinding device for artillery use was the 'telemeter', a system which involved two operators, one at each end of a precisely measured base-line, measuring angles to the target simultaneously. This was adequate against a stationary target but useless against a rapidly-moving one. The single-observer type of range-finder, such as the Barr and Stroud or the Marinden, made an appearance in limited numbers in 1912, as an adjunct to the infantry machine gun, but their short optical base made them unsuited to taking ranges much in excess of 3,000 yards, the inherent error increased with the range, and they were extremely difficult to operate against a moving target.

However (and this was something not appreciated at the time) even knowing the exact range to the target would not have ensured hitting it. The sights of a field gun were calibrated in ranges, and the correlation of the range set on the sight with the elevation of the gun was based on long experimental firings during the gun's development, the object being that with a given range set on the sights and the sights laid accurately on the target, the gun would be elevated so that the shell would strike the ground at the target. If the same range were set on the sight and the gun and sight super-elevated in order to point at an object in the air, the assumption, in 1912, was that the trajectory would then pass through the intersection of the line of sight and the target. Unfortunately, this wasn't so; the trajectory is not a rigid figure which can be waved about in space, and once the target is sensibly higher (or, for that matter, lower) than the gun, the trajectory deforms under the effects of air density and gravity, a deformation which has to be taken into account in the design of the sight.

Thirdly comes the performance of the shell at high altitude. There was, by this time, a considerable body of data on what effect such factors as air temperature, wind, and barometric pressure would have on the flight of a shell, but only in terrestrial shooting where the shell rarely rose more than one or two thousand feet into the air. It was assumed that similar rules would apply at greater heights, but experience during the war was to show that the upper air held a few mysteries of its own, and until these were unravelled anti-aircraft gunnery was going to remain an art more than a science.

Fourthly came the task of arranging for the shell and target to coincide not only in space but in time. The aircraft, then greatly affected by head or tail winds, might be travelling at anything between 20mph and 180mph relative to the ground; assuming still air, a good average speed in 1914 was 75mph, or 110 feet per second. The average field gun of the day – for example the Austro-Hungarian 76mm – had a muzzle velocity of about 1,640 feet per second. This, of course, gradually decreased as the shell flew through the air, and at a range of 5,000 yards the shell took 18 seconds to reach the target. This meant that during the flight of the shell, after it had left the gunner's control, the aircraft had travelled 1,980 feet, or 0.375 of a mile. It was obviously useless to aim at the aircraft, but to aim 1,980 feet ahead of it meant displacing the sight through some 7½ degrees which introduced several technical complications, as well as demanding a considerable degree of faith from the gunlayer.

Finally, as already touched upon, came the problem of observing the target and assessing the direction and amount of the errors in gun-laying from the position of the shell bursts. The trajectory of the shell was invisible, so that only limited conclusions could be drawn; a burst to the right of the target was certainly 'right' but was it 'plus' or 'minus'? And it all depended upon where the observer was standing in relation to the gun.

But even with this formidable body of problems, there was still room for luck. In September 1911 Italy went to war with Turkey, and the Italians used aircraft for reconnaissance in war for the first time. An Italian aeroplane over Tripoli was hit seven times by rifle fire when flying at 2,500 feet, though without being disabled. An Italian observer was later wounded. In 1912 the French employed aircraft in their sporadic war against Moroccan tribesmen and had two aviators wounded when they incautiously flew too low over a hilltop occupied by Moorish riflemen.

Also in 1912 came the Balkan War, between Turkey and the united Balkan states – Bulgaria, Serbia, Greece and Montenegro. The Bulgarians used a number of aircraft, apparently flown by private owners anxious to assist; they were generally commissioned into the Bulgarian or Greek armies, though some appear to have retained their civilian status. A pilot named Constantin, while making a reconnaissance of the Turkish lines at Chatalja, was struck by a rifle bullet and killed. He was found dead beside his crashed aircraft, the wings of which also showed bullet holes. The unfortunate Constantin thus has the melancholy distinction of being the first aviator to die as a result of anti-aircraft fire; he was to be the first of a great host.

2 ARCHIBALD AND THE FLYING MACHINES

The outbreak of war in 1914 found the combatant armies largely concerned with the mechanics of mobilisation and moving to their battle positions on one or other side of the German frontier, but one or two people managed to find time to wonder what the other side's aviation might be getting up to. Some averred that it could only be used for reconnaissance, since the Hague Convention of 1907 said that 'the bombardment of undefended places by any means whatever was forbidden', and the specific 'by any means whatever' had been included in the phrase so as to cover the possibility of aerial attack. But the precise definition of 'undefended places' had never, in fact, been agreed, so there was no firm assertion of what was or was not a permissible objective for aircraft attack. The only guidance was naval practise; the Hague Naval Convention allowed warships to bombard 'military works, military or naval establishments, depots of arms or war material, workshops or plant which could be utilised for the needs of a hostile fleet or army, and ships of war', suggesting that anything else came into the realm of an 'undefended place'.

As a result of this point of view, it was assumed that naval installations, military barracks and arsenals might expect attack from the air, and in Britain this led to the Admiralty calling for some form of defence for their installations and inviting the Army to do something about it. This duality of responsibility had firm roots in a traditional division of labour: the Navy was responsible for keeping the seas open, and in order to do this successfully the Army was responsible for protecting the Navy's shore establishments against attack from the sea – by coast defence artillery – or from the land – by placing suitable garrisons in the vicinity. Stemming from this, the Army thus assumed the task of protecting the shore establishments from aerial attack as well. As one naval officer is reputed to have said, 'If you want the team to win its away matches, then we must have a reliable goalkeeper.'

The first practical move came in early 1913 when the Admiralty expressed concern over the safety of their enormous magazines at Chattenden and Lodge Hill, north of Chatham. Since both the Army and the Navy were still in the course of developing anti-aircraft guns, four 6in 30cwt howitzers were sent to the magazine area. Mounted on their 'Tops, Siege Carriage', these were the only weapons the Army then owned which were capable of elevating to 70 degrees and traversing in any direction, which is probably the only reason for such otherwise unsuitable weapons being selected. Firing a 118lb shrapnel shell they would doubtless have been effective had they obtained a hit, but they were extremely cumbersome devices for their assigned purpose. But this development seems to have spurred on the gun-builders, and a year later, on 11 March 1914, the 3in 20cwt high angle gun was approved for supply and issue, the first 'purpose-built' anti-aircraft gun. Designed by the Navy, it was a high velocity weapon firing a 12½lb shrapnel shell, mounted on the 'Mounting High Angle Mark 1' which allowed 90-degree elevation and unrestricted traverse. This had, in the first place, been designed as a ship-board mounting, but it was easily adapted to mounting on a suitable concrete base by means of a holdfast ring of heavy bolts, and it entered service as a 'Common' equipment, that is, one for issue to Navy or Army as required. Although approved well before the war, manufacture proceeded slowly and by August only four guns were in service; the first two had been sent to Chattenden and Lodge hill (the howitzers being withdrawn), the next one to the Royal Gunpowder Factory at Waltham Abbey, and the fourth to guard the powder magazines at Purfleet.

The Army, during this time, had been working on a design of a 4in gun and this was introduced as the '4in Mark V' on New Year's Eve 1913, though, strangely, it was approved for naval service. Manufacture of this gun moved even more slowly than that of the 3in, and by August 1914 only one was in service, forming part of the defences of Portsmouth Dockyard. By this time too some 25 one-pounder pom-poms had been distributed to various naval establishments, with four of them allocated to defend London. The disposition of these four was somewhat curious; one on top of the Foreign Office, one on Admiralty Arch, one on the Crown Agent's Office in Millbank, and one at Woolwich Arsenal.

It was, of course, realised that air defence was going to be a business shared between guns and aircraft, and before the war an Admiralty Committee had made it clear that attack was the best form of defence when they said: 'the real key to the situation will be found to lie in a vigorous and offensive attack on the enemy's air-sheds and on his aircraft before they reach these shores'. In furtherance of this policy a Royal Naval Air Service squadron was established, immediately after the outbreak of war, at Dunkerque, from which offensive operations were to be mounted, and on 8 October Flight Lieutenant Marix flew from an advanced base near Antwerp to attack the German airship base at Dusseldorf. Achieving a direct hit with two 20lb bombs, he destroyed the shed and the airship inside it, the Zeppelin Z-9. Unfortunately that same day saw Antwerp evacuated in the face of the oncoming German Army, and thereafter the Dusseldorf area was out of range of the aircraft available to the

RNAS detachment.

On the outbreak of war in August 1914 all the serviceable aircraft of the Royal Flying Corps departed for France for service with the Expeditionary Force, and this left Britain stripped of defensive aircraft so far as the Army were concerned. The Royal Navy had, however, foreseen this to some extent and had carefully located their seaplane stations in close proximity to their other bases, magazines and other installations, so that by flying defensive patrols from the air stations they automatically covered all their vulnerable points. The gaps left in this coastal patrol system – notably in parts of Scotland and south-eastern England – the RFC attempted to plug by patrolling with training aircraft. This was obviously a situation fraught with possibilities of misunderstanding and failure, and before the end of August Lord Kitchener, newly-appointed as Secretary of State for War, formally requested that the Admiralty assume the whole responsibility for air defence until such time as the Army had sufficient men and equipment to take it over. The First Lord of the Admiralty was Mr Winston Churchill, and he, anxiously seeking ways of gainfully employing the Navy to the nation's best advantage, willingly took on the task. In fact the responsibility was still divided since the Navy saw no purpose in usurping the functions of the Royal Garrison Artillery, so the few gun defences which already existed in various naval ports and those which arrived later, were manned and controlled by the Army. Only in London itself did the Navy take on the gun committment. On the other hand the provision of aircraft became entirely a naval responsibility, though the RFC agreed to assist as soon as they were in a position to do so.

In September, then, the Royal Navy began to organise the defences into an homogenous whole. Churchill's first action was to direct the Third Sea Lord, Rear-Admiral F. C. T. Tudor, to examine the availability of guns; his report, on 4 September, showed twelve 3in guns were available, 38 one-pounder pom-poms were being converted to high-angle mountings, and about 150 3-pounder and 6-pounder Hotchkiss quick-firing guns taken from the Fleet's reserve stocks were also being assembled on improvised high angle mountings. Admiral Tudor then proposed to defend London by setting up twelve 'gun posts' each with two guns, and eighteen searchlight posts, each with two lights. But this proposal, small as it was, was turned down by Mr Churchill on the grounds that, firstly, the number of guns could not possibly provide effective protection for the entire area of London and, secondly, that there were no really valid grounds for defending London unless every other city and town was also defended. Defence was to be limited to areas of strictly military importance: 'Far more important than London are the vulnerable points on the Medway, at Dover, and Portsmouth. Oil tanks, power houses, lock gates, magazines, airship sheds – all require to have their aerial guns increased in number.' So London retained its four pom-poms and the remainder of the available guns were distributed to Chatham, Dover and Portsmouth, and as more guns (the Hotchkiss guns) arrived they were to be divided between the fleet and its naval bases.

With some action under way Mr Churchill now convened a committee of experts to consider the whole defence question and draw up plans. The members were Rear-Admiral Tudor, Rear-Admiral Singer (Director of Naval Operations), Captain Murray Sueter (Director, Air Department of the Navy), and Colonel L. C. Jackson, (Assistant Director of Fortifications and Works at the War Office). Their first task, in spite of Churchill's opinion expressed on the previous day, was to organise the defence of London and, particularly, to consider a scheme proposed by Captain Sueter. Since defending individual buildings and locations of importance was not practical, the proposal was to delineate an area of Central London stretching from Charing Cross Station to Buckingham Palace as being of vital importance – since it contained the principal government and military offices – and ring it with guns and searchlights. Around this, at about ten miles radius, would be another ring, this time of landing grounds on which aircraft would be stationed. All these guns, lights and aircraft locations would be in telephone communication with a control room on top of the Admiralty Arch.

The scheme was adopted, landing grounds being prepared in Regents Park, Battersea Park and in the grounds of Buckingham Palace for use in case of emergency. A flight of RNAS aircraft were stationed at Hendon, and two new aerodromes were opened at Hainault Farm in Essex and at Joyce Green near Dartford. The gun defences, though, remained at three pom-poms and three pairs of searchlights on the edges of the 'vital area'. The problem of producing the necessary manpower for guns, searchlights and for observers was neatly solved by forming the Anti-Aircraft Corps, Royal Naval Volunteer Reserve and stocking it with volunteers who were sworn in as Special Constables, signing on to perform day or night duties as they preferred and continuing in their civil occupations when not on duty with the defences.

Not surprisingly this demarcation of the 'vital area' led to some criticism when it became known, and before long a deputation, headed by the Lord Mayor of London, requested that the protected area be extended to take in the City. Since more guns were slowly becoming available, the request was granted; 3in guns were sited near Tower Bridge and in Green Park, six-pounders at Waterloo, Nine Elms and the Temple, and pom-poms in St James's Street, Cannon Street, Gresham College, St Helen's Court and Blackfriars, while more searchlights were also emplaced. To make navigation more difficult for intruders street lights were dimmed and some sections completely extinguished to break up the continuity of lights in the longer and straighter roads. Parks and similar open spaces apparently stood out from the dim background as patches of unrelieved darkness, and in order to remove these position-finding clues, lighting was installed in a criss-cross pattern to simulate street lighting. Finally, in December 1914, the use of outside advertising lights was prohibited.

If the city was thus prepared for attack, the problem remained of alerting the defenders that an attack was on the way. To do this a network of observers was needed, and the only organised body available was the police force. So every policeman within a 60-mile radius of London was instructed to keep a watchful eye for airships (since these were still thought to be the only possible hazard) and, upon seeing one, go to the nearest telephone, when the words 'Anti-Aircraft London' gave a priority line direct to the control room at the Admiralty. From here warning was passed to the gun and searchlight sites, to the aerodromes, and also to the War Office, Scotland Yard, the railway companies and to the Speaker of the House of Commons.

Outside London measures were taken to dim the lights, though the precise degree was left entirely to local authorities. In some seaside resorts the feeling was that a dimunition of lighting might well keep visitors away or, worse still, drive them into the arms of other resorts which were better lit. But by the end of the year the level of illumination along the entire coast had been reduced. A small number of guns were dispersed about the coastline, principally in the neighbourhood of naval establishments, and with that the defences sat and waited for the onslaught.

In fact the first German attempt had been made, but had come to an ignominious end; in November 1914 a free balloon carrying one ton of assorted bombs was prepared in Belgium, the object being to release it when the wind was in the right quarter to drift it across the Channel. The wind speed having been estimated, a primitive timing device would release the bombs after a period of time calculated to elapse when the balloon was somewhere over London. On 14 November the wind was judged to be of the correct strength and direction and the balloon was prepared for launching. Unfortunately it failed to leave the ground – probably someone had done his sums wrongly – and after three futile attempts to launch, the idea was abandoned as impractical.

More concrete was the formation, in the same month, of the *Brieftauben Abteilung Ostende Nr. 1* or 'Ostende Carrier Pigeon Detachment No. 1'. This title disguised a squadron formed in order to bomb England by means of aircraft based near Calais. But the war took a sudden turn at the Battle of the Marne, the German advance failed to achieve Calais, and the 'Carrier Pigeons', bereft of their special function, were moved to Metz in the spring of 1915 to take up more normal employment with the armies in the field.

The Zeppelin campaign was slow in starting due to a series of unfortunate accidents and malfunctions, so that in the end it fell to a German aircraft to be the first to violate English airspace. Shortly after noon on 21 December an aeroplane appeared off Dover, dropped two bombs into the sea close to the Admiralty pier, then turned about and headed back to Belgium. There was some speculation as to whether his target was the shipping in the harbour or the obsolete turret on the pier which contained two venerable muzzle-loading coast defence guns, or whether it was merely a gesture of defiance. Three days later another aircraft appeared, crossed the coast, and dropped a single bomb into the fields near the Castle at Dover. Finally on Christmas Day an Albatros seaplane flew up the Thames estuary. It was fired on by a gun in Sheerness dockyard, but continued upriver. Three RFC aircraft took off from Eastchurch, and three RNAS aircraft from Grain, and set off in pursuit; they caught up with the Albatros at Erith, whereupon the intruder turned about and headed back the way he had come. A gun at Cliffe Fort opened fire, and the Albatros retaliated by dropping two bombs which missed the fort by about a mile and a half, landing near Cliffe railway station. After this it departed rapidly out to sea, escaping unscathed.

Eventually, of course, the Zeppelins came. The first airship attack took place on 19 January 1915 when three German Navy airships, L3, L4 and L6, set forth. L6 was compelled to break off its mission halfway across the North Sea when engine trouble developed, and it turned back; L3 and L4 made their landfall on the Norfolk coast, using the Happisburgh light vessel as their navigational aid. L3 flew south and dropped nine bombs on Great Yarmouth, while L4 took a northward swing; after dropping a few bombs haphazardly on various coastal villages it arrived at King's Lynn. By this time it was dark, and the airship commander (*Kapitanleutnant* Graf von Platen), seeing the lights below, assumed he had arrived over the Humber; so in the hope of damaging some of the Humberside industrial complex, he pitched the rest of his bombs overboard, seven 50kg high explosive and some incendiaries. Two people were killed and thirteen injured in King's Lynn. In his subsequent report von Platen stated that his ship had been tracked by searchlights and fired on by anti-aircraft guns, but in fact there were neither guns nor lights in that area and no defence was put up against the Zeppelins at all.

The general feeling in England after this raid was one of indignation rather than anger, and demands for gun protection came in from all quarters. Since there was no possibility of putting guns in every field and village, an Eastern Mobile Air Defence Force was hastily organised. Vickers machine guns and searchlights were fitted to motor chassis, and the force was stationed at Newmarket.

Fresh instructions were given to the police in East Anglia so that if a raider was seen it could be reported to Newmarket and the Mobile Force would turn out like a fire brigade and dash off to pre-arranged sites, hoping to intercept the raider's line of flight. A fortnight after this a Southern Mobile Force was assembled at Caterham, in Surrey, to perform the same function along the southern approaches to London, but later experience showed that raiders rarely appeared in this sector and this force was disbanded in June 1915.

As a result of the Christmas Day flight up the Thames more guns were brought into the London area. Three 3in guns were diverted from the Fleet and positioned on Clapton Orient football ground, One Tree Hill (Honor Oak), and on Parliament Hill. These sites were chosen with some care: Clapton was on a line drawn from the North German airship bases at Nordholz, Tondern, Hage and Seddin; Honor Oak intercepted the line from the bases in Belgium at Gontrode, Berchem and Etterbeek; and the Parliament Hill site offered some protection to the north-western suburbs. More aircraft were also made available; in addition to the London airfields, seaplanes were to be kept in readiness at Dover, Clacton, Felixstowe, Yarmouth, Westgate, Kettingholm, the Isle of Grain, Ramsgate, Chelmsford, Chingford (using the Lea Valley reservoirs as their landing ground) and Maidstone, so that a complete screen could be placed in the air from Dungeness to Felixstowe to cover every line of approach and escape.

During the first few months of 1915 guns were distributed, as they became available, to protect locations of importance in the production of munitions: Sheffield with 6 guns, Birmingham, 5, Coventry, 2, Stowmarket (home of the New Explosives Company), 2, Pitsea (The British Explosives Syndicate), 2, Kynochtown (manufacturing naval cordite), 2, Abbey Wood (to protect Woolwich Arsenal), 1, Chilworth (The Chilworth Powder Company), 1, Middlesbrough, 1 and Darlington, 2, were all armed for the first time, while the existing defences were strengthened. Anti-aircraft guns were also put into coast defence forts and batteries on the Tyne, Forth and Humber, and at Dover and Harwich.

By pure luck, the next Zeppelin raid was on the Tyne; the airship was on a reconnaissance flight over the North Sea, but it had bombs on board, the weather was good, and so the commander decided to turn his trip into a raid on the nearest convenient place, which was the Tyne area. Crossing the coast north of Blyth, the L9 was peppered with rifle fire by a Cyclist Battalion in camp at Cambois, but thereafter managed to evade all defences. Due to the lighting restrictions in force, the commander's navigation was not as accurate as he thought; instead of following the course of the Tyne, he was actually at right-angles to the river and the majority of his bombs landed harmlessly in fields. Only at the close of his run, as he crossed the river at Wallsend, did a bomb land in a populated area.

Nevertheless, his report on the success of his raid cheered his companions, and on 15 April three more airships set out to raid the Humber. None of them reached their objective, flying too far south; one failed to cross the coast at all, the two others dropped their bombs indiscriminately across Norfolk and Suffolk. But this raid was notable for one feature; on returning to base, an examination of the L6 revealed 8 major holes and 17 smaller bullet holes in the fabric. This damage had been done by rifle fire from a Field Company of Royal Engineers at Brightlingsea and by Maxim gun and pom-pom fire from the Garrison Artillery in Landguard Fort opposite Harwich, as the Zeppelin had crossed the coast on its inward journey. It was the first sign of an effective defence, though, of course, the defenders knew nothing of it at the time.

By way of a diversion, the German Airship Service had also decided to raid Paris. This promised to be an easier trip, since the navigation problems were fewer and, because Paris had not bothered with dimming its lights, there would be little difficulty in locating their target from a considerable way off. The French, though, had by this time accumulated a number of excellent anti-aircraft guns; their 75mm M1897 field gun was a high-velocity weapon well suited to vertical fire, and several had been adapted to high-angle mountings and placed on De Dion Bouton motor chassis. These 'auto-canon' were distributed around the northern suburbs of Paris and were in telephone communication with observers in the front line, which the Zeppelins would have to cross. The front line was, in truth, a threefold hazard; the occupants of the trenches were alert and would be unlikely to miss the passage of an airship; they were armed and needed little encouragement to open fire; and the raiders had to run the gauntlet twice, once to get to Paris and once on the way home.

One would have thought that this might have daunted the Zeppelin commanders, but they apparently thought little of it and, on 20 March, three raiders set out from the airship base at Maubeuge. The first setback occurred when crossing the front line, one Zeppelin being hit by ground fire and forced to turn about and limp home. The other two continued, arrived over Paris and dropped several bombs, and then turned for home. Passing over Noyon the Z 10 came under fire from an auto-canon and was severely holed, crashing near St Quentin. The other ship, LZ 35, reached Maubeuge safely but was to be shot down less than a month later while attempting to raid Calais, again victim of an auto-canon.

The first German attack to reach London was that of Hauptmann Linnarz in the Zeppelin LZ38 on 31 May 1915. He approached London across Essex, having crossed the coast near Shoeburyness and dropped bombs in Stoke Newington, Stepney, Poplar, West Ham and Leytonstone, a total of some 30 explosive grenades and 90 incendiary bombs. The Zeppelin flew high and was quite unseen from the ground; not surprisingly, no guns opened fire, and the raider went back the way he had come, leaving 7 killed, 35 injured, and an estimated £18,000 worth of damage. This scot-free run caused some discontent, and on 15 June the Admiralty reluctantly agreed to release another three 3in guns from the Fleet's store, siting them at Blackheath, Finsbury and West Ham.

Until now the Kaiser had forbidden any raids on London west of the Tower, but on 18 June the German Admiralty (who were operating the airships at that time, since the Army ships were not ready) requested permission to abandon this restriction, and after some discussion they obtained the necessary permission on 20 June, with a proviso that historic buildings were not to be bombed. In August several Naval airship raids were mounted, but for various reasons, generally connected with ill winds or poor navigation, few of them achieved any results and none of them managed to get near London. It was not until 17 August that Zeppelin L10 reached the capital, appearing over Walthamstow late at night to drop three bombs. It then flew on to Leyton to drop another 26 bombs, Leytonstone (4 bombs), Wanstead (10 bombs) and then departed. A pom-pom at Waltham Abbey (defending the Royal Gunpowder Factory) managed to get off a few shots as the Zeppelin passed over on its way in to London, but no other guns saw it, nor did four aircraft which hunted for it across Essex. The Leyton bombs killed 9 and injured 48, and damage was done to the railway station and the tramways depot.

On 7 September the German Army Airship Service appeared, intent upon improving on the Navy's achievements. SL2 (a Schutte-Lanz airship, not a Zeppelin) bombed Leytonstone again, flew on to Milwall, Deptford, Southwark, New Cross, Greenwich, Charlton and Woolwich, scattering bombs as it went, to kill 18 and injure 38. Simultaneously, Zeppelin LZ74 approached down the Lea Valley, bombing Cheshunt as it passed; it was fired at by the Waltham Abbey gun (which appeared to have had an alert detachment) and arrived over Fenchurch Street just after midnight. It dropped one incendiary bomb which did little damage but which went on record as being the first enemy missile to land within the City of London. After this gesture, LZ74 joined up with SL2 and the pair flew off in company, both being fired at by the guns at Purfleet as they passed. Blowing out acres of greenhouses at Cheshunt in order to drop one ineffective bomb on the City scarcely made tactical sense, and perhaps somebody in Germany thought so too; in any event, it was the last time a German Army airship attacked London.

The Navy, however, were convinced that bombing could be made effective, and they proved their contention with their next raid, which took place on the following day. Zeppelin L13 crossed the Wash and made for London, passing over Cambridge en route. At 10.40pm he bombed Golders Green and then passed over Euston

Station, Hatton Garden, Smithfield Market, Moorgate and Liverpool Street bombing as he went; 22 people were killed and 87 injured, while property damage was estimated at over half a million pounds. One bomb, which fell in Bartholomew Close, was of 300kg, the heaviest so far developed. All the London guns – by now 26 in number – opened fire, without success, though they drove L13 up to 11,000 feet altitude in order to escape the shells. The Zeppelin commander reported on his return that 'The AA fire was so extensive that in future, with a clear sky, airships will only be able to remain for a short time over the city'.

Londoners, though, had less high an opinion of the defences, and the press were quick to point out that there was obviously something seriously amiss with the system when Zeppelins could sail in and out unhindered. The Admiralty therefore decided to divorce the defence of London from the general air defence scheme of the country as a whole, which was under the control of the Navy's Director of Air Services, and place the London side of it under a separate command, the officer appointed to this task being Admiral Sir Percy Scott, the renowned gunnery expert. Scott's first move was to throw out the pom-poms as being useless and dangerous. He then demanded another 104 guns and 50 searchlights and, although a gunnery specialist, he appreciated the part which aircraft could play. (His declared creed was 'If you are a Gunnery Man you must believe and preach that the World Will Be Saved By Gunnery and Only By Gunnery'.) His plan of defence was to put guns and aircraft well forward so as to prevent an enemy from reaching London, reserving sufficient guns around the capital to deal with any which might get through; his view was that 'the defence of London by aircraft begins over the Zeppelin sheds and the defence by gunfire begins at the coast'.

Unfortunately, as he recalled in his memoirs, the Admiralty 'informed me that they would not give me any more guns at once, and that although they had been experimenting for ten years they had no time fuze suitable for exploding high explosive shells'.

This question of fuzes deserves some discussion, since there have been some considerable misapprehensions in print about the matter, largely on the basis of statements by Commander Rawlinson, Scott's assistant. As we have already seen, the question of projectiles for anti-aircraft fire revolved round three possibles; the shrapnel shell, the high explosive shell, and the incendiary shell. Shrapnel had been the standard field artillery shell for years, and was fitted with a pyrotechnic time fuze which caused the gunpowder expelling charge in the shell to be fired at the desired point, so as to eject the lead balls which formed the filling. High explosive shells, on the other hand, were normally used with howitzers for the destruction of defensive works; therefore they were fitted with impact fuzes. Since nobody could visualise a situation in which it would be required to burst a high explosive shell in the air, there was no suitable time fuze. The fuze used with the shrapnel could not be used; the screwed hole in the shell nose was of a different size and, more important, the time fuze used with shrapnel delivered a flash, whereas the fuze used with high explosive shells had to deliver a detonating impulse.

Scott's claim that the Admiralty has been trying to develop a time fuze for ten years is not borne out by the record; no such work had been done, since there had not been any requirement for one until anti-aircraft fire began to demand the peculiar combination of explosive shell and time fuze. A further complication was the demand that any fuze used with high explosive shells had to be 'bore-safe'; that is, it had to incorporate a centrifugal safety device which would prevent premature detonation should any part of the fuze mechanism inadvertently function while the shell was still inside the gun barrel.

Scott's assistant, Commander Rawlinson, later claimed to have solved the whole problem overnight by incorporating a naval delayed-action fuze mechanism into the design of a time fuze, but no such design has ever been found. At best, this claim is a gross simplification of what actually happened. The Royal Laboratory at Woolwich Arsenal had, in fact, appreciated the problem shortly before the war and had solved it by taking the standard howitzer detonating fuze, which was bore-safe, and screwing it down into the shell, leaving sufficient room above it to allow the shrapnel time fuze to be screwed on top. In this way the explosion of the time fuze fired the detonating fuze and thus, in a roundabout way, initiated the shell filling. This fuze, known as the 'fuze, Time and Percussion No. 80/44' was approved for service on 29 October 1914, almost exactly a year before Rawlinson claimed to have invented it. The only trouble, and the one which was preventing Scott from obtaining supplies of high explosive, was that once the fuze had been designed it was necessary to design a new shell to accept this peculiar combination, and this shell had then to be tested, proved, and put into manufacture; in the meantime, it was shrapnel only.

But in October 1915 the fuze and shell problem was just one of many; Scott had obtained the services of Rawlinson because the latter was familiar with the air defences of Paris which, according to common report, were highly efficient, and Rawlinson was now depatched post-haste to Paris to borrow one of the latest French AA guns and bring it back to England to be copied. Just why this course was adopted is hard to say, since the 75mm gun was inferior in performance to the 3in 20cwt. Its only virtue was that it was provided with a high explosive shell with time fuze, (which, incidentally, was not bore-safe) and its sighting system was more advanced. Rawlinson returned with an 'auto-cannon' and, using this as a pattern, De Dion, Lancia and Daimler lorries were converted into mountings for a variety of British guns. The object in this was to have a mobile column of guns which could be stationed centrally and, upon receipt of a warning of the approach of Zeppelins, could drive out rapidly and position itself across the raider's path to reinforce the static guns in the area. Vickers produced a supply of high-velocity 3-pounder guns suitable for mounting on lorry chassis, and the Coventry Ordnance Works undertook to build duplicates of the French 'auto-cannon' mounting, for which the French Government would supply the guns and ammunition. All this activity of Scott's played havoc with the Admiralty's time-hallowed system of dockets, files, contracts and procurement routines, and he was soon in conflict with the Civil Service. On 18 October he fired off a powerful broadside at the First Lord of the Admiralty, Mr Balfour:

> 'If I am to be responsible for the gunnery defence of London, I must be allowed to do things my own way, and not be interfered with by the Admiralty. If the Admiralty are to settle what guns are to be used for the defence of London and how they are to be obtained, then they become responsible for the defence of London and I resign.
>
> If I am to remain in charge . . . I must have a free hand to procure what is wanted, how and best I can, and not be handicapped by Admiralty red-tape-ism.'

This appears to have had the desired effect; Scott's methods were approved, and he was allowed to get on with the job in his own way.

With all this concentration on home defence, the needs of the British Expeditionary Force were not being overlooked. Immediately upon the outbreak of war the Royal Gun Factory put the provision of mobile anti-aircraft guns high on the priority list and, since time was short, looked at what was already in being and amenable to modification. Their choice fell on what, at first sight, seems a peculiar weapon for the role – the Royal Horse Artillery's 13-pounder light field gun. But this fired a useful 3in shell at a respectable velocity and was a light and handy equipment, so the gun and recoil system were removed from the two-wheeled field carriage and installed on a pedestal mounted on the rear platform of a motor lorry. Since it was now to operate at a high angle, a 'cartridge retaining catch' was fitted into the breech mechanism; at the normal low angles used by field guns, a cartridge loaded into the breech would stay there while the breech-block was swung across and closed, but at high angles it was liable to fall out before the closing movement could be completed; hence the retaining catch. An additional powerful spring was added to the recoil system to pull the gun back into the firing position after recoil; again, at low angles the normal system was enough, but to pull the gun uphill, as it were, demanded an additional spring. On test the '13-pounder 6cwt' as it was now known (to distinguish it from the ordinary '13-pounder Mark 1' field piece) showed itself capable of sending a shell to 17,000 feet altitude with the aid of a slightly more powerful cartridge than normal, and on 16 October 1914 it was approved for issue. (It is not without interest to note that several guns survived the war. In 1919 they were reconverted by removal of the cartridge catch and returned to their field carriages for duty with the RHA. Declared obsolete in 1944, some survived in store, and in 1948 were brought back into service for ceremonial use with the King's Troop, RHA,where they are still in service. The guns which fire salutes in Hyde Park may well have performed more serious duties in France in 1915-16.)

By January 1915 sufficient of these 13-pounder 6cwt guns had been produced to allow the formation of 'AA Sections', each of two guns, with the intention of providing one such section to each division in the field, but this aim was never reached. By July 1915 there were 28 divisions in France but only 13 AA Sections. Nevertheless, the guns did good work until that month, when they suddenly came under a cloud due to a change of ammunition policy.

The shrapnel shell had several advantages as an anti-aircraft weapon, notably the spread of bullets which considerably increased the chance of hitting. But it also suffered from one notable defect, which was that the shell's nose section, complete with fuze – weighing about a pound – and the empty shell body – weighing about six pounds – came hurtling back to earth after functioning in the sky, and in spite of Colonel Bethell's nonchalant dimissal of the problem in pre-war days, when it actually started to happen the luckless soldiers on the ground were not slow to complain. As a result the high explosive shell was hurried into service; this detonated in the sky, producing a shower of fragments to rain down on the ground beneath, and this was considered to be as much of a relief as could be managed.

Unfortunately the manufacture of the early batches of high explosive shells was hurriedly done and inspection of the finished product was cursory, due to the lack of experience in factories suddenly converted to munitions production. Standards of manufacture and tolerances in measurement which sufficed for railway trucks or roof girders were not good enough when it came to the manufacture of explosive devices. As a result, a large quantity of 13-pounder shells were 'high to gauge' or, in non-service English, too wide to go up the gun's barrel; they jammed as they entered the rifling, and this sudden check detonated the explosive inside, destroying the guns and killing or wounding the gunners. There was a sudden reluctance to fire the 13-pounder with high explosive shells and huge amounts of ammunition had to be withdrawn for testing; this, on top of the general shortage of ammunition which obtained in 1915, severely curtailed the activities of the AA Sections and it was not until early in 1916 that confidence was restored with the regular issue of reliable ammunition.

Another gun which was converted from its original role was the 12-pounder 12cwt coast defence gun. This, in spite of its 'smaller' terminology, was a much more powerful weapon than the Horse Artillery piece, since it had been designed as a fixed emplacement gun for shooting at warships. The amount of modification needed was much the same as that for the 13-pounder; the addition of a cartridge retaining catch and a return spring to the recoil system. The coast defence mounting was already a pedestal, and this needed small change to make the gun capable of elevating to 85 degrees. The guns were originally intended to be statically mounted for the defence of dockyards, but a number were placed on motor chassis and sent to France to be emplaced in rear areas where mobility was less important, guarding railway junctions and supply dumps.

On the other side of the front it seemed to the Allied aviators that, as usual, the Germans had better weapons, and they were vociferous in their complaints about the power of the German guns. It was about this period that anti-aircraft guns collected the nickname which was to accompany them until 1939 – 'Archie'. The story goes that a young British pilot flying over the German lines used to express his disdain for the shells which burst around him by using the 'punch-line' from a music-hall song of the day; as his aircraft rocked to the blast, he would sing out 'Archibald – certainly NOT!'. The story got about, as such stories do, and before long all anti-aircraft guns were known as 'Archibald', shortened, in due course, to 'Archie'.

In August 1914 the Germans were, in fact, no better off than anyone else in the matter of high-angle guns; they had six motorised guns, three by Krupp and three by Erhardt, all of which were actually the 1909 Frankfurt show models. There were also a dozen horse-drawn equipments, all of 77mm calibre, from various makers. Once war began the motorised models were given 1,000 rounds of shrapnel each and sent to serve with the field armies. The horse-drawn weapons were dispersed along the Rhine valley, with 2,000 rounds apiece, placed so as to protect the major munitions installations such as the Krupp and Zeppelin factories.

Like the other combatants Germany was unprepared for the enormous demands for weapon replacement and ammunition which the war was to make and, like the others, for the first few months of the war found it difficult to keep up with the demand for standard weapons, let alone to set up production of completely new designs. So the first demands for anti-aircraft guns were met in a rather unusual way. In the first campaigns on the Eastern Front a considerable number of 3in Russian field guns had been captured; these weapons, the Putilov M1903, had the unusually high muzzle velocity of 1,980 feet per second and fired a 14.45lb shrapnel shell. They were therefore converted to pedestal mounting as the 7.62cm *Russische Sockel Fliegerabwehrkanone*: the latter part of the title, which meant literally 'flyer defence cannon', was soon abbreviated in German style to *Flak* and it has remained the standard German term ever since. During the Second World War it spread across to the Allied side, entered the popular terminology, and is now in universal use.

In a similar manner the French 75mm M1897 field gun, when it fell into German hands, was adapted to the high angle role, but in this case insufficient ammunition was captured with them (probably because the French were short of it themselves) and so these guns had the barrels bored out and re-rifled to accept the standard German 77mm ammunition.

In England there was no chance of using captured stocks, since sufficient were never captured, but there was one unusual source of supply – the private gunmakers. Firms such as the Elswick Ordnance Company, Vickers, the Coventry Ordnance Works and Beardmore had all, in some degree, experimented with anti-aircraft gun design and had made guns in small numbers either as a speculative venture or to a contract from a foreign country. On 4 August 1914 all such contracts were voided by Government decree – the Royal Navy thereby acquiring several warships intended for Turkish, Brazilian and Japanese use – and the stocks of weapons, frequently of calibres not standard in British service, were placed in store. In the spring of 1915 much of this stock was offered to the Army and Navy, and some remarkable things came to light.

The Elswick Ordnance Company, for example, had a variety of 3in guns intended for foreign contracts. Six of these resembled the 13-pounder 6cwt but were shorter and were rifled with 24 grooves instead of the service pattern of 18; these were mounted on motor lorries and taken for Army use, one going to guard the Royal Small Arms Factory at Enfield Lock and the other five to France, being officially known as the '13-pounder Mark IV'. Another design, again similar to the 13-pounder 6cwt but with a much different breech mechanism, became the '3in 5cwt' and four were taken for protection of dockyards. Elswick appeared to have had some stock of components for these weapons since another eight were then built and, mounted on lorries, went to swell the AA Sections in France.

A third Elswick gun was one which had been designed for the Russian Navy; it was a 75mm weapon firing a 10.75lb shell and was on a high angle mounting. Twelve of these were taken by the Royal Navy and known as the 'Ten-pounder Russians', but the complication of having to organise a special ammunition supply for the ships which carried them was more than they were worth and they were eventually handed over to the Army to be used in the London defences, the Navy taking a dozen new 3in 20cwt guns in their place.

These were, of course, expedients and were not, as the official phrase had it, 'to be perpetuated in service', because while they could undoubtedly shoot upwards, they were far from being the best possible design. Sir John French, mindful of the complaints from

RFC pilots about German guns, now urged the Army Council to provide a gun of sufficient power to make life equally hazardous for German aviators venturing across the Allied lines. Since the 13-pounder field gun conversion had been a success, the logical move was to do the same thing with the heavier 18-pounder field gun, but this idea fell a long way short of expectations. For a variety of technical ballistic reasons the 18-pounder shell did not perform well in high-angle fire and the project had to be abandoned. In August 1915 the Director of Artillery suggested putting a 3in calibre liner into the barrel of the 18-pounder (which was 3.3in calibre) so that the resulting weapon would use the 18-pounder cartridge to fire the 13-pounder shell. Within a week the idea had been examined and tried and pronounced workable, and fifty 18-pounders were relined, placed on modified 13-pounder pedestals and fitted to Peerless motor trucks. This new weapon had a muzzle velocity of 2,150 feet per second and a ceiling of 19,000 feet, and in order to avoid confusion it became known as the '13-pounder 9cwt'. The first equipments were issued in November 1915 and in due course it replaced all the older 13-pounder models in France; the French were sufficiently impressed with it to ask for 30 guns for use in their own rear areas.

The system which had grown up in France was to establish a line of AA sections some 3–4,000 yards behind the trenches; by late 1915 there were sufficient weapons to provide one section for every four miles of front. The sections prepared a number of sites in their area, reinforcing the ground with logs or stones, and they would drive forward and occupy one of these sites shortly before dawn. As targets appeared, so they would be engaged, but sooner or later the German aviators complained, on their return home, and the location of the offending 'Archie' would be passed to the German field artillery for bombardment. Since the 'Archie' was motorised, it was the work of a moment to wind up the jacks, swing in the stabilising outriggers, crank up the engine and depart, while the field guns were still finding the range, to another of the prepared positions. But this 'shoot and scoot' technique, while popular with the anti-aircraft gunners, was less popular with other units in their neighbourhood who were longer-established and less readily mobile, since the hostile artillery fire intended for the departed 'Archie' landed on them instead.

As darkness fell, flying activity usually ceased and the 'Archie' and crew would then drive back to their billets, usually a farm building or hutment some 3,000 yards further back, and settle down for the night. The guns were placed 'in action' in case a night flyer chanced along, and as the war progressed and night flying became more common, searchlight sections were deployed and a second line of AA Sections was dispersed further back, among the railheads, supply dumps and base areas.

Overlaying all these questions of provision of equipment and deployment of effort was, of course, the technical problem of anti-aircraft gunnery, and as the war progressed it began to look as if the difficulties were piling up faster than they were ever likely to be solved. Shooting was done entirely by eye and the techniques employed were simply extensions of the methods of fire correction used by field and garrison artillery against terrestrial targets, largely because it took considerable faith to imagine any other way of going about it. An aircraft would be seen approaching; its range would be measured by an optical range-finder, usually the two-metre-base Barr and Stroud; the height had to be estimated, and from this height and range a fuze-length was determined for the setting of the shell's time fuze. This was, of course, calculated (by means of a graphical chart) for the *future* position of the aircraft, the position it was hoped it would be occupying when the shell finally got there, some 30 seconds or so after being fired. Suitable deflections were calculated – or guessed – and set on to the gun's sight, so that when the gun-layer pointed the gun at the aircraft, the muzzle would be pointed at the future position. And finally the shell was loaded and the gun was fired.

In field gunnery practice there would now be a pause until the shell arrived and burst, after which a correction would be deduced from the relative positions of shell and target, converted to gun data, passed to the gun, and a fresh round fired. But with the target soaring across the sky at speed, such leisurely methods could no longer be used, and the gun continued to fire, as fast as it could, using the same initial information. After five or six shots had gone, the first would burst in the sky and the observing officer could then make an assessment of the error, recalculate his data, and give fresh information to the gun.

Obviously, there were defects in this system. The initial data were largely based on guesswork, while the subsequent corrections were all based on out-of-date information; it was useless to correct on the relative position of burst and aircraft since, after a few shots had been fired and some corrections made it took a remarkable mental agility to relate the puff of smoke in the sky to a particular set of data given out two or three corrections previously (when the shot had been fired), relate that in turn to the data currently on the gun, and then relate both to what might be the future position of the aircraft by the time the new correction had been applied, the shell fuze set, the shell loaded, fired, and finally burst in the sky. Some people achieved it, just as some people can play six games of chess simultaneously, but gun commanders of that sort of ability were rare.

The first improvement was to modify the range-finder so that it also measured the vertical angle to the target and this allowed the height to be calculated with some accuracy. Next came the Wilson-Dalby Deflection Meter, a telescope controlled by a geared handle;

an observer, looking through the telescope, tracked the target in flight by turning the handle; this allowed the rate of movement of the aircraft to be mechanically measured, and this rate, together with the known range and height, enabled an accurate deflection to be calculated. The process was speeded up by fitting scales to the gun sight matching the readings from the deflection meter. The gun-layer set a pointer according to the estimated fuze-length (derived from height and range) and then set his sight so that the tip of this pointer matched the 'raw' figure from the deflection meter. The correct deflection was automatically worked out and set into the sight without the need to calculate it; but since the gun-layer wanted to keep his eye on the target, another man had to be drafted in to set the deflection on the sight. A further improvement came with a French invention, the Brocq *tachymetre*, which did the same job but electrically instead of mechanically, and displayed the correct deflection on a dial attached to the gun; in this case the calculation was performed electrically inside the *tachymetre*, which simplified the design of the gun sight.

Unfortunately, improvement brought problems in its train. The aviators had discovered, by this time, that flying below 3,000 feet was distinctly hazardous due to rifle and machine-gun fire from the occupants of the trenches; above 3,000 feet this was of no account, and it was the fire of the anti-aircraft guns which counted, so it became their practice to fly at 10,000 to 12,000 feet, and thus avoid all danger from the ground. As the gunnery improved, so the dangerous height crept upward and the aviators moved up to 15,000 feet or so. This was satisfactory for a while and then the danger height climbed again and the aviators went up to 20,000 feet. So far the guns had justified their existence; as a prominent French anti-aircraft gunner, Colonel Pagezy, said: 'The function of anti-aircraft guns is to punish the audacity of aircraft flying in a straight line, hinder and obstruct others in the performance of their duties, and prevent aeroplanes flying at low heights.' And this had been done.

However, once the targets were higher than 15,000 feet the accuracy of artillery fire suddenly became most erratic, and it was obvious that some fundamental research had to be done. The problem was how to find a system of actually measuring the gun's performance; the only way to do this was to be able to locate the shell burst in the sky with great precision, so that the result of corrections or experiments could be accurately measured. In theory this was easy; you set up two or three theodolites and measured the horizontal and vertical angles to the burst, and from this, by using arbitrary coordinates, the burst could be very precisely fixed. The trouble came when it was put to practical test; the field of view of a theodolite was so small that invariably the burst occurred outside the observer's vision. After many false starts this problem was solved by Major A. V. Hill (later to be better known as Professor A. V. Hill,

FRS) and Sir Horace Darwin who, in early 1916, invented the mirror position finder. This was an optically flat and carefully levelled mirror some 30 inches square, laid flat so as to reflect the sky. Two observers watched the surface of the mirror through fixed peep-sights and, upon seeing the reflection of a shell-burst, marked its apparent position on the mirror's surface. From this, by some fairly abstruse geometry and mathematics, it was possible to deduce the position of the burst in the sky with remarkable accuracy. (In fact the mathematics were largely taken care of by graduations marked on the mirror and the shell's position could be determined quite easily and quickly by the operators; like so many devices of this kind, the hardest part was inventing it; working it was much easier.)

With the mirror position finder to give the basic facts, the Ministry of Munitions set up an Anti-Aircraft Experimental Section at Portsmouth, using the gun firing facilities of Whale Island, the RN Gunnery School, and systematic testing of every aspect of the anti-aircraft system got under way. It soon became apparent that the prime cause of trouble lay in the time fuzes.

The fuzes in use at this time were operated by the burning of a train of gunpowder. As the gun was fired an igniting detonator in the fuze struck a fixed needle; the resulting flash lit the end of the powder train which then began to burn at a speed predetermined by the composition of the powder and the density with which it was packed. But it was now apparent that something was upsetting the regularity of the powder at heights over 15,000 feet. The AAES built a vacuum chamber and installed a spinning table inside it so that the fuxe could be operated in conditions of rarified atmosphere and spin exactly like those it would meet in the air when fired, and experiments showed that the burning powder was often extinguished due to the drop in air pressure at great heights. Another defect was the centrifugal force due to the spinning shell, which caused the molten burning area of the powder to detach itself from the rest of the train and thus fail to pass on the ignition. By reformulating the powder and changing the internal arrangements in the fuzes, they were gradually made more reliable, but even when the war ended 20,000 feet seemed to be the greatest height at which a fuze could be relied upon to function with any degree of accuracy.

For several years coast gunners had appreciated that such apparently trivial matters as air temperature, humidity, barometric pressure and wind angle and speed made appreciable differences to the shell's flight, and it was now clear that these factors would have to enter into anti-aircraft gunnery. As Colonel Pagezy put it, 'Don't *correct* anti-aircraft fire – *prepare* it'; if all these variables were taken into account and applied to the data before firing, the chances of the first shot being close to the target were immeasurably increased. The trouble was that by the time all the calculations had been done and the corrections made, the aeroplane was over the next county or even on the way home. Not for the first time, the theory was impeccable but putting it into practise was formidable. Not for nothing did an official manual contain the cautionary words 'In designing AA equipment the technical expert must guard against evolving gear whose adjustment or use may be beyond the experience or state of training of the personnel.' And so, for the time being, anti-aircraft gunnery had to rely on simple systems.

Besides the actual question of shooting at aircraft there was also the question of detecting them; the sooner the target was detected, the more time there would be in which to calculate initial data and the sooner the shooting could start. The only detection method, at first, was the human eye, but this was a highly variable system; two men with identical vision could differ widely in their ability to spot and follow an aircraft. The average aeroplane of the day, it was calculated, occupied about one twenty-millionth part of the sky, and in some conditions of lighting could be virtually invisible at ranges as short as 5,000 feet.

Apart from vision, the only other detectable feature of the aeroplane was its noise, and in 1915 the first primitive sound detector was produced by the London air defences. This consisted of a long pole, mounted so as to rotate horizontally on a pivot, and bearing at each end a gramophone horn. Attached to the horns were rubber tubes which led in to the centre of the pole and terminated in a pair of stethoscope earpieces. The operator placed these in his ears, and by this actually extended the 'base' of his two ears, so that by turning the pole about its pivot until the sound of the aircraft could be heard equally in each ear, he could determine with some accuracy the direction from which the sound was coming. To try to extract the utmost from this idea, blind men were used as operators in some instances, on the premise that a man born blind would have a more highly developed sense of hearing than a man who relied principally on his eysight. It appears to have worked well, but there were practical difficulties in the supply of suitable blind men, and, moreover, the system could hardly have been exported to the battle lines in France.

Sound detectors of more elegant pattern followed, and a vertically-mounted pair of horns allowed an estimation of height to be made. Eventually a three-horn unit was evolved in which the two horns in the horizontal plane gave direction and one horizontal horn with another above it gave height, two operators being used. In still air, with no other noises to distract the operators, these devices could pick up an approaching aircraft at about five miles range, which wasn't a lot better than a good visual observer, but it could continue to do it in cloudy or hazy condition which defeated the human eye. The French Army developed a much more sophisticated device in which a large parabolic reflector collected the sound and concentrated it into an electrical microphone at the reflector's focal point. The sound was then amplified and presented to the operator, and movement of the reflector until the sound was at its strongest allowed height and direction to be determined. It was claimed that an aircraft could be detected at ten miles range with this detector, largely due to its ability to amplify sounds which were too weak to permit an unaided ear to make reliable estimations.

In the battle areas, of course, the desirable condition of 'no distracting noises' was out of the question and the performance of sound detectors was reduced accordingly. A measure of success was reached by careful design of the horns and the provision of insulation and frequency filters which removed some of the worst of the noise and confined the instrument's response to that band of frequencies in which an aero-engine operated.

And what when it *was* heard? Sound travels much more slowly than light, so that an aircraft five miles away moving at 100mph had actually flown 1,150 yards in the 23.6 seconds it took the sound to reach the detector, so a suitable correction factor had to be applied to the detector's figures. There was also the fear that in those 1,150 yards the aeroplane might have speeded up, slowed down, turned, climbed, dived, or any combination of these manoeuvres. But to contemplate such contingencies was quite impossible, and by 1916 the anti-aircraft gunners had settled on the fundamental hypothesis which was to be their one sure touch-stone for evermore; that between the instant the gun data was produced and the time the shell burst in the sky, the aeroplane would continue to fly at the same speed and on the same course. It wasn't always true, but it was true enough for most of the time, and without this assumption anti-aircraft gunnery theory would never have made any progress.

It will have been noted that most of the technical improvements appeared from the defence systems concerned with the protection of rear areas rather than from those in the front line. The reason for this was simply that the front line sections in France had a comparatively simple task, shooting at whatever they saw every day, while the home defences were faced with a more complex form of attack in which aircraft could appear from almost any direction at any time of day or night. Moreover, they were more in the public eye; the odd bomb dropped on the Menin Road was of little remark to the soldiers in the area, but a similar bomb on the Commercial Road or Oxford Street would provoke a mighty uproar in press and parliament. The home defences also had the advantage that they were not constantly in action; there were long periods of inactivity during which they would plan and experiment, try out new ideas and perfect their organisation. On the other hand, these periods of inactivity tended to take the edge off the defence forces, who frequently complained of spending long hours waiting for something to happen and getting bored when nothing did. It was to be a long-standing complaint with anti-aircraft gunners.

The first purpose-built anti-aircraft weapon was Krupp's balloon gun of 1870.

Top left: Evidence of the rising interest in countering military aviation was Krupp's 1909 12-pounder gun. The motor chassis had a 50hp motor and could reach a speed of 28mph.

Below left: Krupp's 9-pounder of 1909; notice how the wheels were pivoted forward to allow the entire equipment to be swung around the point of the trail.

Above: A 1914 proposal for attacking airships by means of a suspended mine. It was never put into practice but was the inspiration of several parachute-and-cable devices in the Second World War.

Above: The Erhardt 5cm balloon gun in fully-armoured car, 1909.

Top right: The Parseval II Military Airship of 1909, a non-rigid type which was superseded by the rigid Zeppelin and Schütte-Lanz designs.

Centre right: Erhardt 75mm gun on motor truck. Note that the whole rear section carrying the gun is capable of pivoting.

Below right: The Erhardt 5cm gun of 1909 on its 'half-armoured car' mounting.

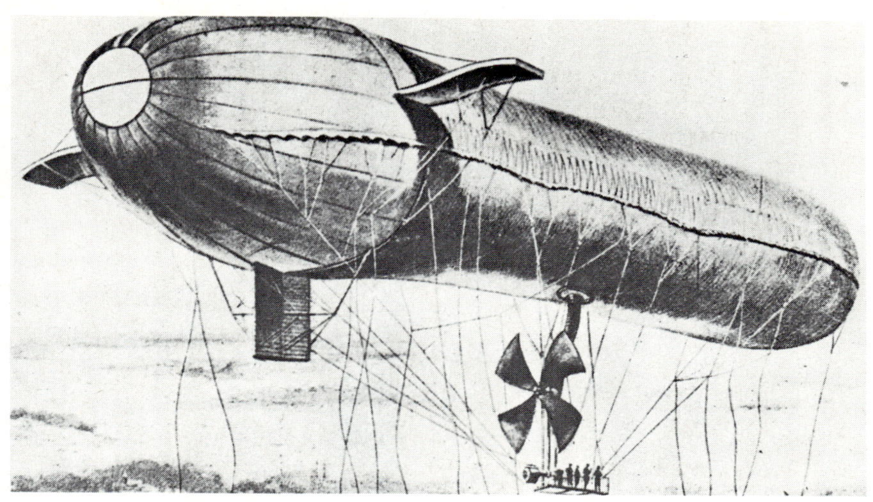

IZ-4259

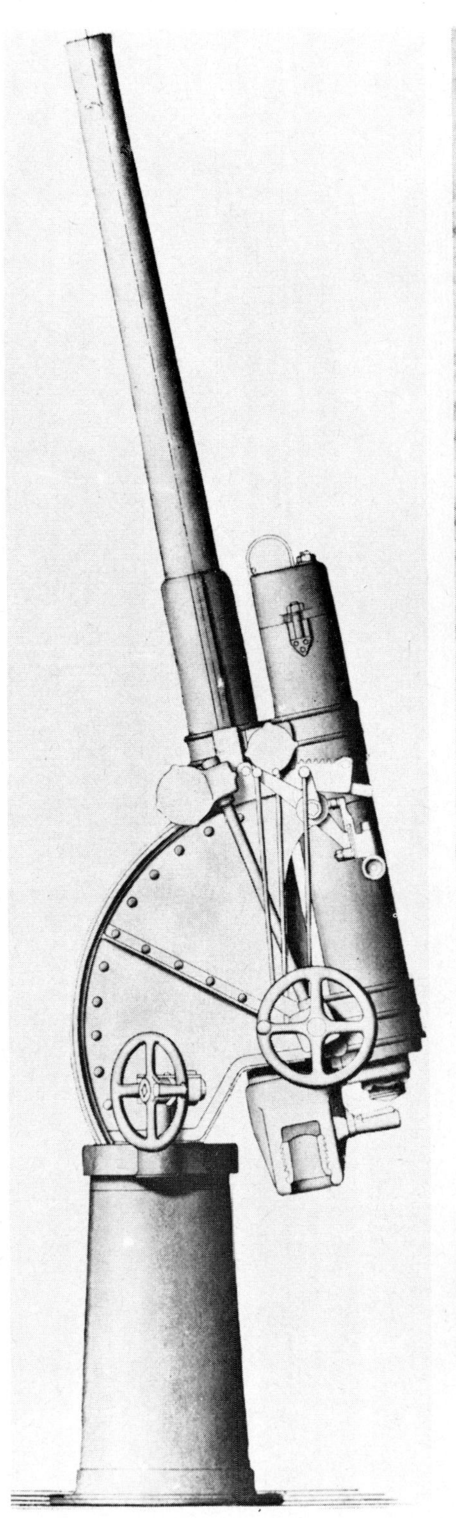

POLICE NOTICE
TAKE COVER

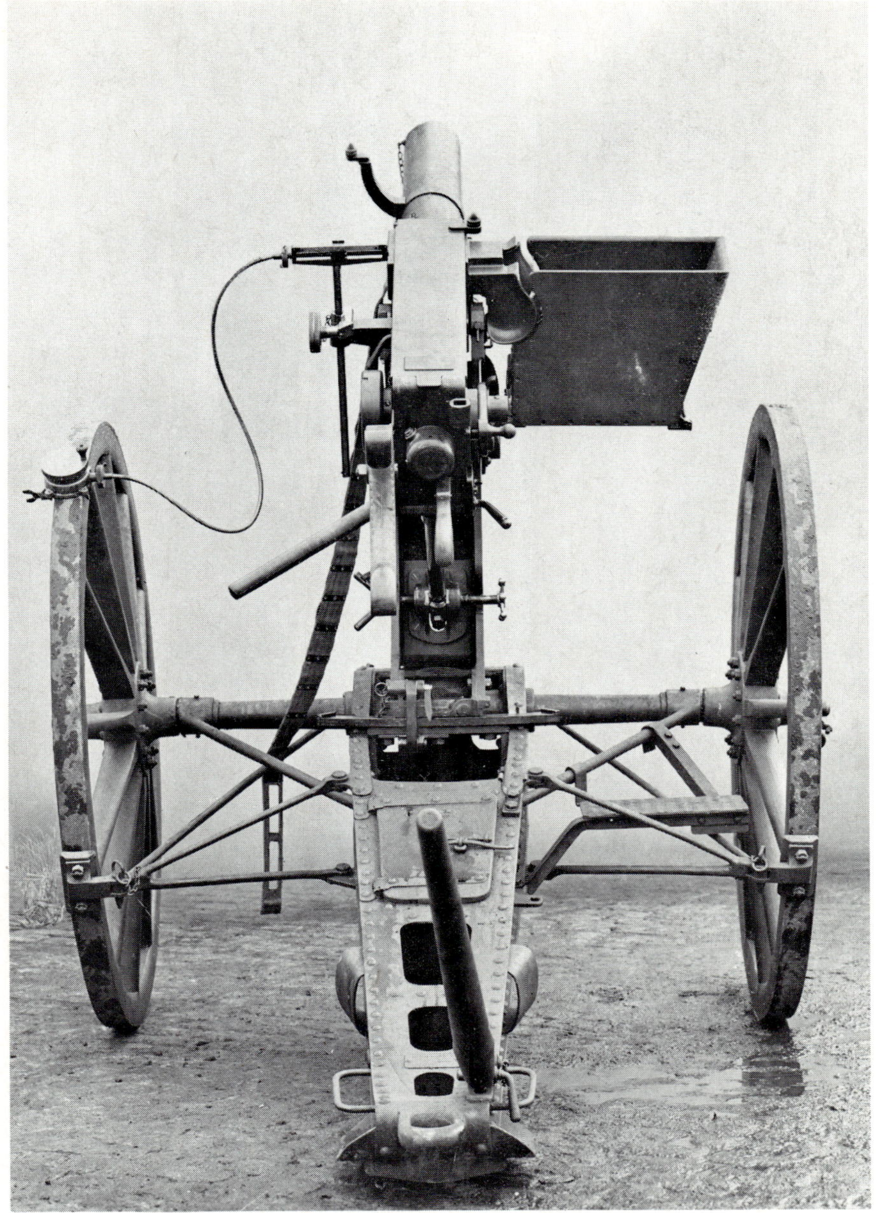

Far left: The Vickers, Son and Maxim 3-pounder balloon gun of 1910.

Left: The police were responsible for observation and reporting of raiders and also for warning the populace, which was done in a manner in keeping with the leisurely spirit of the age.

Above: The British one-pounder Pom-Pom on field carriage, modified for high-angle firing; approved in February 1914, it was the first anti-aircraft gun to enter British service.

Top: An AVRO aircraft of the type used to raid the Zeppelin Sheds at Friederichshavn in November 1914 in pursuance of the policy that an active offence was the best defence.

Above: The 3in 20cwt gun on Peerless lorry; introduced in this form in 1915 it was to remain in service until the early 1940s.

Top: The French 75mm auto-cannon on De Dion Bouton chassis, ready for the road.

Above: The auto-cannon in a prepared emplacement. Notice the complicated sighting apparatus.

Top: The 75mm gun was also adapted to ground mountings, since there were more guns than motor chassis. This was a British improvisation; the Paris defences used similar devices.

Above: The British 13-pounder Mark 4, a commercially-made gun which had been produced for foreign sale and then modified into an extemporary anti-aircraft weapon.

Top: A 13-pounder 9cwt gun in France. Notice that four men are occupied with sight-setting and laying.

Above left: The Brocq *Tachymetre* in use; it might have given an even better answer had the operators levelled it first.

Above right: Elementary sound detection on the German front in 1915.

Top: By 1918 matters had improved; this four-horn sound detector was a French model in use by the American AA Artillery.

Above: The BE2C, the standard fighter used against Zeppelins. No less than five airships fell to these machines.

Top: The Royal Naval Air Service AA gun battery being inspected by Grand Duke Michael of Russia in 1916.

Above: Grand Duke Michael, Sir Percy Scott and Commander Rawlinson at Kenwood House, Hampstead, headquarters of the RNAS guns.

IF ZEPPELINS drop Poison Gas Bombs in your neighbourhood are you and your family suitably protected from the danger of poison fumes? The purchase of a reliable respirator for each member of the household will at least ensure your peace of mind; it may save the lives of those dear to you. Freer's Respirators, which afford real protection from poison gases, are now being sold at COOPER & SON'S ESTABLISHMENT, KING STREET. These little "guardians" are fitted with medicated pads through which the air is filtered. Perfect breathing is, however, assured. These pads have only to be damped to be ready for action. Complete protection is given to the eyes, yet vision is not interfered with.

PRICE 2/6 EACH.

Top: Zeppelin L20, damaged over Scotland in May 1916, crashed into the Hafrsfjord in Norway on the way back to its base.

Above: With Zeppelins and gas in the news, some people couldn't resist the temptation . . .

Right: . . . while others relied on ridicule.

THE ACHIEVEMENT.

Count Zeppelin. "STANDS LONDON WHERE IT DID, MY CHILD?"
The Child. "YES, FATHER; MISSED IT AGAIN."
Count Zeppelin. "THEN YOU HAD NO SUCCESS?"
The Child. "OH, YES, FATHER; I'VE GOT HOME AGAIN."

Top: The Gotha, a more formidable threat than the Zeppelin.

Above: Air raid damage at Warrington Crescent, St John's Wood, March 1918. King George V and Queen Mary can be seen immediately above the left edge of the piano.

The last air raid on London for 1915 took place on 13 October. By this time the AA Defence Staff had come to some conclusions about 'ideal bombing conditions' of moon and weather and, as a result, the defences were placed in a state of readiness from 5th of the month onward. A ring of ground observers was stationed across Hertfordshire and Essex, aircraft were in readiness at Joyce Green, and six 13-pounder 9cwt guns on Peerless lorries, part of an AA Artillery Regiment assembling at Woolwich for service in France, were spaced across the northern edge of London. At midday on 13th five airships set out from Germany and at 17.30hr they were reported by a Naval patrol vessel off the Norfolk coast. Of this five, three reached London and two set off for the Midlands, finding no worthwhile targets and doing little or no damage. Of the London raiders, the first was L15 which was seen and fired on by one of the mobile guns as it passed over Broxbourne; it retaliated by dropping three bombs which landed so close as to blow the gunners off the mounting, though without seriously injuring any of them. It then swung across Edgware and back across Central London, dropping some thirty bombs from Charing Cross to Limehouse, after which it sailed away across Suffolk, heading for the North Sea. L15 had been seen and illuminated by searchlights while over London, and every available gun had fired, but without damaging it. The bombs, on the other hand, did considerable damage; 28 killed and 70 injured, with several buildings in the City and the East End destroyed.

The second airship of the group, L14 now appeared. The pilot had lost his bearings for a time and had passed to the west of London unobserved. He now came in, unexpectedly, from the south, to bomb Croydon, killing nine and injuring 15 and doing a great deal of damage to residential property.

Finally the L13, which had also gone astray, appeared over Woolwich Arsenal and, thinking he was over the Victoria Docks, dropped 5 explosive and 28 incendiary bombs. Remarkably, considering the potential of the target, relatively little damage was done, though four soldiers in a Woolwich barrack-room were killed. Again, all the guns had fired at these last two raiders, but their shrapnel was ineffective. The mobile 13-pounders on the northern outskirts had proved so useful that from then on, the northern environs of London became a 'finishing school' for army AA batteries en route to France, during their final mobilisation and training period at Woolwich.

Although the aircraft had had no success on this night, they were still regarded as having considerable potential, largely because in July 1915 the first aerial defeat of a Zeppelin had taken place over Ostend. Flight Sub-Lieutenant Warneford, flying a Moraine, managed to get above Zeppelin LZ37 and drop bombs on it. A violent explosion occurred and the Zeppelin fell into the sea in flames. This achievement was widely acclaimed, and Warneford was awarded the Victoria Cross. Ten days later, when collecting a new Farman biplane from a rear airfield, he was killed in a flying accident.

Admiral Scott had asked, in September 1915, for a force of 100 aircraft to be spread around London and the south-eastern counties. With sufficient aircraft aloft, no Zeppelin ought to get as far as London, but if any did, then the gun strength would be increased to ensure that such evaders would be given a suitable reception. But 100 aircraft was beyond the capacity of the Royal Naval Air Service and would necessitate the RFC increasing its strength. This, of course, was a golden opportunity for the RFC to expand, and the Army was quick to point out that if they were given the hundred aircraft and the men to operate them, they would be happy to take over the burden of air defence from the Navy, as had always been intended. Those elements of gun defence operated by the RNVR would be absorbed into the Army since, by this time, the naval guns were only a small proportion of the whole defence organisation. They were, moreover, being operated in a somewhat idiosyncratic fashion by Commander Rawlinson, and bringing them into the Army organisation would be an improvement in many ways.

In February 1916, therefore, the responsibility for AA defence passed entirely into the hands of the War Office, and their Home Defence Directorate unveiled a scheme which they had prepared in anticipation of this handover. This divided the country into a number of primary areas which had to be defended because of the targets within them, plus a number of ports and scattered munitions factories outside the defined areas. The distribution of guns was to be such that a raider would meet an increasing volume of fire as he approached the centre of any area. Mobile gun sections would also be deployed, their positions being changed frequently so as to exploit the possibility of surprising a raider who thought he knew where the defences were. In the defence of London Sir Percy Scott's proposals were accepted and expanded, resulting in a double circle of guns around London, five and nine miles from Charing Cross, with slight distortions to the outer circle to take in Woolwich Arsenal, the Royal Small Arms Factory Enfield, and the Royal Gunpowder Factory Waltham Abbey.

Outside the gun rings was an outer searchlight ring, primarily intended to guide defending aircraft by signalling, with the beam, in the direction of any reported raider. The whole scheme demanded 475 guns and 500 searchlights; when the War Office took control they found themselves in possession of 295 guns in the whole of the Kingdom, of which 53 were one-pounder pom-poms (which Scott had been unable to get rid of), 140 were 6-pounder Hotchkiss guns, 20 were 3-pounder Hotchkiss, and two were Naval 2-pounder pom-poms, none of which collection were considered to be of any operational value. In the course of being transferred from Naval stocks were another 80 guns which Scott had organised, but these turned out to be a heterogenous collection of oddities including four 6in guns on railway wagons, ten 4.7in, 28 French 75mm guns some on auto-cannon mounts and some on peculiar extemporised ground mounts, and, of course, the ubiquitous 10-pounder Russians still looking for a home. The Admiralty had also promised another 86 guns, and it is interesting to speculate on what they might have been, but in the event, most of these failed to appear since they were suddenly needed to arm merchant ships against U-Boats – which says much for their anti-aircraft potential.

One ingenious idea which was initiated at this time was the setting up of a 'trap position' or decoy in Epping Forest. A large area was wired off and prohibited to the public, the word being allowed to leak out that the area was now a new and secret explosive factory. In fact, the forest now contained a pattern of dim lights arranged to resemble a factory at night, but all it contained were the mobile guns of the RNAS 'Mobile Brigade', who drove out to man the trap when a raid threatened. They would set up their guns and then light the illuminations, hoping that some curious Zeppelin would be seduced from its path and lured within range of the guns. There is no record of the trap ever working, but it probably represents the first of several similar ideas which were employed during both wars.

So far the defence by aircraft had not been very successful, the reasons being that the aircraft available were incapable of catching or rising above the airships, that if they did get into position they had no suitable ammunition with which to engage the targets, and the pilots were quite inexperienced in night flying. Things gradually improved, but desperate measures were sometimes advocated; the commander of the RNAS station at Hendon published an order which said, in part,

> 'If the aeroplane fails to stop the airship by the time all the ammunition is expended, and the airship is still heading for London and shows no signs of being turned from her objective, then the pilot must decide to sacrifice himself and his machine and ram the airship at the utmost speed.'

Higher up the chain of command there was even more plain speaking, as when Lord Kitchener sent for the Director-General of Military Aeronautics and asked what was being done about the airship raids. Upon being told that the matter was (at that time) the responsibility of the RNAS and not the Army, 'K' replied, 'I don't care who has the responsibility. If there are any more Zeppelin raids and the Royal Flying Corps do not interfere with them, I shall hold YOU responsible.' As a result of that blast, the RFC adopted a similar policy to that of the Royal Artillery, and when squadrons were in their final stages of training, preparatory to going to France, they were sent to stations at Hainault, Sutton's Farm, Farningham and Joyce Green to join the defensive force. In addition, ten airfields around London were specially reinforced with two BE2C fighters each, with the pilots and observers specially trained in night flying.

The principal armament for the flyers at the end of 1915 was the Ranken Explosive Dart or the 16lb Cooper bomb, both of which were supposed to be dropped from above so as to explode in contact with the airship frame, thus puncturing and igniting the gasbags. This method of attack was favoured because of the erroneous belief (carefully fostered by the Germans in magazine articles and reports) that the area between the gasbag and the outer skin of the Zeppelin was filled with some inert gas as a protection against fire-raising by incendiary bullets. It was an academic point anyway, since in 1914 there were no incendiary bullets, but the idea was enough to discourage the use of machine guns and encourage the use of drop bombs. In any case, since machine guns only had solid ball ammunition, the most they could hope to achieve was to riddle the gasbags and so perhaps force the Zeppelin to descend into the sea on his way home.

But ever since the start of the war a Mr J. F. Buckingham, a Coventry engineer, had been working on a design of an incendiary bullet to defeat airships, a bullet which used a filling of phosphorus as the active agent. In late 1915 the design was perfected and issues began. It was followed by a design of tracer bullet developed by the Royal Laboratory at Woolwich Arsenal and subsequently manufactured in a factory owned by Messrs Aerators, Ltd, from which the bullet acquired its name the 'Sparklet' bullet. Primarily intended to give aerial gunners an indication of the track their bullets were taking, it also had a slight incendiary effect. A third design came from Commander Brock of the Brock fireworks family, this one being intended to explode after passing through the outer skin of the Zeppelin and thus defeat the inert gas layer. Finally came the Pomeroy bullet, an ordinary 0.303 bullet with a tiny copper tube containing detonating composition inserted into the nose. By mid-1916 most of these were in production, Lewis guns were carried on aircraft, and the days of the Zeppelin were numbered. The Lewis gun drum was loaded with a combination of bullet types so that the Sparklet indicated the trajectory, the Brock blew a hole in the fabric, and the Buckingham and Pomeroy bullets ignited the escaping hydrogen. Using this combination Lieutenant Leefe Robinson shot down the Schütte-Lanz airship SL11 near Cuffley on 3 September 1916, for which he too received the Victoria Cross. (He later returned to serve in France, was shot down and made prisoner for the rest of the war. He then repatriated to England in December 1918 in poor health, contracted influenza in the great epidemic, and died on 17 January 1919.) A few days later Second-Lieutenant Alfred de Bath Brandon (RFC Special Reserve) shot L33 but failed to ignite the gas; but the airship commander decided that return to Germany was impossible and force-landed the Zeppelin in Essex. For this Brandon added the DSO to his decorations, having previously been awarded the MC for his part in the destruction of L15. And on that same night Second-Lieutenant F. Sowrey caught L32, 'hosed it with a stream of fire', to quote one eyewitness, and brought it down in flames close to Billericay.

In January 1917, confident that the defences now had the measure of the Zeppelin, a reduction in the strength of those defences was proposed. The history of anti-aircraft defence, anywhere and at any time, shows that it never pays to become too efficient, or somebody will inevitably tamper with the winning combination. This time it was the Admiralty demanding a proportion of the gun production earmarked for the air defences so that they could be used to arm merchant ships against U-Boat attacks. The number of guns then allotted to London was 84, and this was now reduced to 65, all guns above that number being removed. By February the strength stood at 48 3in, 16 75mm mobile and static, one 12-pounder and one 3.5in (an odd weapon which appears in no artillery records and was probably an experimental weapon). In similar manner, the aircraft strength was reduced by sending two squadrons to France.

The Zeppelin raids were declining, as the Germans came to realise that the airship was no longer a viable weapon, and the last was to take place in October 1917. But something worse was on the way; the twin-engined Gotha bombing aircraft. On 25 May sixteen Gothas appeared over the Essex coast, turned south because London was obscured by heavy cloud, and bombed Folkestone and Shornecliffe with heavy loss of life. While this was still being discussed and argued about, on 13 June 1919 a squadron of 14 Gothas flew up the Thames in broad daylight, in diamond formation. They bombed Eltham, the Royal Albert Docks, Liverpool Street Station, Southwark and Dalston. In the space of two minutes, 72 bombs showered down on Liverpool Street. The Upper North Street School in Poplar received a 50kg bomb through the roof which tore through the building to ground level before detonating; 18 children were killed. The Cowper Street School in the City Road had a remarkable escape when a similar bomb passed through five crowded floors and failed to detonate. A total of 162 people were killed and 432 injured in this brief raid. Ninety-two pilots took to the air but few saw the raiders and fewer still came within range of them; the raiders escaped unhurt.

As might be imagined, this raid set the country in an uproar. Plans were put forward for increasing the strength of the Royal Flying Corps, but little concrete action was taken other than to shuffle some of the guns around to give better protection to the eastern approaches to London. Before much else had been done the Gothas returned on 7 July, 21 aircraft flying across the East End and the City bombing as they went. Fifty-four were killed and 190 injured, though subsequent analysis revealed that 10 of the dead and 55 of the injured had been victims of falling shell splinters or unexploded shells from the AA defences. Again, 95 pilots in 21 different kinds of aeroplane took to the air, but only one Gotha was shot down and that almost accidentally; it was found limping along the coast near the North Foreland and was shot into the sea by an aircraft of 50 Home Defence Squadron, a formation which was not, in fact, concerned with the defence of London at all.

The result of this second daylight assault was an even greater public uproar. The War Cabinet met immediately and demanded the return of the two squadrons of aircraft from France. Haig, predictably, protested that the whole of the Western Front would collapse about his ears, the request was halved, and one squadron was returned, while another which had been about to leave for France was diverted to home defence. The next response of the War Cabinet was equally predictable; they set up a committee to look into the matter.

And just this once, this stereotyped response was probably the best thing they could have done, since the 'committee' virtually finished up as a one-man show in the person of Lieutenant-General J. C. Smuts, a remarkable man by anybody's standards. Smuts had the right kind of trained, analytical mind and the report he drew up was one of the fundamental documents which led to the foundation of the Royal Air Force in the following year. He pointed out that the prime fault in the system of defence was that it had been built up against the Zeppelin which was, in many respects, an easy target. Searchlights could easily find it, could easily hold it; it was a big target for the guns and a vulnerable one; and if one aircraft, with incendiary and explosive ammunition got within range, it was as good as destroyed. Aircraft, on the other hand, were a harder proposition; more difficult for searchlights to find and follow, more difficult for guns to hit, faster and more agile, and by no means an easy target for a lone fighter if, as was usual, the bombers flew in formation. Smuts' solution was to fire massive barrages of shells into the track of the bombers so as to break up their formations, and to deploy the fighters in formations instead of singly, so that they too could break up bomber groups and then pick off individuals while protecting each other.

Action followed rapidly. Brigadier-General E. B. Ashmore was brought home from France to become the head of the new London Air Defence Area (LADA). Ashmore viewed his new appointment with a wry sense of humour; in his memoirs he observed that 'we of the Expeditionary Force were inclined to look on the troubles of London somewhat light-heartedly. The fact that I was exchanging the comparative safety of the front for the probability of being hanged in the streets of London did not worry me.'

Ashmore's first step was to set up a barrier line of guns some twenty miles out of London to the east. Moving the guns out to this distance meant that the fighters had a free hand on both sides of the gun line; they could, if they could find them, attack raiders coming over the coast, while other fighters on patrol behind the gun line would be able to pick off the Gothas one by one as their formations were broken up by gunfire. Searchlights and gun sites were provided with large moveable arrows, easily visible from the air, which were to be pointed towards any enemy aircraft in sight. This took advantage of the superior visibility of the ground observers over that of the pilots and ensured that fighters could be steered in the right direction.

To make sure that there would be fighters, three new squadrons began forming: 44 Squadron (Sopwith two-seaters) at Hainault, 61 (Sopwith Pups) at Rochford and 112 (Sopwith Pups) at Throwley, south of Faversham. Additional Home Defence Squadrons in Essex and Sussex were nominated as part of the London force and placed at Ashmore's disposal. A final innovation was to detail a number of wireless-equipped aircraft as 'trackers' whose sole job was to keep on the trail of the raiders and wireless their position and course back to the ground at intervals.

Lieutenant-Colonel Simon, RE, who was the AA Defence Commander, London, had on 21 June put forward a scheme of improvement involving 45 more guns on the outskirts so as to present an enemy with a barrier of shells, but this had been turned down. On 16 July he put forward another scheme for locating a ring of guns on a 25-mile radius from Charing Cross to break up enemy formations and allow the fighters to deal with them more easily. Lord French, Commander-in-Chief, endorsed this scheme and pressed it strongly to the War Cabinet, requesting 110 additional guns, but the Cabinet replied that the flow of guns to the Merchant Navy could not be impeded, and if French wanted guns he had better go and find them from places less likely to be attacked. Eventually 34 guns were found, 10 from the west side of London and 24 from the provinces.

These new measures had immediate effect. On 12 August a nine-Gotha flight found a squadron of fighters rising in its path, turned about, jettisoned its bombs and fled. On 22 August a force of Gothas crossed the coast at Margate and met with such a hot reception that they abandoned their plans and set about getting rid of their bombs on any target which presented itself on their way home. Two were shot down by aircraft from Manston, another fell to the Thanet Gun defences, and a constant stream of gunfire pursued them along the coast to Dover, where more fighters appeared and chased them back to Belgium. This reception so daunted the German commander that he reported that 'the increased strength and better organisation of the defences has now made it inadvisable to attack unless with machines which can fly loaded at over 10,000 feet or under cover of darkness'. This marked the virtual end of daylight raiding.

The defences were alert to the possibility of air raids taking place at night – intelligence sources had reported that one German bomber squadron was already practising night flying – but they were not looking forward to the idea with much enthusiasm. In the first place the aeroplanes which had operated successfully against the Zeppelins were incapable of catching the faster Gothas, and the scouting and fighter planes with the necessary higher performance were, in official eyes, not suited to night operation because of their higher landing speeds. This theory was, fortunately, refuted by some practical pilots who took Sopwith Camels (probably the most touchy of all the fighters) and flew them at night, landing successfully in darkness relieved only by paraffin flares. Another problem was that of attempting accurate gunfire from the ground, but this was solved by developing a barrage system. Colonel Buckle, in charge of the Chatham Gun Defences evolved a method of deducing the raiders position from sound bearings and then distributing the gunfire to place a 2,500-foot high curtain of bursting shells across their path.

The first indication of the new German technique was revealed on 3 September with an attack which was spotted at 10.35pm off the North Foreland. Shortly afterwards three or four Gothas appeared over Chatham; due to some unexplained delay in passing the warning, no alarm had been sounded and two 100lb bombs landed on the Drill Hall of the Naval Barracks, killing 130 naval ratings and wounding another 88. Several guns opened fire and sixteen fighters were sent up, but they saw nothing of the enemy. Among these fighters was Major Murlis-Green of 44 Squadron accompanied by Captain Brand and Lieutenant Banks, all flying Sopwith Camels. This was the first time that fighters of this type were flown at night and, much against general expectation, they landed the machines safely, thus clearing the way for future development of high-performance machines at night.

On the following night a force of 10 Gothas attacked London, while another 16 bombed a variety of targets in south-east England including Dover and Margate. It was in this raid that a bomb landed close to Cleopatra's Needle, leaving marks which can still be seen today. Eight hundred shells were fired by the defences and one aircraft was brought down by a gun at Chatham. Eighteen fighter aircraft, including four Camels, went up but none made contact with the enemy.

The next day saw a worried War Cabinet discussing what could be done and calling for a further report from General Smuts. He, as had Scott before him, forthrightly observed that the best defence would be to go out and attack the German airfields and aircraft factories, but in default of that he suggested a balloon barrage, a line of balloons carrying an 'apron' of wire in the sky to force the aircraft so high that accurate bombing would be impossible. Moreover, the sudden appearance of balloons in their path would break up formations so that the fighters could pick them off more easily.

This idea was not entirely new; it had been suggested, several times in fact, by some of the myriad amateur inventors who besieged the Munitions Inventions Department with bright ideas, but they had all proposed hanging a huge steel net around London, and no balloon was capable of supporting that sort of load. (General Ashmore had more than his fair share of lunatic notions passed to him by the MID; of one, which proposed floodlighting the whole of southern England to silhouette the raiders for the benefit of fighters above them, he observed that it would have been cheaper and easier to move London. Another suggestion was to blow carborundum powder into the air to foul the engines of raiders. An engine was set up and started and carborundum was blown at it. 'The more the engine got, the better it liked it', Ashmore reported.)

But the new idea was simply to tie a number of balloons together with long horizontal wires and then hang vertical wires beneath in the form of a screen; less weight, but still a formidable obstacle, especially at night. Twenty 'aprons' were proposed and authorised, but only ten, of five balloons each were installed on a line between Tottenham–Wanstead–Barking–Plumstead and Lewisham. The remainder of the planned ten were victims of a form of parsimony frequent in defence spending; a raid in May 1918 was severely mauled by the defences and, as a result, the Air Council decided that what they had was good enough and there was no call to implement the remaining aprons.

While this system was being implemented, a new scheme of barrage fire was worked out. The London sky was divided into squares and patterns of barrage were calculated for each square to produce a curtain of shell bursts some 2,500 feet deep at various heights. These areas were declared 'out of bounds' to aircraft, and any aircraft seen or heard in them was assumed to be hostile and could be shot at instantly and without question.

Colonel Thompson of the Thanet Gun Defences devised an improvement to this, a system of height observation and control which, when he put it into operation, proved so effective that his guns shot down two Gothas. Strange to say (or perhaps not) he was immediately rebuked by the War Office for using an unauthorised method, but General Ashmore stepped in and took responsibility. The War Office then retaliated by forbidding the use of barrage fire at all and hamstrung some of Ashmore's gunsites by refusing to provide them with telephones. At this point Lord French intervened and gave General Ashmore a free hand. Colonel Thompson's system was standardised and, indeed, was to remain the standard system until it was replaced by radar sets in the latter part of the Second World War.

On 19 October 1917 a Zeppelin raid was mounted against England which was to go down in history. Eleven airships set out, intending to raid Sheffield and the north Midlands, but unknown to the airship commanders the weather began to deteriorate rapidly, and extremely high winds began to blow in the upper air levels. At 16,000 feet, at which the Zeppelins were flying, a wind of 80mph was blowing almost due north-south. Yet at ground level there was hardly any wind and a thick layer of mist which prevented the airship navigators from seeing the ground, thus checking their progress. As a result the airship's course took on a distinct southerly bias; their rendezvous point was Flamborough Head, but they actually made their landfall just north of Skegness, about sixty miles too far south. After turning inland, they assumed that they were on course across Yorkshire for Sheffield; in fact they were being swept south-west across Lincolnshire and were set fair for London at high speed.

The alarm was passed to the defences, but due to the dense mist, the searchlights were unable to pick anything out of the sky; conversely, there was a strong probability that the lights would have a floodlighting effect in the mist and thus announce their presence, and hence the presence of a target, to the raiders, so General Ashmore ordered a general dousing of searchlights. This had the desired effect; the Zeppelin navigators could see nothing below them except odd small patches of diffused light and were unable to make any assessment of their position. But it had an unfortunate byproduct when the exasperated commander of L45 decided to try to 'wake up the defences' by pitching out bombs at intervals; this, he hoped, might result in a display of lights or gunfire and might help them to fix their position. As it happened L45 was actually over London when this decision was taken, and the pitched-out bombs landed on a line from Hendon to Cricklewood, outside Swan & Edgar's in Piccadilly, to Camberwell and Lewisham, killing 34 people and injuring 49. There was a good deal of ill-feeling on the following day, when questions were asked about the apparent failure of the defences to retaliate; eventually Ashmore was able to explain his policy and the critics were satisfied.

The other airships of the raid missed London completely, but the weather had them in its grip and their adventures were by no means over. One managed to struggle home across the North Sea, two crossed Holland and one Belgium to get home safely, while three made wide southerly swings across northern France and crossed the front line to reach home, though one was damaged on landing. Two were shot down in France; a third, seeing one of the shot-down ships on the ground, assumed he must be home and began to land alongside. At the last moment he realised his mistake and ascended rapidly; he then crash-landed rather roughly a few miles away and tore off one gondola in the process, the commander and fifteen of the crew leaping clear of the wrecked car. Relieved of this weight, the ship soared into the sky again and was blown south across France, finally crossing the Mediterranean coast; it was never seen again. The last of the raiding force also found itself in the south of France, ran out of fuel and landed, just in time to see the carless drifter pass overhead on its way out to sea. What began as a raid ended as an expensive fiasco which almost put an end to the Zeppelin as a viable weapon.

Early in December 1917 a new threat appeared; the German Air Force had now begun to use the Giant Gotha, an enormous four-engined biplane. These could carry a bomb-load of 2,000kg either as individual 100kg bombs or as a brace of 1,000kg bombs slung externally and were well-endowed with protective machine guns. Whether this latter feature led to feelings of self-sufficiency is not recorded, but certainly the first 'Giant' to attack England did so as an individual, crossing the coast near Ramsgate on the night of 5/6 December and dropping a few ineffectual bombs before returning home again. Some hours after this a force of 15 Gothas approached the coast, then split up, some going the usual route up the Thames Estuary to bomb Sheerness while six swung in a loop across Kent and managed to get to London while the defences were concentrating on the river route. One unusual feature of this raid was that it was much later than usual; the raiders did not cross the coast until 2.00am, by which time most of the defence forces had decided that there was nothing likely to happen and had settled down for a quiet night. Another unusual point was that the bomb-loads were mostly incendiary bombs; as a result the loss of life was minimal but the damage to property sizeable.

The defences did very well; the barrage fire had discouraged the Sheerness raiders from coming further up the river, and two Gothas were damaged sufficiently for them to have to make forced landings. One landed near Canterbury and was burned by its crew; the other landed near Rochford and was inadvertently burned by an RFC airman who, placed on guard, succumbed to curiosity and pressed the trigger of the German flare pistol 'to see if it was loaded'. It was. A third Gotha was seen to fall into the sea after clearing the coast and is assumed to have been damaged by gunfire.

It was 18 December when the first 'Giant' reached London, accompanied by six Gothas; the Giant dropped a single 300kg bomb which landed in Eaton Square and made a large hole without doing any more damage. One of the Gothas was shot down over Folkestone by Major Murlis-Green, the Camel pioneer.

Unfortunately, this one success was by no means the sort of return which had been expected from the night fighters. After this raid Ashmore did some analysis which showed that for 131 sorties flown the pilots had only managed to see the enemy on eight occasions, which produced three combats, of which only one was successful. In his words, 'A large number of pilots were risking their necks for pitifully small results'. His conclusion was that while the aviators were as efficient as could be expected, once they got into the air, they were being let down by poor support from the ground.

While this was being considered an interesting technical point appeared. On several occasions in January and February 1918 the Giant Gothas came over England and were attacked by fighter aircraft; although they closed, aimed and fired their guns, the Giants flew on unharmed. It was eventually realised that the fault lay in the form of gunsight in use, two vertical posts set a fixed distance apart. When the wingspan of the Gotha filled this gap, the pilot opened fire and his bullets struck their target. But the early Gotha had a wingspan of 75 feet, so that when the Giant Gotha was 'fitted in' between the two posts, due to its much greater wingspan it was actually about three times further away and the trajectory of the bullets fell below it.

General Ashmore now reasoned that the tools of the defence, the actual guns and aircraft, were as good as they were ever likely to be; the flaw lay in their application. In spite of arrows on the ground by day and searchlight indicators by night, the fact remained that once the fighter got off the ground he was no longer under anyone's effective control, and any interception he made was more by luck than good management. What was needed was wireless communication with the pilot, and by the beginning of 1918 experiments in progress showed that this was no longer a pipe-dream but something which could be made to work. If it could be made to work, the next problem was what to tell the pilots; because the biggest flaw in the whole system was the method of reporting the movement of raiders. The distribution of observers was uneven, and so was their performance; as Ashmore later said, the receipt of a report from an observer told him that there was an aircraft in that area, but the absence of a report from an area was no guarantee that there were no aircraft there. By collating reports gathered from observers it was possible, two or three days after a raid, to produce an elegant and accurate plot of exactly where the aircraft had been at any moment, but the information was no use by that time; it was wanted while the raid was on, and the telephone reporting system then in use could not produce that sort of result. In theory, the distant observer should have been able to pick up a telephone, give the priority call 'Air Bandit', and be connected directly to the report centre at Horse Guards in London; but delays in connection meant that the best reporting time was three minutes and the average was ten or twelve minutes. General Ashmore now set out on a massive re-organisation of his observer and reporting system, a task which, in many ways, was a preview of his work six years later in setting up the Observer Corps.

Other moves made at the end of 1917 were the hastening of the balloon aprons around the eastern outskirts of London, setting them at 8,000 feet to force the bombers up and thus keep them into a

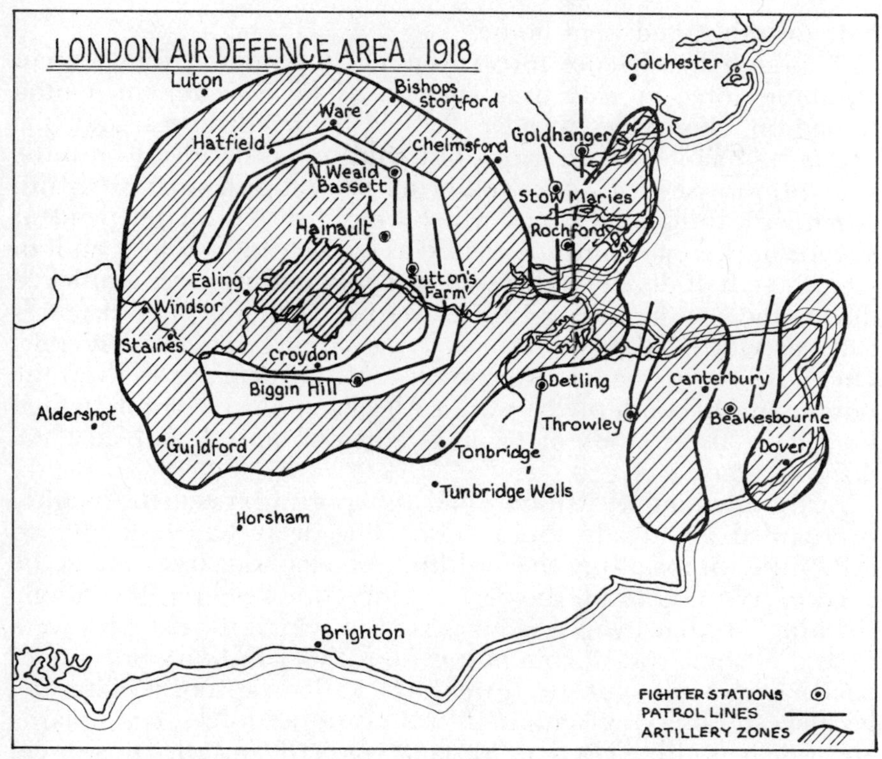

relatively restricted belt of altitude, which made less sky for the fighters to search. Patrol lines were set up for the fighters, crossing the most likely enemy approach lanes and patrolling at 8, 9, 10 and 11,000 feet, and the area beneath these patrol lines was emptied of guns but packed with searchlights. In an endeavour to make the searchlight units more efficient by better motivation they were placed under command of the local squadron for tactical training.

As 1918 began the London Defences mustered 249 guns, 323 searchlights, 89 day fighters, 63 night fighters and a number of wireless-equipped 'trackers'. And on 28 January raiding began again when three Gothas flew up the Thames, spread out on both sides of the river to confuse the listening posts. One was shot down as it was returning to the coast after dropping its bombs. Shortly after this a single Giant flew in, heading for London. It was caught over Essex by a Bristol Fighter, one of the newer machines used by the defence squadrons, but the Giant carried five machine guns and was a steady gun platform, and the fighter was beaten off, sustaining a punctured fuel tank and a wounded observer. After this the Giant continued in to Central London and dropped a number of bombs, one of which landed on a public air-raid shelter in Long Acre killing 37 and wounding another 89 people. It then turned about, evaded two lots of barrage fire, escaped another fighter, sliced through a balloon cable, and went home.

Although the defence forces were not to know it, the German bombing force at this time was at its lowest ebb; the Gotha Squadron, Kampfgeschwader 3, had suffered losses and the surviving members were worn out, and it was decided to rest the squadron for several weeks and bring it up to full strength again. Meanwhile the Giant Gothas, which were formed in an independent squadron, were to continue to raid as opportunity offered, and, in fact, these half-dozen Giants were the only raiding force employed during the early months of 1918. Nevertheless, they kept the defences fully stretched, for, certainly at first, they appeared to be invincible. On 16 February one Giant penetrated all the defences to drop the largest single bomb of the war, a 1,000kg explosive bomb, which landed in thegrounds of Chelsea Hospital and demolished the doctor's house.

By the late summer Ashmore had his reporting system thoroughly overhauled and ready to function. The delay had been due to difficulties in installing the multitude of telephone lines and to the need to try to build up the new system while keeping the old one working, so that there was no period in which the defences were devoid of some sort of communication. Every military unit under LADA command – gunsite, searchlight, balloon apron, aerodrome – became an observing station, as well as police forces, coastguards and, where nothing else was available, specially installed posts were manned with either police or medically downgraded soldiers. All these myriad of eyes were connected by telephone to one of 25 'sub-control points'. Each sub-control featured a large-scale map laid on a table, around which were a number of 'plotters' who were in direct communication with a group of observers. As the observers reported sight or sound of aircraft, so the plotters would place markers on the map to correspond, moving them to keep pace with the constant flow of information. One important feature of this system was that every telephone line was permanently connected; it did not pass through any telephone exchange, there was no possibility of being disconnected, and there was no waiting for connections.

Above the map table sat 'tellers' who were, in their turn, in direct communication by telephone with the LADA control room. This duplicated the sub-control but on a larger scale, with a map table which encompassed the whole of the LADA area. The plotters at this table were being fed with information from the tellers of two or three sub-control rooms, and they also placed markers on the map to indicate the progress of the raiders. An ingenious detail was the provision of a large clock, its face divided into coloured segments; as the minute hand entered a segment, so the markers placed on the table were of that particular colour, so that watchers could immediately distinguish new information from old.

In a gallery overlooking the table sat Major-General Ashmore, accompanied by officers controlling the gun defences and the fighter aircraft, as well as representatives of the police and fire sevices. From the picture built up on the map, instructions were sent to guns and fighter airfields, to the balloon aprons, and to police stations for warning purposes. From the fighter commander in the gallery a direct line ran to a powerful wireless transmitter near Biggin Hill from which orders were relayed directly to flight commanders in the air, for by the end of May the long-awaited wireless link had been perfected and was installed in selected aircraft. This arrangement was satisfactory for day work, since it would get the flight within visual pick-up distance of a raid; at night, a further refinement was the provision of short-range transmitters on the flight commander's machine and receivers in every fighter, so that the commands emanating from LADA control would be relayed to every machine in the air in a matter of minutes. Frequent exercises of the whole system soon tuned it to a perfect pitch, but, unfortunately, the whole splendid machine never went into action in earnest. The last German bomber had flown over England on 19 May 1918, four months before the LADA system got into operation. The last sortie of all was, remarkably enough, by Zeppelins. In August, five Zeppelins appeared off the Norfolk coast, and one actually crossed the coast for a few minutes, near Yarmouth. All the bombs dropped landed in the sea, and the flagship, L70, which was commanded by Fregatten-Kapitan Strasser, Commander of the Naval Airship Service, was shot down in flames; a second ship, L65, had a close escape when the fighter's guns jammed as it was closing in, a misfortune which prevented the fighter's crew, Major Cadbury and Captain Leckie, from achieving the distinction of downing two airships in one sortie.

Although no raider crossed the English coast after that, one more Zeppelin was to be shot down by a Royal Air Force fighter, and that in unusual circumstances. By way of moving the defensive system outwards, an experiment had been set up in conjunction with the Royal Navy, in which a destroyer patrolled the North Sea towing behind it a barge with an extended flat deck upon which sat a Sopwith Camel fighter. When an enemy aircraft was seen, the destroyer clapped on all speed to build up a rush of air over the barge, and the Camel took off to give battle. Once battle was over, the fighter then flew to either England or Belgium, whichever was closer, and landed on a convenient aerodrome, while the destroyer went back to port to collect a fresh Camel. On 11 August this combination was on patrol in the North Sea when a Zeppelin was sighted. Whether it was heading for an attack on England or merely doing a routine patrol over the North Sea is not clear, but in any event the destroyer did not wait to ask; Lieutenant S. D. Culley took off from his barge and shot the Zeppelin into the sea near Borkum Reef.

3 THE DOLDRUMS

While the raids on London waxed and waned and the defenders found their feet, a similar process was taking place across the Channel. Although the German Army owned a handful of guns at the start of the war and had rapidly converted several hundred captured weapons, they had no sort of defensive organisation. A French bombing raid on Freiburg in December 1914 caused a considerable outcry, particularly from factories involved in war production, and in the words of one critic 'local defences were hurriedly provided for the individual places that made most noise' without much thought being given to building up a systematic organisation. One bar to progress was the division of Germany into semi-autonomous states; each was responsible for its own defence without reference to its neighbouring states, and since the telephone system was similarly fragmented the passage of information across the country to warn of coming aircraft was a good deal slower than the aircraft themselves.

In the middle of 1915 an Inspector of Home Air Defence was appointed. But since he had no staff and little material at his disposal, and since the post was advisory rather than executive, he had an uphill task in persuading the various authorities to take heed of his ideas. Eventually his limitations were recognised, and he was given a staff and some authority, and his first major step was to set up a double cordon of trained observers behind the German front line to spot and report incoming aircraft. These observers, though, were primarily allied to the Army anti-aircraft artillery in the battle zone. Once aircraft passed this barrier they were relatively safe, since observers in the interior of the country were few, poorly trained, and with poor lines of communication. On seeing an aircraft all they could do was report it to the nearest military unit, and if that unit was not directly concerned with air defence – and few were – then the message was passed on until it finally arrived in the hands of someone who could do something about it. Frequently this chain collapsed – messages were garbled in repetition, or failed to get far enough, or arrived too late – and there were several occasions when French aircraft raided an unwarned target.

In 1916 therefore there was a sweeping reorganisation when the *Luftstreitkraft* – Air Combat Force – was founded on 8 October, with

General von Höppner in command. All the various armed service branches involved in aerial warfare – the Air Force, Army Zeppelins, balloons, meteorological service and anti-aircraft artillery – were brought under a single commander and welded into a new arm of the services. Included in von Höppner's brief were the Home Air Defences, and the Inspector of Home Air Defences was now given executive powers. A school of air raid reporting was set up to train observers and establish a nationwide reporting system, while a gunnery school was set up at Ostend to which the home defence batteries could be sent to obtain practice against live targets – British and French aircraft. Nine squadrons of fighters were earmarked for home defence, and these were split up into flights and sited near likely targets and vulnerable points. At first they were as disorganised as their British equivalents; they took off on the intimation that raiders were about, and once their wheels left the ground they became a bunch of individualists, hunting around the sky for a target. But improvements in communication were rapid and soon aircraft fitted with radio were provided for patrol leaders. This enabled directions to be given after take-off and the leader could then command his patrol by simple visual signals and take them to the scene of a raid. The greater flexibility allowed by this system permitted aircraft to be concentrated at a smaller number of airfields, since concentration in a threatened area could be achieved quite quickly and with greater certainty than under the scattered flight system.

A form of balloon defence was also instituted but since it consisted solely of individual kite balloons, without the inter-linking apron of the British system, it was of little use. It seems to have deterred some Allied pilots from low level attacks and forced them up to a height at which the gun defences could deal with them, but it was not as effective an obstacle as the London apron.

By the end of the war the Germans had 2,576 guns deployed in addition to the fighter aircraft, and the Allied air forces had suffered in proportion, their average losses being 4.6 per cent by day and 1.5 per cent by night. Had the situation within Germany not deteriorated during 1918, with shortages of raw materials and fuel, drafting-out of skilled men to make up numbers at the front, and similar obstacles to success, the Allied losses might well have been greater.

On the other side of the front the French seem to have put more faith in artillery than they did in aircraft, though this arose largely because the output of aircraft was never sufficient to supply the squadrons at the front and have a surplus to provide a defensive force. In 1915 Commander Rawlinson reported to the Admiralty on the defensive system protecting Paris, with a view to using this as a guide to setting up the London defences, and he noted that at that time there were 127 guns, 88 machine guns and 41 searchlights in use, with another 80 guns about to be added. There were also 60 aircraft, some flying standing patrols over and around the city with others in constant readiness, but this number dwindled rapidly as they were taken for replacement of front-line squadron losses. The guns were gradually moved so as to form a belt some distance from the city to the north, only eight guns remaining inside the city itself. A balloon defence system was provided, but, according to contemporary observers it was of little use since it did not use aprons and was incapable of reaching an effective height. Fortunately the Germans, after some attacks in 1915 and 1916, left Paris alone for a long period, and it was not until early 1918, after a particularly bad raid had killed and wounded over 200 people, that interest in the defences was rekindled. Now the roles were reversed, and General Ashmore was sent to Paris in order to give the French the benefits of British experience, largely in the matter of observing and tracking organisations. While many of his suggestions and recommendations were approved, little was done before the war ended.

As an omen of things to come, though, the contrast between German air raids and German long-range artillery is worth remarking. The total casualties attributable to air raids on Paris throughout the war were 266 killed and 603 wounded. The 28cm Paris Gun, firing at a range of 76 miles, dropped 303 shells in and around the city in the course of 44 days of bombardment in 1918 and killed 256 people, wounding 620.

In contrast to their Allies, the American Expeditionary Force had a hard row to hoe in order to catch up in the air defence field once they got into the war. During 1915-16 the US Army had placed great reliance on the 3in M1916 field gun, with its 53-degree elevation, to provide defence for the field army, while the Ordnance Department had adapted the 3in M1902 seacoast gun to a static high angle mounting for use around dockyards and naval bases. In May 1916 contracts for this gun were placed and by April 1919 one hundred and sixteen had been built and emplaced. But even before the Americans entered the war it was apparent that the M1916 field gun was unlikely to proved an efficient answer to the mobile defence requirements, and so the Modified Improved Anti-Aircraft Gun Carriage M1917 was devised, a structure of steel girders set on a turntable into which a field gun barrel could be fitted to give adequate elevation and all-round traverse. As a static device it would probably have been no worse than some of the similar improvised mountings then in use in Europe, but this was meant to be mobile, transportable on a trailer. In fact the operative word was 'transportable' rather than 'mobile' since it had to be carried partially dismantled and then erected at the desired site. But since nothing better was available, 50 were built in 1917; they were completed after American entry into the war and were then shipped to France to be fitted with 75mm M1897 gun barrels, provided from

French stocks.

The next design was to mount the 3in M1916 gun on a pedestal on the back of a 1½-ton White truck; twenty-six of these were built and sent to the AEF in France, while numbers of 75mm auto-cannon were purchased from the French to complete the AEF's organisation. The problem of manning was solved relatively simply; since anti-aircraft gunnery was entirely new, there was no point in taking any of the few experienced artillery officers from posts in which they were irreplaceable, so 25 newly-commissioned officers were sent to France in the autumn of 1917 to attend the French anti-aircraft school. Upon graduating, most of them went to take charge of AA sections in the AEF, while some went back to the United States and began instructing more officers at Fort Monroe, the Coast Artillery School, in February 1918. In this fashion the US Army AAA (Anti-Aircraft Artillery) rapidly reached a high standard of proficiency. Figures, we know, can be manipulated to prove or disprove anything, but it is an indisputable fact that the AEF's AAA service in France had an average score of one aircraft brought down for every 1,055 shots fired. The French average, over the entire war, was one for 3,225 shots, and the British one for 1,800; the difference between these figures is largely a measure of the amount of area to be defended and the length of time spent in doing it.

When the war ended, high resolve filled the air. In February 1919 Mr Winston Churchill, Secretary of State for War and Air, presiding over a War Office conference, said: 'It is essential to keep alive the intricate and specialised art of air defence.' But even as he spoke the defences had begun to shrink; from 286 guns in November 1918 they were cut to a proposed establishment of 164 by January 1919. By June it was down to 42, by September 32, by December 8. And as General Ashmore later wrote, 'The finale . . . came in 1920 when a reporter happened on a gun station near London with a real gun and real soldiers (two caretakers). The subsequent outcry was too much for the authorities; the few remains of the London Air Defence Area were hurried away and hidden . . . near Aldershot.' And as a final indignity, the Whitehall Warriors decreed that the gun and searchlight detachments who had guarded them so faithfully and shot down several would-be attackers, had not, in fact, participated in combat at all and were not, therefore, entitled to the award of any war medals. The RNVR ratings who had manned guns, being administered by the Admiralty, did receive the War Medal, but even that example failed to move the War Office. It was a sorry piece of humbug which rankled with anti-aircraft gunners for many years and which, astonishingly, was to be repeated after the Second World War.

In Germany the anti-aircraft defence system was entirely dismantled by the Allied Disarmament Commission, in accordance with the provisions of the Versailles Treaty. All that was left to the

German Army was a handful of guns in the Fortress of Königsberg, while the German Navy was permitted to retain high angle guns on its ships. To comply with the letter of the Treaty, if not quite the spirit, a number of AA guns escaped being broken up for scrap; their elevating gear was modified so as to prevent them being pointed skywards and the AA sights were removed, thus converting them into field guns of a sort. These were then issued as the armament of seven motorised batteries, one of which was attached to each of the seven artillery regiments permitted to the Reichswehr. The *Flieger Abwehr Artillerie* became dormant.

The story was the same in France and in the United States; in 1919, assertions that air defence must never again be neglected were followed by a rapid run-down of men and equipment, until by 1923 there was hardly a serviceable AA battery left in the world. But then came a change of heart; no longer was it quite certain that the First World War had ended all wars. Instead came the uneasy generalisation that there would at least be a breathing space before the next one, and from that came the so-called 'ten-year rule' of the British government, the edict that there would be no war for the next ten years. Although formulation of this belief was entirely British, it seems to have been accepted by others as well, and it formed a sort of framework for subsequent military and political development. With such a time-scale postulated the planners could put forward ideas and point to the ten year rule as evidence that they were adhering to an official policy and not simply war-mongering. The only fly in the ointment, so far as Britain was concerned, was that the ten year rule was tacitly accepted as a permanent fixture, the ten years always starting from the moment of speaking and being gradually extended year after year.

In 1923 the British government began to consider building up an air defence system once more. Overall control of the defences was given to the Air Ministry, though the War Office was still to be responsible for the provision of guns, searchlights, and the men to operate them. A committee was set up in 1923 to produce a coordinated defence plan, based on an Air Force strength of twenty-three squadrons, nine of which were to be fighter squadrons for home defence. Their report, known as the 'Steel-Bartholomew Plan' after the committee's principal members, was an expansion of the 1918 dispositions in many ways. It envisaged a chain of sound-locating stations on the south-east coast, backed by a belt of advanced observation posts. Behind this, protecting London, was an Outer Artillery Zone, and then an Aircraft Fighting Zone stretching from Duxford in Cambridgeshire around London and across to Salisbury Plain. This zone was divided up into eight sectors, each the responsibility of one fighter squadron. Within the curve of the Aircraft Fighting Zone, London was to be covered by an Inner Artillery Zone, and that area of the Thames which included much of

Dockland and Woolwich Arsenal was specially marked for defence by both guns and aircraft.

It was hoped that the London area and the approaches to the south-east would be fully manned and equipped by the summer of 1925, but in June 1923, after a government reshuffle, the Cabinet approved a further expansion of the Royal Air Force, this time to a total of 52 squadrons, of which 17 were to be fighters. This additional strength was to keep parity with the forecast expansion of the French Air Force, and it is worth remarking that all the defence schemes of this period laid emphasis on the south-eastern area of England, the assumption being that the only country capable of producing an air force big enough to constitute a threat was France, and, moreover, that the only country within flying distance of London was France.

In view of the new figures, the Steel-Bartholomew Plan had to be abandoned before it had begun, and another committee was set up in 1924 under Major-General F. C. Romer to study systems of command, warning and communication, and to prepare a fresh air defence scheme. So far as organisation went, Romer's recommendations were based on the Steel-Bartholomew Plan, with two more fighter sectors tacked on to the western end so as to extend the Aircraft Fighting Zone to the Bristol Channel, using 14 fighter

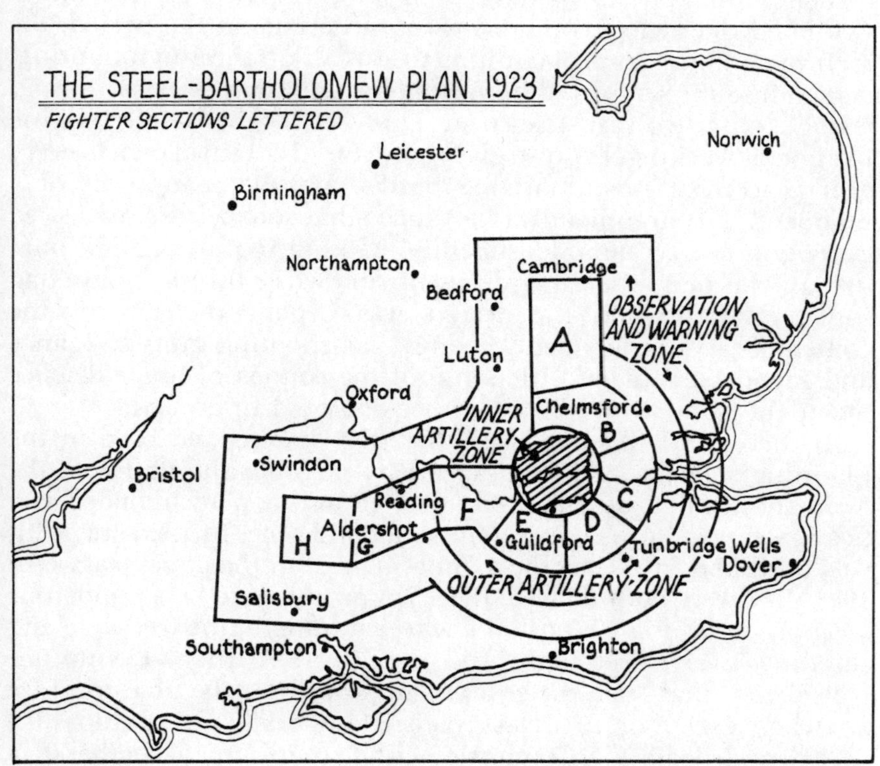

squadrons altogether. Three further squadrons were to be deployed forward, close to the south coast. The artillery zones were much the same, and eight Artillery Brigades, totalling 192 guns, were allotted.

Allotting 192 guns was simple; finding them would have been more difficult and manning them impossible. The Army had been run down to a minimum strength and most of the guns from the defences of 1918 had either been scrapped or disposed of overseas. This had been done for two reasons; firstly, the motley collection was, as we have seen, composed of a number of guns which were obsolete but which had been given an extended life since they were at least capable of shooting; so as soon as the war was over they were unceremoniously consigned to the scrapyard where they were long overdue. And secondly it was intended to replace them with one standard gun, designed for the job. This was to be the 3.6in gun, which had been designed early in 1918 and approved for service in September of that year. Two mountings had been designed, a static pedestal and a tracked trailer, but before production could be organised the war ended and no more than a handful were in existence. Nonetheless, it was the approved and latest pattern, which would go into production as and when the need arose, and so the older equipments were ruthlessly culled, only the 3in 20cwt guns remaining in service.

The 3.6in appears to have been an excellent weapon, but it exhibited one defect common to most designs of the period; the sighting and fire control equipment was all on the gun mounting, demanding the services of five gunlayers and sight-setters to aim it, though only two men loaded it. This was a grossly uneconomic method of working, because giving five highly-trained men to every gun placed an unsupportable burden on the manpower of a regiment. The argument was advanced that such a system allowed every gun to operate independently, without requiring additional fire control personnel or equipment, and while this may have had some validity when the design was begun, in view of the contemporary employment of single eye-shooting guns in France and Flanders, it made little sense in the context of home defence where the guns would invariably be deployed in groups.

At the end of the war two other gun designs had been in the planning stage, a 3.3in envisaged as a possible alternative to the 3.6in should that design come to grief, and a 4.7in intended as a heavy weapon for use in rear areas and at home. In 1920 one 3.3in was built and fired, but the 4.7in remained in the paper stages. In 1923 they were both revived; the 4.7in promised to be a ponderous weapon, weighing 27 tons on a wheeled trailer, nine feet wide and standing twelve feet high, and the Royal Artillery Committee considered 'that such an equipment would not be able to move anywhere except on first-class roads. Many bridges would not take such an axle load. The Committee wish to be informed whether they are to proceed further with this question'. There is no record of what the Committee were told, but the 4.7in gun seems to have been quietly abandoned from then on.

The Director of Artillery next minuted the Royal Artillery Committee (RAC) to 'forward a definite recommendation as to which gun, 3.3in or 3.6in, should be developed as the forward gun in mobile warfare in place of the 3in 20cwt'. The official specification for the replacement gun demanded the heaviest shell consistent with efficient hand loading, a rate of fire of at least 20 shots a minute, a minimum height of 20,000 feet at 4,000 yards from the gun, the shortest possible time of flight of the shell to that range, and 'mobility equal to that of the troops', a splendid phrase which could be construed to mean almost anything. And so, in view of these demands, the RAC came down in favour of the 3.3in design; work on the 3.6in stopped, and it was officially made obsolete in 1927.

The 3.3in project was based on the 18-pounder field gun. It will be remembered that wartime attempts to convert the 18-pounder into an AA gun had failed, due to the ballistic inefficiency of the shell. Since then there had been much fundamental research into the design of projectiles, and a new streamlined shell had been developed for the 18-pounder. A new gun, the 18-pounder Mark 5, was now produced, to be mounted on a self-propelled carriage based on the Vickers tank chassis. This became better known as the 'Birch Gun', named after General Sir Noel Birch, then Master-General of the Ordnance. A limited number of these were made and issued to the Experimental Mechanised Force in 1926–28 as self-propelled field guns, but it is less well-known that they were dual-purpose weapons capable of 80 degrees elevation and sighted and equipped for anti-aircraft firing. Unfortunately the whole idea of the mechanised force ran into problems and it was eventually disbanded. The Birch Guns went with it, being made obsolete in 1934, and the 3.3in forward area AA gun evaporated, leaving the Army back where it had started with nothing more than a collection of elderly 3in 20cwt weapons in stock.

In October 1928 the Director of Artillery wrote once more to the RAC.

> 'Assuming a war in which all the existing stocks of 3in guns are used up, is it recommended that replacement should be carried out:
> (a) by the same type of gun, or
> (b) by a new design?
> In view of the low shell power and ceiling of the present 3in 20cwt equipment, would it not be advisable to go into the question of a design of a gun firing a heavier shell? . . . Any new design must be suitable for the equipment of Mobile AA units.'

To which the RAC replied:

> 'The Committee are of the opinion that in the present 3in equipment the limit has been reached as regards shell power and ceiling combined with the mobility

> required by AA units in the field. If, however, a less mobile but more powerful equipment is required . . . the Committee consider that a 3.7in gun firing a shell of 25lb with a ceiling of, say, 28,000 feet would be effective.'

After some discussion this brief specification became the starting point of a fresh design project.

Meanwhile another major step had been taken. In January 1924 the Committee of Imperial Defence appointed an Air Raid Precautions Sub-Committee, and they, in turn, called upon General Ashmore to give his views on the organising of a force of observers. In April of the same year Ashmore was appointed General Officer Commanding the Territorial Army Defence Formations and

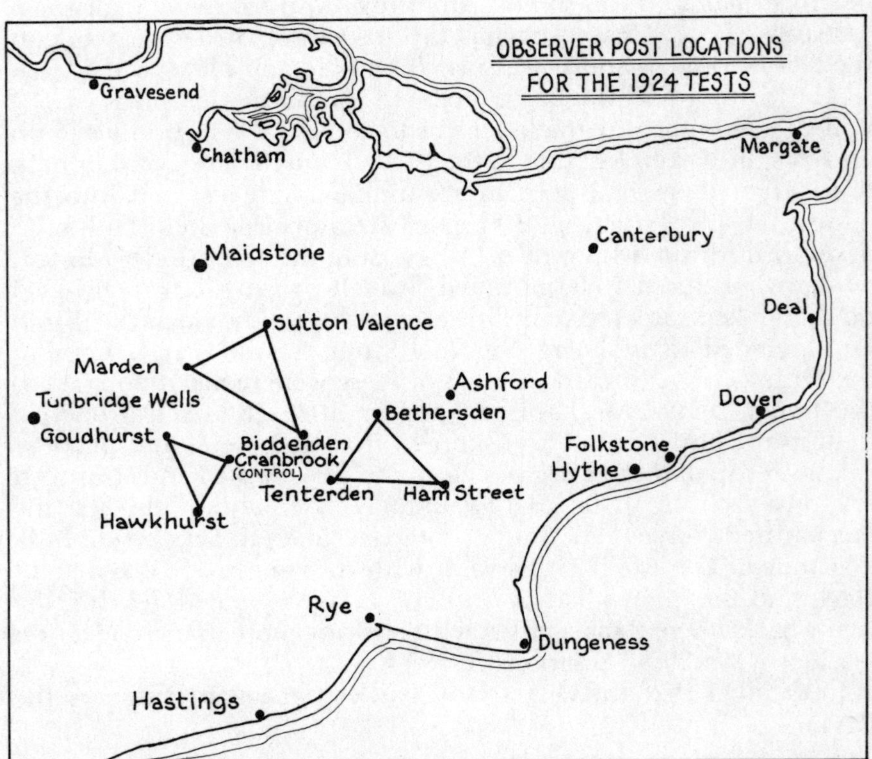

Inspector-General of Anti-Aircraft, a position which gave him the opportunity to conduct some practical tests. He began by arranging experiments to try to determine systems of reporting and observing aircraft, principally in order to establish the best method of spacing and grouping observers so as to obtain a thorough coverage of a given air space in the most economical manner. Remembering that much of the observing and reporting during the war had been done by the police, Ashmore spent the summer in touring the South Downs, talking with Chief Constables and other police officers and discussing his ideas with Post Office engineers. Finally he set up a simple layout of nine observing posts in three groups in the Weald of Kent, south of Maidstone, covering an area about 12 by 18 miles. During August and September 1924 four day and two night tests were conducted, the posts being manned by Special Constables and a control post being set up in the Post Office at Cranbrook. The 'target' was a solitary Sopwith Snipe biplane, the pilot of which kept a precise log of his movements. At the conclusion of the tests, Ashmore compared the pilot's reports with the plots made by the control post on the basis of the observers' reports. The correlation was, in most cases, exact, and the general result so excellent that Ashmore was encouraged to expand the system during the following year, organising 24 posts in two groups, one centred on Maidstone and the other on Horsham. One 22 June 1925 a three-day exercise began, using three squadrons of aircraft. Once again the results were excellent and, on 29 October 1925 the Committee of Imperial Defence gave their approval for the formation of the Observer Corps. Two further groups, covering Hampshire and Essex, were organised, and by the end of 1926 the four south-eastern counties had a working network of observers and reporting centres, though, of course, this network was not regularly manned.

The Romer Committee plans slowly took shape, much more slowly than had been intended. In 1925 the whole of the 52 squadron scheme, together with the gun defences and the reporting system, was brought under one head as the 'Air Defence of Great Britain' (ADGB). Recruiting for the Territorial Army began, since the manning of home defence guns was beyond the capability of the Regular Army who, in the event of war, would form the British Expeditionary Force. Communications networks had to be set up on a permanent basis, beginning with a portable telephone attached to a tapping box on a convenient pole near the humblest observer post, and running partly over public lines and partly over specially laid wire to reporting centres, sector headquarters, searchlight posts, and eventually to fighter airfields and gun sites. The problems were immense; in late 1925 there was talk of abandoning the whole scheme as impractical and unnecessary. The usual compromise was reached; continue, but slowly. Instead of completing the organisation by 1930, it would be completed by 1932. This later slipped to 1934, then 1936, and then to 1938, so that by 1932, when there should have been 52 squadrons in being, there were only 42. Only half the gun batteries had been formed, due to lack of equipment, money and recruits. The only component of the whole scheme which was functioning as planned was the Observer Corps, largely because it was an all-volunteer unpaid force operating on the proverbial shoe-string.

It was, and still remains, a mystery to many of my generation how the Observer Corps managed to survive and function so efficiently

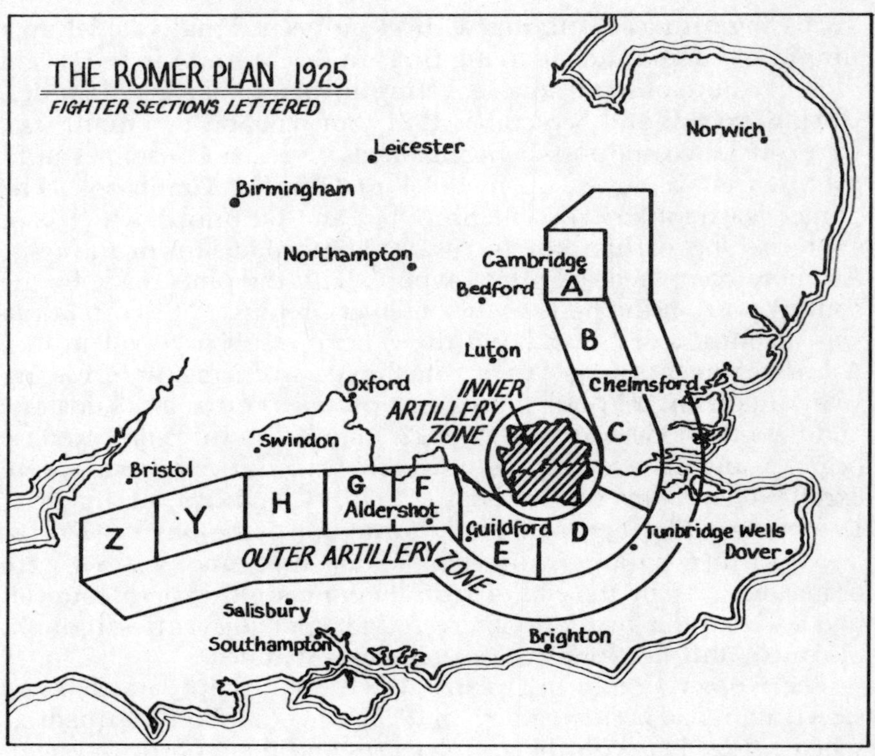

and, above all, how it managed to find recruits, for it seemed to be about three shades more secret than the Secret Service. By 1931 the Air Ministry was treating the whole organisation as a state secret; it was no longer mentioned in the newspapers or technical press when the annual RAF exercises were reported. The observers themselves never spoke about their activities. In the Hertfordshire village in which I lived, an inconspicuous card would appear in the window of the local Post Office, which read: 'Forewarned is Forearmed; 7.30pm Tuesday', which announced, to those in the know, a forthcoming training exercise. ('Forewarned is Forearmed' was the motto of the Corps.) In the local telephone exchange, in the Post Office, when 7.30pm Tuesday arrived, a special cord with two plugs connected the observer post to a specially marked junction connection on the switchboard which ran nobody knew where; this arrangement ensured that messages by-passed the exchange and could not be overheard by a curious operator. I know, because I was the operator and I was consumed with curiosity. It was months before I discovered that my elder brother was one of the observers and responsible for putting the card in the window.

In 1933, however, the idea spread, and a similar system, though thinner on the ground, and less well organised, was set up in Germany in order to feed information to the AA defences which were then being resurrected. In 1925 the officers of the converted AA/Field gun batteries had been attached to the German Navy for several months, ostensibly as liaison officers but in fact to be trained in anti-aircraft gunnery techniques on the Navy's authorised guns. In 1928 the converted batteries were quietly re-equipped with real anti-aircraft guns, 75mm weapons built quite legally by Krupp for export but then, by middlemen and other devious shifts, spirited away to reappear in Reichswehr gunparks. The re-equipped batteries then vanished into the wastes of East Prussia and other out-of-the-way places to practice their new role, and in 1932 they reappeared in Germany under the guise of 'Transport Units', heavily mechanised but without guns. At the same time the *Deutscher Luftsportverband* (German Air Sports Association) was formed to give gliding instruction to air-minded youths, and under the cover of this organisation AA machine gun companies were formed and trained.

By 1932 there was considerable argument in the German services as to which arm should be responsible for air defence. The Army said that artillery was their responsibility, while the Air Force (which didn't officially exist) pointed to 1916 and said that all air defence was in their province. In 1933 the Reichs Defence minister gave his decision: protection in the field – that is, in a combat zone – was the responsibility of the Army; protection at sea or on the coast, that of the Navy; and protection of the Reich itself, that of the Air Force. This was followed, in October 1934, by a decree which removed the seven 'Transport Units' from the Army and placed them under the command of the Air Ministry; they were brought up to full strength in men and equipment and their guns suddenly reappeared. Finally on 1 April 1935 the creation of the German Air Force was publicly announced, and on that day all air defence troops, together with signal units and the observer network, were officially transferred into the hands of the new Luftwaffe.

While all these organisations were being perfected and types of armament being discussed, a third question to require attention was the basic one of hitting the target. The years following the Armistice saw a rapid rise in the efficiency of aircraft. Speeds doubled, heights increased, aircraft were larger, more manoeuvrable and, in short, became even more difficult targets. The basic problems were the same – the need to calculate firing data based on the future position of the aircraft, given the assumption that it would continue to fly at the same speed and on the same course.

Once the urgency of war had died away it was possible to sit down and think about less hasty and more elegant solutions to the problem. The British 3.6in gun, with its five gun-layers, illustrated the defect of trying to provide every gun with its own means of calculating aim-off and fuze-setting, and the French 'Central Post' system, developed in 1918, had indicated the advantages of concentrating all the calculations into one central point and simply telling the guns at what bearing, elevation and fuze-setting to open fire. This had the virtue of putting all the mathematicians under one controlling eye and clearing them away from the gun, which at least let the gun detachment get on with their work unhindered and improved the rate of fire.

A similar situation had obtained years before in another artillery application concerned with firing at moving targets – coast defence artillery. In the earliest days shooting at ships had been a highly individual matter, each gun captain assessing his aim, firing, and then correcting by observation of the strike of his shot. But as ranges increased and ships moved more rapidly this was abandoned in favour of a central determination of firing data, transmitted to the guns by various means. A similar system, 'director firing', was adopted by the Royal Navy, in which a central controlling point determined the range and other gun data and transmitted it to the guns. Once this basic principle was adopted, experience showed that there were a number of influences on the flight of the shell which predisposed it to inaccuracy: the physical separation of the gun from the control point, for example, meant that the data had to be slightly corrected to compensate for this displacement. Such matters as air temperature, wind speed and direction, the drift of the shell due to the gun's rifling, small changes in the gun's muzzle velocity due to gradual wearing away of the bore with each shot, all these had effect and one by one these factors were isolated, correction factors calculated, and graphs and scales prepared so that the fire controllers could make allowances in their calculation of gun data.

The next step was to devise mechanical plotting machines which would automatically do all the sums and include all the various factors, machines such as the Royal Navy's 'Dreyer Fire Control Table', the Royal Artillery's 'Dumaresque' and the American Coast Artillery 'Pratt Range Board'. They differed in appearance but they all worked in more or less the same way: the position of the target was plotted graphically, after which the various corrections could be set on scales and dials eventually to produce a set of fully-corrected gun data for the future position of the target.

This system was now examined again in the light of the anti-aircraft problem. The cases were not strictly analogous: the aircraft was moving much faster than a ship and the target area was three-dimensional; the plotting and calculating had to be a good deal faster than was needed in naval or coastal gunnery, and there was not the opportunity of making adjustments to the plotting machine by observation of the fall of shot close to the target. Nevertheless it formed a basis upon which to begin, and in government establishments, as well as in the laboratories of such companies as Vickers Armstrong, Sperry, Zeiss, and Barr and Stroud, the scientists set to work. The devices they produced were to be known variously as 'predictors' in Britain, 'directors' in the USA, and *Kommandogerat* (command equipment) in Germany, all names which indicated their use, and they were all very similar. A telescope enabled the target to be tracked, and this act of tracking was converted into an angular velocity. A range-finder delivered range and height, and this, fed into the predictor, reacted with the angular velocity to give the target's speed. Values for temperature, drift, velocity, and other factors were set in by means of knobs and dials, and the predictor then calculated a future position and displayed the bearing, range and fuze-setting necessary to place the bursting shell there.

All this, it must be emphasised, was done mechanically; a few factors lent themselves to being represented by varying electrical voltages, but others did not, and the performance of arithmetic by electrical currents was far in the future. The majority of the correcting was done by motors, differentials, cams, wormwheels and similar agencies. As a result, predictors tended to be heavy and required several men to operate them; the German *Kommandogerät* 36, for example, needed 13 men to operate it, while a later model, the *KdoG 40*, contained 35 differentials and 24 electric motors and weighed 1½ tons. The American Sperry T8 of 1937 contained no less than 3,500 individual components.

But this complexity was still in the future in 1923, when work on predictors began in earnest; the manufacturers and designers were wise enough to proceed at a walk before running, and the early models were restricted to simple determination of a future position based upon course and speed, without adding any refinements. Once that had been perfected the other factors could be added one at a time. Often the incorporation of a new factor had a sorry effect on those already there; some predictors proved to be excellent at 'smoothing' all the factors relative to flight but made a nonsense of calculating the future position, while others performed elegant mathematical exercises to produce highly erratic answers.

Allied with the predictor was the means of getting the answers to the gun and applying them when they arrived. The simplest answer was to have someone read them off the predictor and call them over a telephone link direct to the gun-layers, who set their sights and fuze-setters accordingly. This was good at first sight, but one very basic drawback was that if the predictor man spoke directly to the gun-layer, the gun captain knew nothing of what was going on, which could never be allowed. A more technical objection was that if predictor data were read direct to the gun, the displacement correction would have to be applied by the gun-layer, constantly adding or subtracting a figure from the data he was being given; the opportunities for disaster are obvious.

An electrical system which would display the data on a dial at the gun was the obvious answer, but this took some development. A simple voltmeter looked attractive, the voltage varying as, for example, the range. But voltmeters to the necessary degree of accuracy had never been made, and any slight fluctuation of voltage due to faulty connections or poor insulation would produce a serious error. The solution lay in the development of self-synchronous motors, electrical rotors which transmitted angular displacements of a dial reading without being effected by voltage fluctuations. The predictor had a dial with two pointers, one of which was positioned by the predictor mechanism to indicate, say, gun elevation. The operator, by turning a handwheel, matched this pointer with a second one, and as he did so, transmitted an electrical signal to the gun which set a receiving pointer to a similar position. Finally the gun-layer operated the elevating handwheel of the gun, raising the gun barrel in the air and actuating a second pointer on the gun dial until it, in turn, matched that position of the transmitted data pointer. Once this initial setting had been made the predictor operator merely kept his pointer aligned to send the latest data to the gun, where the layer, in turn, followed the movements with *his* pointer; which gave rise to the general name for this system – the 'follow-the-pointer system'.

The ideal, of course, was to remove the human element from the chain as much as possible, and thus remove areas of potential error. If the predictor could be designed so as to do its own pointer-setting, and if, at the gun, the received data could be made to actuate motors to elevate and point the gun and set the fuze-setter, then all the men at the gun would have to do would be to throw ammunition into the breech as fast as possible. The American Army set its heart on this very early in the 1920s, but the production of suitable controllers, to convert the small electric currents from the predictor into powerful movements of several tons of machinery, and do this to a fine degree of accuracy, took a great deal of time and research. By 1930 an experimental 3in gun with remote power control had been built and tested at the Aberdeen Proving Ground in Maryland, and while the results were good enough to encourage more research, they were a long way from being good enough to incorporate into a service equipment.

The last link in the complicated chain of equipment was the fuze fitted in the shell in order to burst it at the predicted place in the sky. Wartime improvements had made the fuzes more accurate, but basically they were still no more than convenient casings in which to carry a length of burning gunpowder, and even with all the improvements this was still an inaccurate way of measuring time. In 1916 the German firm of Krupp had produced a clockwork time fuze which was taken into service use, though not for anti-aircraft fire since it was impossible to manufacture the immense number which would have been needed. Instead, it was used for long-range shrapnel fire by heavy guns and, inevitably, the day came when one failed to operate and was picked up whole by an Allied intelligence officer. It was sent to England to be dismantled and examined, and by November 1917 the Cambridge Scientific Instrument Company had manufactured and tested a mechanism based on the Krupp design. It was, in essence, an extremely robust watch mechanism with a pre-wound spring and a hair-spring regulator; on firing a trigger was released which allowed the spring to drive a hand round at regulated speed. At the end of the set time (a maximum of 60 seconds) the hand released a firing pin on to a detonator which, in its turn, detonated the shell.

The advantage of this mechanism to AA fire lay in its regularity; such things as air density, humidity and temperature, which affected powder-burning fuzes, had no effect on the mechanical type. Centrifugal force could be overcome by careful placement of the gears on the axis of the fuze, and robust design took care of the problems associated with the sudden shock of discharge. Whereas the powder fuze had an accuracy of about 2 per cent of the total time of running, the mechanical fuze cut this to about half of one per cent. This meant that a shell moving at 2,000 feet per second, fitted with a powder fuze, might burst anywhere on its trajectory from 400 feet short to 400 feet past the target; a mechanical fuze cut this to 100 feet each side.

In the post-war years many designs of mechanical fuze were perfected, but while it was feasible to perfect and hand-build enough fuzes for tests and demonstrations, production of the number needed for practical gunnery was out of the question. Special factories, special machinery and skilled workmen were needed, and none of them were forthcoming in the 1920s. Although Britain produced and approved the 'Fuze, Time, No. 205' for the 3in 20cwt gun in 1925, only a thousand were ever made, for use solely in demonstrations and trials. The mechanical time fuze was another luxury for which the gunners would have to wait.

If aeroplanes were flying higher and faster and giving the gunners problems, they were also flying lower and faster, and this began to worry the gunners as well. Ground 'strafing' had become common in 1917–18, but the aircraft of the time were still slow enough to be targets for riflemen and ordinary machine guns pointed upward. But by the end of the 1920s the speed of such attacks had more than doubled, and several countries began examining the prospect of a light, fast-firing gun which could deal with these targets. The gun had to be light so that it could be elevated and swung rapidly to keep pace with the target; this meant that the shell would have to be a small one; from this followed the need for a high rate of fire in order to get as many hits as possible during the brief action. Time fuzes were out of the question; they were impossible to make in small calibres, and it would be impossible to set them before firing at the rates of fire demanded. Simple impact fuzes had to be used, relying on a direct hit for their effect; this brought the problem of what happened to the shell when it missed. It would go on and eventually come back to earth and detonate. To prevent this a 'self-destruction' device was used, which would burst the shell well past the target in the event of a miss. The easiest way to do this was to fit the shell with a tracer, necessary in any case to allow the gunners to see where the shots were going, and arrange for the tracer to ignite the shell's filling as it came to the end of its burning time. Another method, favoured by the Germans, was to incorporate a short length of gunpowder in the fuze to act as a fixed-time fuze and burst the shell after a few seconds of flight.

Several countries elected to use rapid-firing 20mm guns, using the designs of Oerlikon, Hispano-Suiza or Solothurn. The German Navy, for example, adopted in 1934 the Solothurn gun designed by Rheinmetall, and the Army followed suit in the following year. Typical of its class, this was an extremely light weapon on a three-legged mounting which could be quickly transported by a special two-wheeled trailer. It was little more than an over-sized machine gun, but it fired an explosive shell of just over three ounces at 120 rounds per minute, and could reach up to 2,000 metres altitude before the tracer destroyed the shell.

There were other opinions in this field, though; one criticism of the 20mm guns was that the projectile was too small to do much serious damage without multiple hits. Far better, it was felt, would be to increase the calibre slightly to obtain a more lethal shell, but without decreasing the gun's ability to point and shoot quickly. The foremost protagonists of this theory were Aktiebolaget Bofors of Sweden – respected (if little known) gunmakers. In 1928 they drew up a design for a gun of 40mm calibre, obtained financial support from the Swedish government, and in 1930 produced their '40mm Automatic Field Gun L/60', a lightweight automatic cannon firing a 2lb shell to 5,000 metres at a rate of 120 rounds per minute. It was adopted by the Swedish Navy, and in 1932 Bofors began to sell it overseas. By 1939 eighteen countries had adopted the gun and eleven had taken out licenses to manufacture it themselves, including Britain. Even now, 50 years after the first line was put on paper, improved versions of this gun are in use by over 20 nations. The Bofors Gun (the name became synonymous with the 40mm AA gun – the other products of AB Bofors were ignored) was one of the most successful gun designs ever built.

4 THE STORMCLOUDS GATHER

The 40mm L/60 gun was not the only famous design to come out of the Bofors drawing office in the late 1920s, though the other one was not, in fact, a Bofors responsibility, nor was it ever publicly credited to that company. During the 'Versailles' years in Germany the Krupp company, its gunmaking activities severely restricted, had sent several gun designers to foreign companies in order that their talents could be kept alive until such time as Krupp would be in a position to re-employ them. The 'cell' who went to Bofors passed their time in designing a new medium anti-aircraft gun; with plenty of time at their disposal they were able to modify and redesign until it was well-nigh perfect, and in 1931 they returned to Germany to supervise the construction of a prototype gun. This was demonstrated to the Army in 1932, approved, and by 1933 production had begun. This new design was the '8.8cm *Flugabwehrkanone* 18', which was to go down in military history as 'The Eighty-Eight'.

Contrary to opinions expressed in later years, there was nothing magical about the 88. It was soundly conventional, as were most Krupp designs, and was carried on a cruciform platform with two two-wheeled limbers. It fired a 21lb explosive shell fitted with a mechanical time fuze, had a maximum ceiling of 32,400 feet, and could fire at a rate of 15 rounds a minute. At the time of its introduction it was certainly the best gun of its type in the world, but by 1939 it would have slipped to second or third place. Where it gained immeasurable advantage was in the date of its introduction; its competitors were not even on paper when the first 88s went into service, and by the time the war came there were over a thousand of them in use.

The arming of the flak units, followed in 1935 by the official announcement of the Luftwaffe's formation, caused considerable agitation in the rest of Europe. Indeed, the portents had been under discussion for some time, and in 1934 Britain threw out the uncompleted '52 Squadron' scheme and set about expanding the RAF and overhauling the defences. The most obvious need now was to shift completely the emphasis of the defensive system; it had originally been based on the assumption that the only practicable direction of attack was from France. Now the balance of power, and of probabilities, had shifted to Germany and the defences had thus to be moved round from the south of England to the east. The Aircraft Fighting Zone was now aligned to run from the River Tees in the north, down to and around London, and then across to Southampton. In front of this lay the Outer Artillery Zone, and London itself formed the Inner Artillery Zone. Twenty-five fighter squadrons were allotted, gun and searchlight strength was increased, and the Observer Corps was expanded to cover the new area, as far north as the Tyne, across the country to Preston, and then down to Bristol and Plymouth, a total of 16 groups which were to be fully operational by March 1939.

The artillery defences were to consist of 58 batteries of guns and 100 searchlight companies. At that time an AA battery consisted of eight 3in guns and twelve Lewis machine guns for close defence, while a searchlight company had 24 lights and 24 Lewis guns, which meant a total of 464 guns and 2,400 lights. Unfortunately while the plans were accepted by the government, no money was available and the usual compromise had to be reached; the plan would be tackled in stages. The first stage would be 17 batteries and 42 light companies, (136 guns and 1,008 searchlights) by March 1940, and the entire plan would be completed by 1946.

In furtherance of this scheme the 1st AA Division was formed in December 1935 to embody the first stage proposals. It was to consist of 5,200 men and be split up into four groups – London, Home Counties, Thames and Medway, and East Anglia. Some idea of the problem confronting the Army can be gauged from one set of figures; of the 1,008 searchlights the Division was supposed to have, only 120 existed, throughout the entire Kingdom. Furthermore the production of 5,200 officers and men was not to be achieved overnight, and much of the strength was obtained by converting many of the London area Territorial Army volunteers into AA gunners. This led to some heartache as infantrymen turned into gunners overnight, but by various administrative stratagems the regiments managed to retain their identities and avoided vanishing into numbered anonymity. As a result, there were some odd-sounding titles, when one discovered that such units as the 4th City of London (Royal Fusiliers), the 7th City of London (Post Office Rifles), or the 21st London (1st Surrey Rifles) were all, in fact, Royal Artillerymen.

It might be noted that the projected defences consisted entirely of 3in guns; there was no mention of any form of light weapon for low level defence, because in January 1935, when the plan was promulgated, no decision had yet been reached about such a weapon. Nor, for that matter, was anything said about a replacement for the 3in, for that was also waiting to be settled; the RAC's tentative recommendation of 1928 had been enshrined in a formal specification issued in 1933, calling for a 3.7in gun weighing 8 tons, capable of being towed at 25mph and going into action in 15 minutes. In 1934 designs were put forward by Vickers-Armstrong and by the Design Department of Woolwich Arsenal, but it was not until late in 1935 that the Vickers design was selected and it was to be April 1936 before the first gun was built and tested.

More important than the guns was the ever-present problem of finding them a target, and by this time the performance of contemporary aircraft was leading to some frantic straw-clutching in all quarters. Not only was a detection system vital for the guns, it was needed equally desperately for the fighter aircraft; they needed a

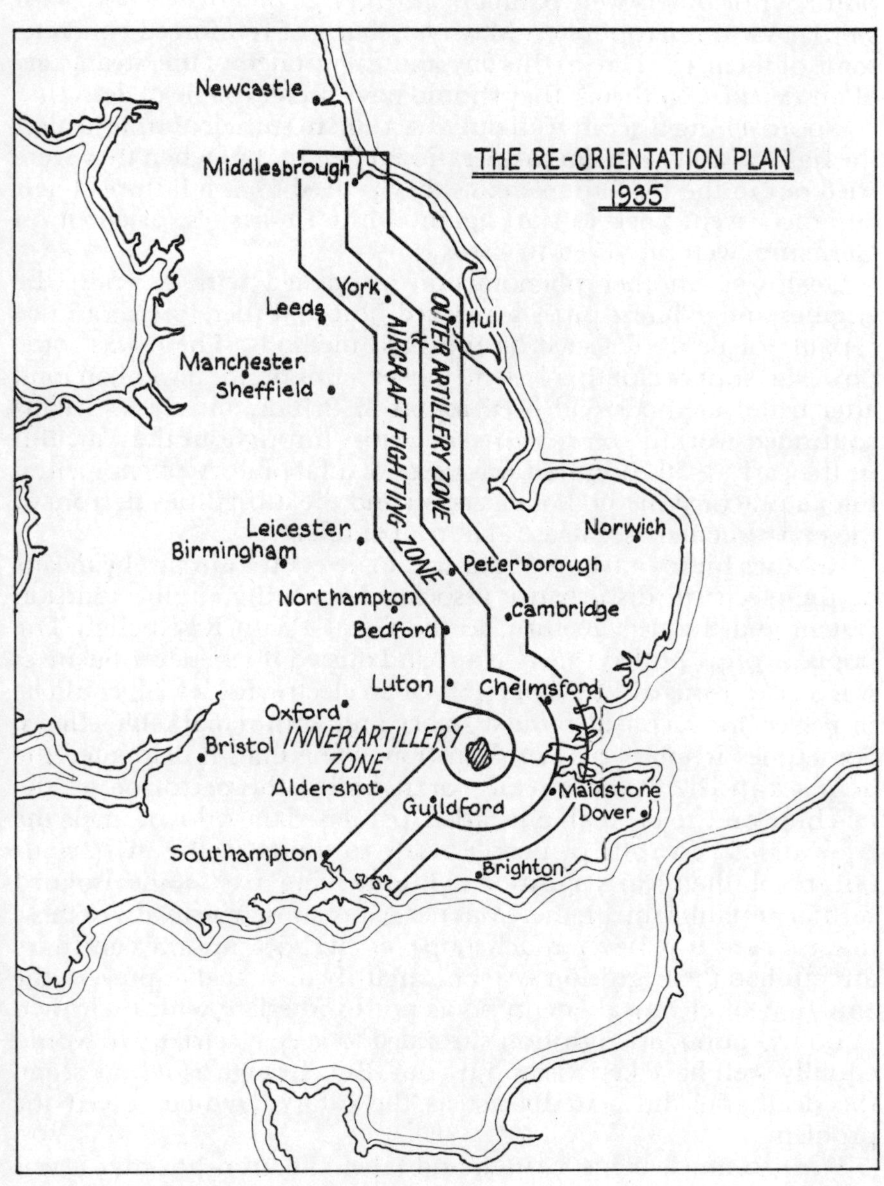

finite time in which to take off and climb to a suitable height in order to intercept the incoming raider, and the point had now been reached where, if the warning was given as a bomber crossed the coast, it would be over London long before the defenders could get up to it.

Sound was still the most obvious choice, and in 1934 a group of enormous 'sound mirrors' were built in the Romney Marshes, oriented towards France. One was 200 feet long and 36 feet high, curved so as to reflect sound into a microphone located at the focal point, while others were parabolic mirrors, 20 or 30 feet across, with similar focal microphones. Massively built of reinforced concrete, some of them are there to this day, mute reminders of the 'steam age' of air defence. In theory they should have been capable of detecting an approaching aircraft well out to sea and in sufficient time to alert the fighters and get them to operational height, but when they were tried out in the 1934 air exercises they proved to be a failure. Their designers went back to start again, while fresh sites, oriented on Germany, were surveyed in Essex.

Heat was another phenomenon associated with aircraft; the engines and exhaust pipes generated heat and therefore should be capable of being detected by infra-red methods. There was some powerful support for this system; indeed, support for it went on long after better methods had been found in Britain and the Germans continued working on infra-red detectors throughout the war. But in the early 1930s infra-red was more of a laboratory phenomenon than a practical method of detection and the difficulties in front of the experimenters seemed to be insuperable.

Another highly-favoured idea was to detect the aircraft by means of the electrical disturbance associated with the engine ignition system and this led, in turn, to the Great Death Ray Belief. The popular press pulled this one out and dusted it whenever business was slack; it was always some sort of an electric ray which could be projected for a considerable distance and with remarkable effects. Sometimes it interfered with ignition, sometimes it detonated the bombs carried by the aircraft, or it boiled the petrol or set the machine on fire or, if all else failed, paralysed the pilot or made the crew airsick. In spite of people ready to testify to the mysterious failure of their car's ignition while driving past some isolated military establishment, there was never any substance in any of these tales. There was never much hope in the idea anyway; military aircraft had their ignition systems carefully insulated to prevent the emission of electrical energy so as not to interfere with their own radio reception, and ignition shrouded to keep electricity in would equally well have kept death rays out. But, strange as it may seem, the death ray did actually act as the catalyst which solved the problem.

With so much being written and talked about death rays it was inevitable that, sooner or later, some government body would want an expert opinion on the viability of the idea. Moreover, by 1934 it had become necessary to make some concerted investigations into the various methods of detection being suggested and get some expert scientific opinion. So in January 1935 the Committee for the Scientific Study of Air Defence (CSSAD) was constituted, and a radio-physicist named Robert Watson-Watt was asked to examine the death ray idea and pronounce upon it. Calculations by Watson-Watts's assistant, A. F. Wilkins, soon demonstrated that the delivery of sufficient power by radio methods was quite impossible and that the death ray was a scientific non-starter, but Watson-Watt, not to be satisfied with merely handing in a negative report, began to consider whether or not there were other aspects of radio technique which could be put to use. It appeared to him likely that, in his own words, 'radio detection as opposed to radio destruction' might be feasible, and he reported this to CSSAD. It immediately came back with a request for mathematical proof (it was that kind of committee); Mr Wilkins did some more sums which showed that if a radio signal was directed at an aircraft, a surprisingly large amount of the energy would be reflected from the surface and it would be possible to detect this.

Finally, in February 1935, Watson-Watt submitted a report to the CSSAD entitled 'The Detection of Aircraft by Radio Methods' in which he laid out, in considerable detail, a potential system of detecting aircraft by relfected radio waves and, for good measure, extrapolated beyond this bald fact to build up a possible defensive system and he outlined the possible future developments which he thought could be reasonably expected; the measurement of range, bearing and height, the possibility of surrounding the entire country with warning devices, the identification of friendly aircraft, the possibility of radio counter-measures, and much more.

Action followed with a swiftness rarely seen in weapon development before or since. Within a week Watson-Watt had carried out the now legendary experiment with a cathode-ray oscilloscope, detecting the reflection of a BBC signal from Daventry radio station as a Heyford bomber flew across, thus demonstrating visual proof of his theories. Within a month the then enormous sum of £10,000 had been granted for further research and a site at Orfordness in Suffolk had been selected as being suitably remote to allow development to proceed in secret. By the middle of May work was in progress there, and by the middle of June detection of aircraft at a range of 17 miles had been achieved.

It should be borne in mind, in contemplating the speed at which the new 'Radio Direction Finding' (RDF) was developed that the work was a great deal more difficult than is easily imagined today. This was, to all intents, the birth of electronics, and Watson-Watt and those who followed him were working in an area so recondite as to be comparable with, say, holography today. The radio itself was barely out of the novelty stage and the cathode-ray tube had never been seen outside a scientific laboratory. The apparatus with which these early researchers worked would be considered primitive today, even the measuring equipment and the very tools with which they worked had to be designed from scratch, and yet in five months they progressed from an idea on a sheet of paper to a detection system which actually worked.

But at the same time as the Orfordness station was being formed, the same idea had occured to other people. In 1934 a Dr Kühnhold of the German Naval Radio Research Establishment had begun experiments with radio, having been moved to this by the study of reports dealing with radio signals being 'bounced' from the upper atmosphere in weather research, reports which had been published in scientific journals in the late 1920s. Late in 1935 he apparently made the same sort of experiment as had Watson-Watt and had reached similar conclusions, though he does not seem to have had Watson-Watt's breadth of vision. Nevertheless, he raised sufficient interest to cause the German Navy to give a development contract the the GEMA company in 1936, which resulted in the 'Freya' early warning set. The success of the first pilot models of this set led to the Luftwaffe showing interest, and they gave contracts to the Telefunken and Lorenz companies to develop early radio detection warning equipment.

In the United States similar conclusions had been reached from similar processes of thought. In 1930 US naval scientists had discovered that a received radio signal showed distortion when an aircraft passed between the transmitter and the receiver, and work began on turning this phenomenon into a practical system of detection. In 1933 the US Army Signal Corps joined in the investigation, and by 1936 both services had produced prototype detection sets, the Army model being an experimental set which later became the SCR-268 and the naval equipment being installed in the destroyer *Leary*. (SCR meant Signal Corps Radio, a non-committal form of nomenclature which survived until 1945, when it was replaced by the present-day inter-service system.)

All the experimenters had much the same row to hoe, but in Britain the work moved much more quickly because of the ever-present threat of Nazi Germany across the water. In Germany it moved less rapidly because it was a 'defensive' system and thus rated a lower priority than tanks and aircraft, which were 'offensive' weapons. In the USA valuable time was lost in attempting to use simple continuous-wave radio transmissions before this line of research was dropped in favour of pulse transmissions, and, again, the absence of a potentially hostile air force over the horizon removed much of the urgency from the programme. But in a remarkable example of faith, the RAF threw all its resources (scant as they then were) into a new and untried scientific theory and made it work.

The basic principle of radar is now, of course, common knowledge; a short pulse of radio energy is transmitted, strikes its target, and a portion of the energy is reflected back into the receiving aerial of the set. At the instant the pulse leaves the transmitter a synchronised line – known as a 'time-base' – begins to be drawn across the face of a cathode-ray tube. When the echo returns it deflects the beam on the tube so as to make a vertical line. The distance between the start of the time-base and the vertical line is thus a measure of the target's range, since the speed of the radio pulse is known. But in 1935 there were several aspects which tend to be forgotten today. In the first place, the transmitter sent out its signal in all directions like a ripple spreading out on the surface of a pond. So that while the echo gave its indication of range, that was the only certain factor. The operator could see that the target was ten miles away, but he had no idea of the direction. The only solution to this, at first, seemed to be simultaneous measurement from two stations; if circles of the measured range were graphically plotted, then the intersection of the circles would give the position of the target. Unfortunately this system gave two positions, which rather reduced the potential accuracy. Moreover it meant building a lot of stations in order to ensure adequate coverage.

Fortunately this, and similar, problems proved more amenable to solution than was feared. By building what amounted to two sets of aerials side by side and feeding them with signals slightly out of phase it was possible to get two return echoes on the cathode-ray tube; by advancing or retarding the phase change the two echoes could be made to vary in size as the energy effectively 'swung' across the sky, and by adjusting until both echoes were the same size, an indication of direction could be obtained. By similar methods the height of the target could also be determined.

By December 1935 plans had been approved for the construction of five stations to protect the approaches to London: Bawdsey in Suffolk, Great Bromley and Canewdon in Essex, Dunkirk and Dover in Kent. It was hoped to have all these working by midsummer 1936 in order to give them a thorough testing during the annual RAF exercises, but delays in the construction of the 200 feet high aerial towers prevented this. When exercise time came round only the Bawdsey station – which was now the home of the development establishment which had moved from Orfordness – was functioning, and that in an unsatisfactory fashion. Nonetheless it managed to produce some reasonably good results after furious modifications and patching by every available scientist in the place, and the results were enough to warrant the continued faith of the RAF. Investigation began into the possibility of fitting equipment into aircraft, while the Army and the Royal Navy began to take an interest, weighing up the possibilities of adapting this new idea to their own needs. The Army sent a scientific civil servant to Bawdsey in 1936 who reported back that there seemed every possibility of developing a light and mobile equipment which would detect aircraft at ten miles range with an accuracy of about five degrees in azimuth. This was a good deal better than could be expected from sound detectors, and on the promise of this and with the successful completion of the five early warning stations, the plans for the fresh set of concrete mirrors were torn up.

With a workable detection system in view, if not fully operational yet, the next question was of the best way to utilise the information being produced. The bearing and range of a target measured from an RDF set at Dover was of little use to an anti-aircraft gun in Greenwich or a fighter aircraft somewhere in Hertfordshire. This 'raw data' had to be turned into something more useful before it could be fed into the reporting system. As it happened the Army had been confronted with a similar problem with their 'fixed azimuth' system of gun control by sound locators. A network of locators, some manned by the Army and some by the Observer Corps, listened on specific bearings and reported when aircraft crossed their set azimuth. This azimuth and the time of report were then compared with reports from other stations to obtain a fix on the aircraft which then became a range and bearing; to convert this to a map reference suitable for plotting the Post Office Engineering Department had invented a computer, using standard 'uniselector' multiple switches, part of the normal apparatus of an automatic telephone exchange. The system, however, had several drawbacks, particularly as it applied to the Observer Corps, and the computers were no longer required. They were now passed to the RDF stations, modified, and they became the standard method of converting 'raw' data into positional information suitable for reporting, plotting and display.

Even with the aid of this device there was still the problem of the sheer volume of information which, pouring in from all the various observing stations, threatened to swamp the system. With perhaps two RDF stations and half a dozen observer posts all reporting the same aircraft at slightly different times, there was every chance that mistakes would be made and, in any case, the plotting system would become chaotic. In the summer of 1936 a 'Commandant, RDF Training' was appointed to Bawdsey, an RAF officer with the task of training service personnel in the operation of the RDF installations and, as an extension of this, developing some system of utilising the information and presenting it in its most useful form to the actual flying squadrons. Practical trials soon showed the dangers referred to above, and indicated the need to intercept the information flow before it reached the fighter sector operations room so as to resolve ambiguities and remove superfluous reports. This led to the idea of the 'filter room' in which trained operators could weed out surplus and overlapping plots and then pass the useful information to the operations room plotters. Information from all sources passed into these filter rooms, was distilled, and passed out to form a graphical plot from which it was possible to discern the movements of the attacker and alert the defending force accordingly.

At that stage the whole wondrous system ground to a halt; for the only response to the threat was either gunfire or the same standing patrols of fighters, flying from A to B and back again to A in the hope that the incoming raiders would appear in their sector. This might have been satisfactory in 1918 when aircraft were slow and economical, but by this time the RAF had issued a specification calling for 8-gun monoplane fighters, and that sort of machine, travelling at high speed and burning up fuel at unheard-of rates, was hardly suited to standing patrols.

The answer to this came as an extension to the RDF development programme. Henry Tizard, the first chairman of the CSSAD committee, and one of the most active supporters of the RDF policy, proposed a system in which the fighters would remain on the ground, conserving fuel and manpower, until a target was detected. Then the fighter would take off and, by means of tracking by the RDF stations and radio communication from the operations room to the pilot, would be guided by a controller on the ground until he came within visual range of the target. Tizard's proposals were received with faint enthusiasm, due probably to the fact that the entire concept and function of the RDF system was so secret that few people outside the Bawdsey circle knew of it or appreciated what it could do. Eventually permission was obtained to conduct a series of trials in August 1936. They were complicated by the security ban on RDF which prevented the pilots from being told how they and their targets were being monitored, and it required some strenuous acts of faith by all concerned. But over a period of weeks it became clear that this was a viable system which, with practice, could put the fighter in contact with the bomber almost every time.

Since the fighter aircraft was seen, quite rightly, as the first line of defence, once the control system was proven the provision of the necessary equipment to provide a complete screen around the country had the first priority, and the coastal stations – now known as the 'RDF Chain Home' – were extended northward to the Yorkshire moors and across the south coast to the Isle of Wight. This, together with the refinement of design which was a continuous process in the early days, took all the available facilities, as a result of which the promised lightweight detection and warning set for use by the AA guns never materialised and the guns were still having to rely on sound locating equipment, the Observer Corps, and an eagle-eyed 'spotter' on the gun position. But if they didn't have their own RDF set, at least they had the prospect of some new guns.

In April 1936 the pilot model of the 3.7in AA gun had completed its acceptance trials and proof firing. Production was authorised in April 1937 and the first production gun appeared in January 1938. It was an advanced gun for its time, mounted on a rather luxurious and complicated carriage, but much heavier than the specified 8 tons and, as a result, it was not well received by gunners used to the handier 3in 20cwt gun. But its performance – it fired a 28lb shell at 2,600 feet per second to a maximum ceiling of 41,000 feet at a rate of ten shots a minute – was in advance of anything else in the world at the time, and this went a long way to compensate for its bulk. While the handy 3in remained the preferred weapon for AA batteries with the field army, the 3.7in was earmarked for service in the air defence of Great Britain, though production was painfully slow.

A ceiling of 41,000 feet – seven and three-quarter miles straight up – sounds extremely impressive, but this is a deceptive figure. This 'maximum ceiling' is the height to which the gun, if set perfectly vertical, would project a solid projectile of 28lb weight before the pull of gravity halted it and returned it to earth, and although it looks good on paper it means very little. A more honest figure is the 'effective ceiling', that height to which the gun, at its maximum designed elevation – which may not be 90 degrees – will project a service high explosive shell carrying a time fuze set to the maximum operating time. At the end of that time the fuze bursts the shell, and for all practical purposes the gun cannot send a projectile any higher. In the case of the 3.7in gun in 1936 the controlling factors were the maximum elevation of 80 degrees and the 25 seconds burning time of the Fuze Time No. 199, an elderly powder-filled pattern. Applying these factors brought the ceiling down to about 28,000 feet.

But even this figure is a deception; the ability to put one shell in the sky at this maximum point ignores the fact of the target's movement since, obviously, that performance could only be of use if the target aircraft happened to be in that particular spot in the sky which coincided with 80 degrees and 25 seconds; let the aircraft move to a point where the gun is elevated to, say, 75 degrees and simple geometry shows that the 25 seconds fuze will not allow the shell to reach the same height. And so a third value, the 'practical ceiling' appears; the greatest height at which it would be possible to engage an aircraft target for a reasonable length of time. Just what constitutes this reasonable period is a changing question based on the gun's rate of fire, the speed of the aircraft, the system of fire control and the ammunition in use, but in 1936 it was defined as the height at which the gun could engage an approaching target travelling at 250mph for twenty seconds before the gun's elevation reached 70 degrees. Under this criterion the ceiling now fell to 23,000 feet, almost half the impressive 'maximum ceiling'. It is only fair to add that in later years, with improvements in fire control, fuzes and rates of fire, the practical ceiling of the 3.7in gun was to increase to 32,500 feet.

For the moment, then, raiders at heights over 23,000 feet were relatively safe from anything but a lucky shot, and since the contemporary German bombers could fly rather higher than that, something more powerful was needed to reach up to them. For some years the War Office had been experimenting with a 4.7in gun, but with the 3.7in just getting into production the prospect of obtaining money and facilities to build a 4.7in as well was remote. It was then suggested that the Army might consider adopting an existing design, a naval 4.5in gun; its ballistic performance was close to that of the projected 4.7in, it was a tried and tested design, and facilities for its production were in being. Furthermore, since most of the localities in which the Army had intended to employ their heavy gun were close to naval installations, it would be possible to provide ammunition through naval supply sources in cases of emergency. The proposal made sense, and in 1938 the Army adopted the 4.5in. It had a maximum ceiling of 41,000 feet and a practical ceiling of 26,500 feet, using a mechanical time fuze. Firing a 54½lb shell at a rate of 8 rounds per minute, it completely dominated the sky to the maximum service ceiling of any known bomber of the day.

With the upper air secured, the Army now turned to contemplate the lower part of the sky and the provision of a light gun to deal with low-flying raiders. Once more the question was affected by considerations of production and availability; it would doubtless be possible to design a suitable equipment from scratch, but finding the money and facilities to set up production was a hopeless prospect, and the time element argued against a development programme and in favour of finding a ready-made solution.

Once again the Royal Navy had a solution; they had, for several years, used a Vickers 2-pounder 'pom-pom', a direct descendant of Maxim's 'pom-pom' which had been the first light AA gun. Being designed for shipboard mounting it would have to be emplaced in concrete and it was a cumbersome device with two barrels each firing 60 shells a minute to about 6,000 feet. But for static mounting around defended ports and other vulnerable points it seemed suitable and, like the 4.5in gun, it was available virtually 'off the shelf', and so in April 1937 a decision was taken by the War Office to adopt this 2-pounder complete with its naval mounting and then to design a more portable form of mounting solely for Army use.

In 1936, however, the Bofors 40mm gun had been brought to the Army's attention, and at that same meeting in April 1937 which settled on the 2-pounder, a decision was also taken to buy 100 Bofors guns and half a million rounds of ammunition from Sweden in order to provide the field army with a mobile light weapon. Experience was soon to show that the Bofors was far superior to the

2-pounder and in 1938 the 2-pounder decision was rescinded after 60 equipments had been delivered. Meanwhile, in 1937, negotiations with AB Bofors resulted in obtaining a license to manufacture the 40mm gun in Britain and, in addition, a further quantity of guns were bought from Poland; the Poles had obtained a license in 1935 and after providing their own services with guns they had gone over to producing them for export.

By the middle of 1937, therefore, the anti-aircraft armament situation in Britain was that a range of guns, light, medium and heavy, had been approved, but the production facilities were such that it would still be some years before the planned gun strength was reached. And time, it seemed, was running short.

In 1935, when the expansion of Britain's air defences was first mooted, the likely future delay in the production of guns was immediately appreciated by the War Office, and the Research Department of Woolwich Arsenal was asked to investigate the use of rockets as a possible cheap and effective anti-aircraft weapon. The only guide-line they were given was that whatever they produced had to have a performance comparable with contemporary AA guns up to a ceiling of 10,000 feet.

Published information on rockets was worthless in this context, so the Research Department had to set out from first principles. The size of the rockets was determined very simply by the question of what propellant to use; a solid stick of cordite was the chosen fuel and, fortunately, there existed in service a type of solventless cordite which could be extruded in long sticks suitable for the task. Mathematics indicated that a two-inch diameter stick was the smallest which would produce an efficient rocket, while the largest stick which could be made by existing machinery was three inches in diameter. From these simple factors the 2in and 3in rockets appeared. And for the sake of secrecy they were no longer to be called rockets; they were to be known an 'unrotated projectiles' or 'UPs', while the department responsible for them became the 'Projectile Development Establishment' or PDE.

The design was kept as simple as possible; a long tube formed the 'motor', inside which was the stick of cordite and an electric igniter. At the front of the tube a high explosive warhead carried a fuze, and at the rear end four fins gave directional stability. Even with this degree of simplicity there were formidable problems, some of which were so basic as to be scarcely believable. The motor tube, for example; since special materials and production facilities were denied to the experimenters (it had to be cheap and simple) a suitable commercially available tube of nickel steel was adopted. This had to be abandoned when it was found that the makers invariably left the tube lengths with a slight curve, scarcely noticeable to the eye but soon apparent in the erratic flight of the rocket. The next choice was a slightly thicker tube of carbon steel, but again, the standard of manufacture was below that demanded for munitions; instead of being circular the tubes were usually oval and the distribution of metal eccentric. The eventual solution devised by PDE was to fabricate tubes by rolling sheet steel and welding the seam, then cold drawing it through a die to get the correct dimensions, and finally heat-treating it to obtain the required strength.

By late 1937 the 3in model, carrying an 18lb warhead, was selected as the future anti-aircraft weapon, and development continued, delayed by the need to initiate fundamental research into almost every aspect of design in order to find answers to the problems which appeared at every stage. By late 1938, however, there was sufficient confidence in the design to initiate an extensive trial which was carried out early in 1939 in Jamaica, 2,500 rockets being fired in secrecy to obtain information on flight characteristics and ballistics.

The greatest problem lay with the design of a projector. The services, for reasons best known to themselves, were insistent that the rocket launcher should be a tube with a closed breech – probably because of the possible hazards from the back-flash when the rocket ignited. Furthermore it was not only to look like a gun but be operated like one, with similar fire control systems. This design proved to be unsatisfactory, since the blast from the rocket, reflected from the closed breech and ejected from the muzzle of the tube, severely disturbed the airstream around the rocket fins and caused erratic flight. The problem was insoluble, the General Staff were not satisfied with the weapon, and in mid-1939 ruled that 'the requirement no longer exists'. In fact the requirement certainly did exist, for the supply of guns was nowhere near satisfying the demand, but adopting this phraseology gave a lever to exert more pressure for greater gun production while allowing development of rockets to continue on a low priority in the hope that accuracy and performance could be improved to a level comparable to that of guns. The way of the rocket pioneer was never an easy one; it is worth recalling the comment of Colonel Boxer, Superintendent of the Royal Laboratory at Woolwich in the 1860s when he was attempting to eliminate some of the defects of the Congreve rocket: 'If the rocket had been invented first, what a wonderful improvement we would consider the gun to be.'

While Britain worked, if not furiously at least with some urgency, to prepare for the forthcoming battle, others were doing the same. In Germany, with the 88mm gun in volume production, thoughts turned to the same question which had led the British Army to adopt the 4.5in gun, the problem of bombers which could fly above the 88's practical ceiling. At the end of 1933 a specification for a 105mm gun to fire a 32lb shell and with full power operation had been issued, and development contracts were placed with both Krupp and Rheinmetall. Each company was asked to produce two prototypes, one with electric power control and one with hydraulic, and four of each were to be made and handed to a special experimental battery for a series of comparative tests. In October 1936 the Rheinmetall design with hydraulic power control was selected as the production weapon, and it entered service in the following year as the 10.5cm Flak 38.

With the 10.5cm project safely under way, the Luftwaffe were still apprehensive of the future and drew up draft specifications for even bigger guns; a 12.8cm to fire a 60lb shell and a 15cm to fire a shell of about 90lb weight. The Rheinmetall company received the contract for the 12.8cm model and, taking the simplest course, produced a design which was little more than the 10.5cm suitably enlarged. The prototype was ready in 1937, completed its trials satisfactorily, and went into production as the 12.8cm Flak 40. While it was a good enough gun when emplaced, moving it was another story, since for travelling it was necessary to remove the barrel from the mounting and carry it on a special transporter. This had, in fact, been written into the specification and had been approved during the acceptance trials, but practical use soon showed that such an arrangement had no place on an anti-aircraft gun. In 1938 the Luftwaffe circularised a number of commercial vehicle companies, inviting them to submit designs which would allow the gun to be moved in one unit. The Meiller company produced a solution which involved a new platform with outriggers and two four-wheeled limbers, one at end end, which lifted the platform by hydraulic power. It was a good technical solution but the resulting load was 49 feet long and weighed 26 tons, which was hardly the mobile weapon the Luftwaffe had in mind.

In the light gun field both the German Army and Navy had a profusion of 20mm automatic weapons, but the Army wanted something more powerful and adopted a 37mm gun in 1935. It was little more than an enlarged version of the 20mm cannon, but the designers took the bit between their teeth and produced a carriage which copied the cruciform pattern used by bigger guns, complete with folding outriggers and two two-wheeled limbers. The result was a clumsy weapon in which far too many things seemed prone to malfunction or breakage and after the summer manoeuvres of 1935 the Army expressed their dissatisfaction, terminated the production contract, and asked for something more mobile. The carriage was scrapped and replaced by a simple platform carried on a two-wheeled trailer, again little more than a scale-up of the existing 20mm pattern. This was far more to the Army's liking and went into service as the 3.7cm Flak 38.

The practical ceiling of the 37mm gun was about 6,000 feet; the 88mm gun found it difficult to swing fast enough to track fast-moving low flyers below about 9,000 feet. So that there was a belt of sky some 3,000 feet deep in which attackers could operate with comparative immunity – at least, in theory. To try to plug this hole in the defences, in 1935 Rheinmetall were given a contract to develop a 50mm gun with high speeds of traverse and elevation and a practical ceiling of about 15,000 feet. This turned out to be a more difficult problem than anyone had expected; it was to take them five years to produce an answer, and when it came the answer would be a poor one.

The French Army was burdened with a vast amount of equipment left over from the First World War. As is well known, the greater part of French defence spending in the between-wars years was poured into the Maginot Line, leaving little for such mobile forms of defence as tanks, aircraft or guns. Over 900 of the 75mm guns of 1918 were still in service, some mobile and some static. An attempt had been made to improve their performance by removing the 1897 barrels and fitting new, longer, 75mm barrels made by Schneider, but the number was pitifully small and the intention was somewhat negated by the obsolete carriages with their old-style sights and fire control gear. Two relatively modern guns had been designed by Schneider, the 75mm Modele 1936 which used a modern design of mounting, off-carriage fire control and had a ceiling of about 22,000 feet, and the 90mm Modele 1926 on a three-legged platform and with a ceiling of about 30,000 feet. But shortage of money meant that few of these were in service; in spite of the 90mm having been officially introduced in 1926 there were only 17 guns in service fourteen years later.

In the United States the wartime 3in gun had been somewhat improved by a more modern design of mounting, expressively nicknamed the 'Spider Mount' from its long, folding, outriggers. The 1920s had been occupied by planning and designing two heavier weapons, a 105mm and a 4.7in, for the defence of rear areas. The 105mm design, a static mounted weapon was approved for the first time in 1927, but before any could be built there was a change of opinion over the design and it was changed in the interest of cheaper and easier production. This set the programme back and it was not until 1933 that the new model received approval. Little more happened until 1937 when some money was made available and fourteen guns were built. Most of these went to the Panama Canal Zone Defences and production then came to a halt because better things were in the air.

In 1919 the Westervelt Board had recommended the development of a 4.7in AA gun, and General Pershing had put his weight behind the proposal. A prototype gun was actually built and tested, but in 1925 the project was shelved. In 1938 it was revived with the intention of providing a heavy mobile gun for use in rear areas and in the continental United States, and once this project got under way, enthusiasm for the 105mm gun evaporated, since the 4.7in promised a considerable increase in performance for a relatively small increase in bulk. But the greatest need of the US Army at that time was for a mobile gun which could accompany a field army. The 3in gun, when all was said and done, was an 1898 design of seacoast gun, and a forty-year-old gun was no longer in the premier league. In 1938 the Coast Artillery Board (who were responsible for anti-aircraft artillery) asked for a new design, firing a shell of at least 21lb weight, the upper limit of calibre being set only by the requirement that the gun had to be loaded by hand. Fifty pounds is the generally accepted maximum weight for a complete round of ammunition capable of being loaded by a man for a continuous spell of firing, and with this in mind the Ordnance Department produced a design for a 90mm gun firing a 24lb shell, the complete round weighing about 42lb. Development of a gun to this specification was formally approved in June 1938, and with that one on the drawing board, the major nations had completed their preparations.

5 WAR IN THE AIR

During 1938 and 1939 Europe rang with the sound of shovels, as air-raid shelters were excavated in every major city. Conditioned by statements in the press and on public platforms by people claiming to have expert knowledge, it became a general belief that declaration of war would be followed very rapidly by the appearance of an enemy air fleet showering high explosives and poison gas in all directions. Some credence had been given to this view by the much-discussed bombing of Guernica in April 1937, by the German 'Condor Legion', a 'volunteer' Luftwaffe force sent to Spain by Hitler. To this day debate and controversy rage around this incident, as it does about almost every facet of the Spanish Civil War, since the simple tactical facts are thickly overlaid by ideological embellishment. The only certainty is that in a matter of three hours some 45 tons of bombs were dropped on the town, killing about 300 people and injuring a like number, but the propaganda and counter-propaganda which followed inflated the casualty and damage figures beyond all recognition. As a result, the more alarming the prophecies about aerial warfare, the more likely they were to be believed. Official circles in Britain did calculations based on the tonnage of bombs dropped in London during the First World War and the number of resulting casualties, and came to the conclusion that fifty people would be killed or injured for every ton of bombs dropped. Then the strength of the Luftwaffe was estimated, its bomb-carrying capacity similarly estimated, and the official conclusion was that 100,000 people would be killed and 200,000 injured every month once war broke out. Defence was farthest from the civil service mind; their principal concern appears to have been the tidy disposal of the bodies. But with the same sort of arithmetic being done in every country in Europe, the obsession with digging becomes understandable.

Nobody was particularly surprised, therefore, when air-raid-warning sirens sounded within an hour of Mr Chamberlain's historic broadcast on that September Sunday morning, and when no shower of bombs materialised, people felt somehow cheated. In fact the 'raider' was a civil machine returning from France which had failed to notify its flight plan to the appropriate authorities. It was not until 6 September that indications of a serious attack began to percolate through the warning and reporting network, with the plotting of a mysterious aircraft approaching across the North Sea. Fighters were despatched to intercept; more raiders were notified, more fighters flown off, and the incoming force gathered in strength. An hour later, after the RAF had lost three machines, the truth of the matter emerged; the initial sighting had been of a British fighter inland, on a training flight, but by some unexplained mistake (it was later proved not to be a technical fault on the radar) it had been plotted 180 degrees out of position. Subsequently the fighters were also plotted in the wrong area, apparently adding to the raiding force and thus generating more fighters which in turn .... A gun battery in the Thames Estuary reported shooting down a twin-engined enemy machine, which turned out to have been an RAF Blenheim, while the other two casualties were Hurricanes shot down when two fighter squadrons met. It all went down in RAF history as the 'Battle of Barking Creek' and it was to serve as a horrible warning of what could happen when things went wrong.

As the first winter of war closed in, the absence of air attack plus the quiescent state of the front line in France led to the 'phoney War' or *Sitzkrieg* period in which people at home began to forget that there was a war on at all, but at least it gave the defences some valuable breathing space together with the finance and manpower to bring the various schemes of defence something closer to their planned strength and efficiency. One problem which made an early appearance was that the Chain Home system of radar was incapable of dealing with targets which chose to fly low, below about 5,000 feet. This had, of course, been known for some time, but it had been put to one side in the excitement of getting the Chain working; now that war had arrived it had to be dealt with fairly rapidly.

At this point the somewhat liberal system of operation at Bawdsey came to the rescue. Work had been in progress for some time in developing a coast-watching equipment for Army use in conjunction with coast artillery; another group had been working on a design for naval use; and a third were studying the Army's requirement for a lightweight anti-aircraft early warning set. In the course of off-duty discussions these three projects cross-fertilised each other and the immediate result was a set with a rotating aerial array (rotated by an airman on a wheel-less bicycle frame who provided the motive power for hours on end) which filled the gap in the defences by being able to detect both low-flying aircraft and ships at sea. This was perfected just as war broke out and the winter of 1939–40 was occupied by the construction of a chain of these sets, known as the 'Chain Home, Low-flying' or CHL.

Guns made their first score on the day after war was declared. On 4 September the RAF attacked the heavy cruiser *Admiral Scheer* and the cruiser *Emden* in the Heligoland Bight. Due to poor weather conditions the 19 attacking bombers had to go in at minimum height, well within the range of even the 20mm guns which both ships carried in generous numbers. As a result, seven aircraft were shot down, an inauspicious beginning for Bomber Command.

The turn of the British gunners did not come until the following month, since the Luftwaffe were less quick off the mark to begin their bombing campaign. But on 16 October a number of German aircraft swept up the Firth of Forth making for two warships close to the Forth Bridge. A gunsite on the south side of the Forth was engaged in gun-drill when the alert was sounded and, rapidly discarding dummy ammunition for live, they engaged the raiders and shot away part of the tail of one Heinkel He III bomber. It limped away to be finished off by a Spitfire, so the first German aircraft to be brought down over Britain was a combined affair by both arms of the defensive force.

The *Sitzkrieg* was finally ended by the German attacks on Norway and Denmark and then the advance into the Low Countries and France in May 1940, and the propagators of the cataclysmic theory of bombing found new support for their fears on 14 May when the Luftwaffe bombed Rotterdam. The bombing was accompanied by an artillery bombardment and the damage and casualties were again severe, but the confused conditions of the time ensured that the tale lost nothing in its telling and, taken together with pseudo-nuns descending by parachute, lady hikers in jackboots and similar rumours, served to sharpen apprehensions of an airborne attack on Britain.

In spite of the factories turning out guns during the winter months, the defences were, in fact, little better than they had been on 3 September. Guns had to be sent to France with the British Expeditionary Force, and the greatest absorber of armament was an insatiable Royal Navy who, in their role as Senior Service, took good care to seize the lion's share of any weapons which were available. In December 1939 they demanded 255 guns to protect fleet anchorages, at a time when the London area had only 96 guns and a target of such vital importance as the Rolls-Royce aero-engine factory had but 8 guns to protect it. Although the overall command of the air defence of Great Britain was in the capable hands of Air Marshal Dowding, and the AA Artillery under General Pile, neither were consulted as to the allocation of gun defences, which was now in the hands of the Deputy Chiefs-of-Staff Committee, some of whose decisions defied rational explanation. In January the Admiralty suggested sending the 3.7in guns of ADGB to France to replace the 3in guns of the BEF, these 3in then being sent back to Britain and presented to the Royal Navy. Such a move would have practically stripped what defences remained in Britain, but fortunately it was scotched by the BEF refusing to have the 3.7s; they preferred their more-manoeuverable 3in guns for mobile warfare.

The lack of light guns – in March 1940 there were only 108 Bofors guns in the whole of the United Kingdom – led to a wholesale issue of obsolescent Lewis light machine guns; they were relatively useless apart from their value in raising morale by allowing the troops actually to shoot back. Over 3,000 of these were issued, with makeshift mountings, but in February 1940 the Navy demanded 800 of them, raised their demand to 1,300 in the following month, and then asked for another 1,600, which would have effectively removed the Lewis gun from ADGB by midsummer.

While this was still being argued the German invasion of Norway took place, resulting in a fresh Admiralty demand for another 800 Lewis guns in order to arm Norwegian and Danish merchant ships, plus a demand from the planning staff of the War Office for 144 heavy and 144 light guns to be sent to Norway forthwith. This was patently impossible; it was thought that, at most, 95 guns of all types could be made available by pruning ADGB to the bone, but before that step could be taken it became obvious that Norway was a lost cause and the requirement was cancelled.

In July 1940, with the Army recovering its breath after Dunkirk, a quick stock-check revealed the gun strength in Britain to be 1,280 medium (3.7in and 4.5in) and 517 light (2-pounder, 3in and 40mm). This may sound reasonable until the figures are compared with the strengths actually planned: 3,744 medium, 4,410 light and over 8,000 rocket projectors. Total deficiency: 2,464 medium, 3,893 light and over 8,000 rocket launchers. There was a long way to go. But before much else could be done the Luftwaffe at last began the all-out attack on Britain which had been so confidently expected in the previous September.

Much has been written about the Battle of Britain, and there is doubtless more to come, though the current tendency appears to lean towards disputing whether it ever happened and if so, who won it. I know it happened, since much of it took place over my head, but I was not, at that time, privy to the higher councils, so no searching analysis of motives and actions need be expected here. Indeed it must be dealt with relatively briefly, since it was but one facet of the history of air defence, but it was a facet which revealed the wisdom of some aspects of pre-war planning and also some of the weaknesses; while the Battle of Britain certainly saved the country in 1940, it is equally certain that by focussing everyone's eyes on the air and the necessity for defence, and thus accelerating the development and production of equipment, it went a long way towards building up the defensive apparatus which was to save the south of England from certain destruction in 1944.

The first German moves came in the form of increasing attacks on coastal areas, Dover in particular being a frequent target and the guns there scoring considerable success. One result of this sudden increase in activity was that guns in the coastal area were having to be manned for 24 hours of the day, and this sort of demand had not been envisaged by those who had planned the manpower structure of an anti-aircraft battery; the establishment had been predicated on short bursts of activity in daylight, with infrequent activity at night, a regime which allowed the men to sleep, eat, maintain their guns, fetch ammunition and so forth. But the constant alerts, together with the other day-to-day demands on manpower – guard details, ammunition supply, routine chores, sickness – left little time to eat or sleep and units were threatened with the prospect of coming to a standstill out of sheer fatigue. In the worst cases it was found necessary to draft more men in and double the pre-war strength of a battery so as to provide enough officers and men to operate a non-stop shift system.

The observing and reporting network set up by General Ashmore now began to show its worth, as did the infant radar network. By this time the Chain Home system stretched in an unbroken barrier from the Isle of Wight to the Orkneys and the Chain Home Low-flying system covered the eastern and south-eastern coasts. From a range of over 100 miles the CH stations were able to see the assembly of German aircraft into raiding formations over their French airfields, track them, and alert the defenders, so that when the raiders closed with the English coast they found a suitable force of fighters, well disposed tactically, waiting to deal with them. The only defect, at the beginning, was the inability of the radar operators to estimate the strength of the incoming raids, since they had not had the opportunity of seeing such quantities of aircraft on their screens before. Thus, when a radar in the north of England warned of an approaching 'thirty plus' force of aircraft, No. 72 Squadron RAF flew to meet them over the North Sea, and signalled back to the Operations Room: 'For 30 read 170, one hundred Heinkel 111 and seventy Messerschmit 110'. For all the disparity, 72 Squadron fell upon the raiders, split up the formation and severely punished them. But that sort of error soon became a thing of the past as, with more practice, operators soon became uncanningly accurate at assessing numbers from the appearance of the echo signals on their screen.

By this time the Germans had realised that some form of radio detection was in use, though since their own system was at an early stage of development they had no inkling of the immense scope of the British network. On 12 August, therefore came a systematic attack on five radar stations, from Dunkirk in Kent, to Ventnor on the Isle of Wight. They were glaringly obvious targets, with aerial masts towering 300 and more feet above them, but they were singularly difficult to put out of action except by complete destruction. Within six hours of the attack all except one was back in operation, the exception being Ventnor which had had a scattering of delayed-action bombs and had to be evacuated until these could be dug up and rendered safe, a task which took ten days. On the day after this attack, the German raiders were greeted by RAF fighters in the customary fashion, which led the Luftwaffe to the conclusion that there was no profit in attacking radar stations; yet had these attacks been followed up in systematic fashion, putting the stations out of action day after day, there is little doubt that the warning system would have been severely reduced in its efficiency. But the quick rebound of these first stations gave an impression of impervious omniscience which did the trick.

The attack then turned to fighter stations, ten of Fighter Command's eleven fields being bombed and machine-gunned on 13 August while the radar stations were untouched. Again, had this line of attack been followed up the consequences would have been extremely serious, but again the plan was abandoned for something else. The reasons for this change were many, but two were particularly significant: the rate of attrition of German bombers and the fact that their escorting fighters were limited in their operational range. Once the scene of action moved further inland from Kent, the escorting fighters had to turn about and head for home, otherwise they were liable to run out of fuel, and once the escort was gone, the bombers were sitting targets; on 15 August the Luftwaffe lost 75 aircraft. On that night, though, the bombers returned under cover of darkness, bombed, and went home unscathed, and after considering the implications of this, the Luftwaffe gradually swung its main effort into night raiding. The daylight attacks continued, for they were part and parcel of the 'Sealion' plan to invade England, which depended on the Luftwaffe attaining air superiority over the English Channel, but on 7 September the German tactics took a new turn as 350 bombers, escorted by over 600 fighters, roared up the Thames estuary late in the afternoon. Assuming another attack on the fighter stations, the RAF controllers had deployed their forces accordingly, so that only a relatively weak screen of fighters covered the route to London. These were soon swept aside by the massive escort; London's dockland was set ablaze, while the Germans lost 10 bombers and 22 fighters to the RAF's 29 fighters lost. The blazing Thames-side acted as a beacon for a fresh force of 318 bombers which appeared over the target shortly after 10.00pm and, free of interference, systematically pounded London until 4.30am. The following day saw heroic efforts by the London Fire Brigade, but many fires were still burning as night fell and they marked the way for a fresh attack. And so it went on, for 65 successive nights.

While the defences had been well pleased with their performance during the August–September day battles, the change to night attacks soon put their feet back on the ground. The inadequate defence of London by guns and the inability of fighters to find targets at night were both revealed in the most violent manner. Within 48 hours the gun strength was increased to 371 barrels by bringing in guns from all over Britain, but even this addition had little effect; in the first four nights only four aircraft were brought down by gunfire. The most noticeable thing to Londoners, though, was that while there seemed to be a lot more guns around the place, there didn't seem to be much increase in the amount of firing going on, and some gunsites were observed not to fire at all during raids. There was a good deal of criticism of the AA defences on this score, but what the public failed to appreciate was that in several cases the guns were silent in order to let RAF fighters have a free run. Nevertheless, much of the trouble stemmed from the fire control system in use, an extension of the fixed azimuth system previously mentioned. This relied on a network of sound locators which had been installed just before the war when it was apparent that Army RDF was at a low priority. This system produced a predicted path of the raid based on those aircraft which appeared more or less on the centre of the listening zone; from this a future position was deduced and passed to the guns on the raid track, which then opened fire. But it meant that raiders which, by luck or good judgement, evaded the sound locators were not predicted and the guns in their path, in the absence of data, were unable to open fire.

On 10 September, General Pile decided to abandon the precise inaccuracies of the fixed azimuth system. He called a meeting of the commanders of every gun position in and around London, assembled them in the Drill Hall in Brompton Road, and gave instructions that henceforth all guns would fire every possible round, pointing at an approximate bearing and elevation based on whatever information the site commander could obtain and on his educated guess if no data were forthcoming. No searchlights would expose and no RAF aircraft would enter the area; everything which flew was to be fired at without question or hesitation. Not only would defences be operating, they would be seen to be operating.

> 'The result was as astonishing to me as it appears to have been to the citizens of London – and, apparently, to the enemy as well. For, although few of the bursts could have been anywhere near the target, the heights of aircraft steadily increased as the night went on, and many of them turned away before entering the Inner Artillery Zone . . . it was in no sense a barrage, though I think by that name it will always be known . . .'
>
> (General Sir Frederick Pile; *Ack-Ack*)

In addition to this, the Admiralty produced a number of elderly 3in guns on motor lorries, manned them with naval ratings, and sent them around the streets; whenever they saw an air-raid shelter they would screech to a halt and blast a few shells into the sky, just to cheer up the occupants of the shelter. It was good for morale, and they had about as much chance of hitting an enemy aircraft as did the more regularly employed guns. (One of these guns, operating in the St Albans district, actually hit a bomber one night. The crew never had to buy a drink for several weeks afterwards.)

While the citizens of Central London were ecstatic at the noise and fury of the guns, those in the outlying suburbs were less enchanted, due to the number of bombs jettisoned at random by the raiders. General Pile recorded one of the many complaints which reached his office in the next few days: 'The council of an outer suburb wrote to say that council house lavatory pans were being cracked by gun vibration and could we please move the barrage somewhere else.' But on the whole, the 'barrage' was a popular move until people began to realise that there seemed to be very few crashed aircraft as a result of all the noise.

It was far from an easy time for the gunners. *Roof over Britain*, an official account of AA published in 1943 by the Ministry of Information, recorded the experience of a battery brought into the London area from the Humber defences. Within 25 hours of receiving orders to move, it had arrived in London and had to begin by clearing a bomb-blasted site in order to provide a gun position. By 7.30pm the guns were ready; at 8.15pm they went into action until 6.00am next morning. The guns were then cleaned, ammunition stocks replenished, and the gunners went to bed at 9.30am, to be roused 30 minutes later by a daylight alert. The gunners continued this routine for eight days, 'with so little sleep that at times the gunlayers were almost unconscious as they tried to keep their eyes focussed on the dials'. On the ninth day the men were relieved by a recruits' battery who had never fired the guns before and had to be given a quick course of instruction before they could be left in charge.

The balloon aprons of 1918 had been revived in a different form in 1936, when the Air Staff laid plans for a ring of balloons around London, without the connecting apron, spaced at about ten balloons to the mile and requiring 450 balloons. This plan was rapidly changed when it was realised that a ring of balloons merely forced an attacker high in order to cross the ring, after which he could come down to bombing height once more, and 'field siting', an irregular pattern all over the area, was adopted.

An interesting experiment was the idea of an aerial mine-field, a drifting barrage of small balloons, some 55 miles long, 7 miles wide and 4,000 feet deep. These balloons were fitted with contact mines sufficiently powerful to blow the wing off a bomber, and they were to be released from sites on the outskirts of London in the hope that they would drift across the approach lines of the raiders. Needless to say, the whole scheme depended upon favourable winds, but, conditions being ripe, it was tried on 27 December 1940. It did not go well. Communications with the various release points were poor, so that when the order to release was given, the balloons straggled up piecemeal for over an hour instead of being released *en masse*. One-third of the balloons proved to be defective, many of the mines detonated prematurely, others descended shortly after release, and the whole barrage appeared to rise too high. Since the Germans chose not to attack in large numbers that night, the barrage was called off after two hours. No results were achieved, though German pilots, it was afterwards discovered, reported the presence of 'parachute mines'. Further attempts were made in 1941 but no useful results were ever achieved and the plan was later abandoned.

It was the gun barrage which caught the public's fancy, though there were plenty of people ready to dispute the choice of description. Professor A.V. Hill, whose association with AA gunnery and its problems went back to the invention of the mirror position finder, was quite forthright: 'One cubic mile of space contains 5,500,000,000 cubic yards. The lethal zone of a 3.7in AA shell is only a few thousand cubic yards and exists for only one-fiftieth of a second. The idea of a 'barrage' of shells is nonsense. The word ought to be dropped; it gives a false impression. Nothing but aimed fire is any use.' He was, of course, perfectly correct, and the AA gunners knew it well enough, but it was one thing to define perfection and quite another to achieve it with the limited technical aids available at the time. This was brought home during the raid on 15/16 October, when 235 aircraft attacked London; the guns fired 8,326 shells to destroy two and damage two.

By the spring of 1941 radar began to appear in serviceable form and useable quantity, in ground control interception sets which allowed RAF controllers to track raiders and fighters and command the fighters, by voice radio, into the area of the enemy; in airborne intercept sets carried in fighters which allowed them to make contact in the dark; and in GL (gun-laying) sets which could provide the AA predictors with accurate information on the target height, range and bearing. The GL sets at first displayed some peculiar aberrations, which were eventually traced to irregular signal reflections from the surrounding ground. This was cured by laying a flat screen of chicken wire around the set to give an artificial plane from which the signals could reflect in an orderly manner. Even this seemingly simple solution raised problems; it demanded some 300 miles of chicken wire, all there was in the country, and there were many people who, intent upon keeping a few chickens to augment their rations, were somewhat baffled to find that such a peaceful commodity had vanished from the market.

One of the most irritating gaps in the defences was the River Thames itself; it lay like a directional sign pointing the way to the capital, and its mouth was so wide that guns positioned at either side could not bar the entrance. In 1941 the Admiralty became concerned with this gap since it was being exploited not only by bombers but also by mine-laying aircraft, and they invited a Mr G.A. Maunsell, a noted civil engineer, to consider the construction of some sort of artificial island upon which anti-aircraft guns could be mounted. Artificial sea forts were no novelty in British defences; they had been built in Plymouth and Portsmouth harbours in the 1870s and in the Humber estuary during the First World War, but these structures had taken years to build on their selected sites, a course which was obviously impractical in this case since the first sign of construction activity would invite attention from the Luftwaffe. Maunsell therefore proposed building the forts in dry dock, complete in every detail, then towing them out to their location and there sinking them to rest on the sea bed.

Each fort consisted of a boat-like concrete pontoon 168 feet long, 88 feet wide and 14 feet deep, on top of which rose two cylindrical concrete towers 24 feet in diameter and 60 feet high. On top of these towers was a four-decked steel superstructure to accommodate a crew of 120 men, two 3.7in and two Bofors 40mm guns, together with radar, searchlights, living quarters, kitchens, and every other adjunct necessary to make each fort a self-contained unit.

Once the fort was built, it was manned in dry dock by its crew, who then familiarised themselves with the equipment and put the fort into commission, after which the dock was flooded. The fort now floated on the concrete pontoon and, when wind and tide were right, it was towed into place by tugs, accompanied by minesweepers and an anti-aircraft frigate to protect the operation. On reaching the site the pontoon was flooded, and in fifteen seconds the fort had sunk until the pontoon was sitting on the sea bed, with the tops of the towers and the superstructure above the waterline. In one case enemy aircraft appeared within minutes of the operation being completed and the fort went straight into action.

Three Maunsell Forts were built and were located on the Tongue Sand, north of Margate; Knock John, off the Essex coast; and Sunk Head, near Clacton-on-sea. Shortly after their interception the War Office, less concerned with mine-laying than with bomber attacks, obtained Mr Maunsell's services to design a different pattern of fort to be sited to cover the Thames and the Mersey estuaries. These forts used a concrete base surmounted by four hollow concrete legs holding a two-floored steel superstructure. These units were taken out to their locations by tugs and sunk in patterns in which a central unit was surrounded by six others, after which the individual units were joined by footbridges. The central tower carried the radar and predictor, while of the ring of six, four held 3.7in guns, one a 40mm Bofors for local defence, and one a searchlight. Three of these combinations were built across the mouth of the Mersey, known simply as Mersey 1, 2 and 3, and these were followed by three more in the middle of the Thames estuary, off the Isle of Sheppey, known as Forts U5, U6 and U7. They effectively corked the approaches to both London and Liverpool and proved of considerable value in barring the raider's approach.

The saturation tactics of the bombers during the winter of 1940/41 caused second thoughts among those who had earlier rejected the rocket. It will be recalled that 2in and 3in rockets had been developed, but the Army had rejected the 3in since its accuracy was not up to gun standards. The Navy had taken the 2in, using it on a 'parachute-and-cable' device intended to counter dive-bombers. The rocket was fired vertically, carrying a length of cable behind it, two parachutes and a small bomb. When the apparatus had deployed fully, the result was a bomb suspended on a long wire, supported by a parachute, with a small stabilising parachute close to the bomb. If an aircraft struck the wire, the whole assembly slid over the wing due to the drag of the upper parachute until the bomb struck the aircraft's wing and detonated; there was sufficient explosive in the bomb to remove the wing. As well as being used by the Royal Navy, these 'Apparatus, Air Defence' were also laid in rows alongside airfields on land, and at least one such layout, that on the fighter airfield at Kenley, managed to greet an attack with a salvo of well-timed rockets which caught a Dornier bomber and brought it down. Possibly as a result of reports from their aviators the Luftwaffe developed a similar device, the *Kurzzeitsperre* (short time barrage). This did not use an explosive bomb, but fired a rocket into the air which dragged a wire behind it. The end of the wire was attached to the launcher, so that when the rocket reached the end of the wire it pulled free, deployed a parachute, and allowed the wire to sink slowly back to earth. The wire was of hard steel, 1.8mm wide and 0.7mm thick; when struck by an aircraft it would spin and saw its way through the airframe, cutting through the average bomber wing in less than a second. Two versions were made, one which reached to 1,000 metres altitude, and a smaller one to reach to 300 metres. There is no record of any British aircraft being brought down or damaged by this device.

The most important thing to come from the 2in rocket was the realisation that an open-rail launcher was quite sufficient and that the back-blast was nothing like as deadly as had been feared. As a result an open-rail launcher for the 3in rocket was designed and approved for issue in the summer of 1940. The designer's aim was to provide a launcher so cheap and simple that it could be built in large numbers without the need for elaborate production facilities, and which could be used with little or no previous training. A good deal of trial had to be done to evolve a system of shielding the crew from the rocket blast, but this was eventually overcome and several thousand Projector Rockets 3in No. 1 Mark 1 were built, beginning in late 1940. In November 1940 a twin projector, the No. 2 Mark 1, was also approved.

The first use of these rockets was as a defence against dive-bombers, using a proximity fuze on the rocket so as to do away with the need to calculate and set fuze lengths. This fuze, the 'Pistol No. 710', was developed in 1939/40 by the Projectile Development Establishment under Dr Alwyn Crowe, and it relied on a set of photo-electric cells 'tuned' to average daylight. When the shadow of an aircraft fell across the cell, as the rocket closed with its target, the change in the intensity of the light triggered an electric circuit which detonated the rocket warhead. Like all first attempts this, the first proximity fuze ever to see service, had its defects, notably a tendency to react to clouds and stray birds, and when the principal German effort turned to night bombing it was, of course, outflanked and rendered useless. So the projectors were now gathered together to form massed batteries, normally of 64 twin projectors, and fired in salvos to give a barrage effect. Normal powder-burning time fuzes were fitted and set so as to burst the rockets at various heights to give a screen of metal in the air. The prime drawback was that shortly after the launch of 128 rockets into the night sky, 128 tail units – each 55in long and weighing 18lb – fell back to earth. Therefore the siting of a rocket battery had to be done with this in mind, ensuring that the spent tail units would not fall into a populated area and do more damage than the unimpeded bombers. One such battery was on the sea front close to Cardiff, and whenever a salvo was fired, the sentry on the coast defence battery on Flatholme Island, in the Bristol Channel, sounded the alarm, since the tail units invariably landed in the battery's gun emplacements.

By this time, the RAF was engaged in bombing Germany and the German defences had begun to demonstrate their efficiency. This defence rested primarily on the 88mm and 105mm guns, several hundred batteries of which were distributed across Germany. Their information came largely from ground observers and sound location, with early warning provided by a handful of Freya radar sets. In addition there were several hundred searchlight batteries, each equipped with three lights and a sound locator. The full strength in September 1940 was impressive: 2,870 heavy guns, 7,970 light and medium guns, 2,540 searchlights and 380 balloons; and these figures did not include naval weapons emplaced on shore around dockyards and naval bases.

The German organisation was headed by a *Flug Wachkommando* (Air Watch Commando), a form of control centre which received warning information from the Freya radars forming part of the *Flug Meldestellen* (Air Reporting Posts), and also from a network of ground observer posts. In the *Wachkommando* information was assessed and the appropriate *Flak Gruppen* covering districts likely to be the target of an oncoming raid were warned. These, in their turn, passed the information to the *Flak Untergruppe* which had direct command of the flak batteries, and the guns would receive a preliminary warning when a raid entered a circle of 200 kilometres radius around the gun site.

The Freya radar had a range of about 100 miles and was a sound early-warning detector but too imprecise to be of much use to the guns. It was, in fact, a German naval set; the Luftwaffe's radar development programme had fallen behind and, after a bitter wrangle, a few Freyas were handed over to the Luftwaffe early in 1940. The Luftwaffe's own design, developed by the Telefunken Company, eventually came into service as the *Würzburg*. The prototype had been demonstrated to Hitler in February 1939, and it went into production in April 1940, but like most innovative devices it took some time to make the production models perform properly and to train people to extract the best from them. Shortly before production got under way an experimental model was developed, with a greatly improved method of measuring target height, and once this had been perfected production of the first model (*Würzburg* A) was stopped after some 200 had been made and its place was taken by the new *Wurzburg* C, of which 1,000 were eventually made and installed. *Würzburg* was a far more advanced and precise instrument than Freya and could direct gunfire quite accurately, but it was to be the middle of 1941 before it came into widespread use.

In the absence of radar the Luftwaffe had placed a great deal of faith in infra-red radiation as a means of detecting targets. This system, relying on detecting the heat emitted by aircraft engines, had been briefly touted in Great Britaïn in 1935–36, but the evident superiority of radar soon put it out of the running. This was due to the relatively close watch and tight grip of the CSSAD Committee, who were able to assess the relative merits of the systems, discard the one and concentrate all the available effort on the other. But in Germany there was no comparable guiding hand and numerous hares were started in the late 1930s, some of which ran until they dropped and some of which were still running in 1945. This diversification of effort ran through all German research and development and was particularly rampant in the air defence field.

The interest in infra-red came about partly from a logical appreciation of the obvious and partly by a misapprehension. Several British inventors took an interest in the infra-red field in 1936–38; none of their work was in any way official and a number of patents for detectors were taken out. These patents were noted in Germany and were adduced as evidence that the British would make considerable use of infra-red during a war – on the assumption that if these things were being published openly, what might be hidden behind the scenes? As a result, German research into infra-red was stepped up. In fact Britain made practically no use of infra-red until the latter part of the war when 'Tabby', an infra-red night driving aid, was introduced.

In Germany, though, a number of devices made an appearance. At least a dozen, bearing names such as 'Popeye', 'Frogs-eye' 'Buttercup' and 'Wunsdorf' were designed for installation in fighter aircraft so as to detect the hot exhausts of the Allied bomber engines. Most of these were abandoned in 1942 when radar development had reached the point of airborne equipment, but one device, known as 'Kiel' and made by Zeiss, was in production when the war ended. This used a lead sulphide detection cell mounted in the focus of a parabolic mirror and was claimed to be able to detect targets up to 5 kilometres away.

For use by AA guns and searchlights, *Adlergerat, Kormoran, Mucke, Obi* and *Walter* were all varieties of infra-red telescope to enable exhausts to be picked up visually in darkness and thus provide data for insertion into a predictor or for aligning a searchlight before switching it on, ensuring rapid acquisition of the target and less chance of evasive action by the aircraft. Most of these equipments failed to come up to expectations, though the *Adlergerät* was in fairly wide use in 1940 and 1941 before the *Würzburg* radars appeared.

The original disposition of German defences was much as

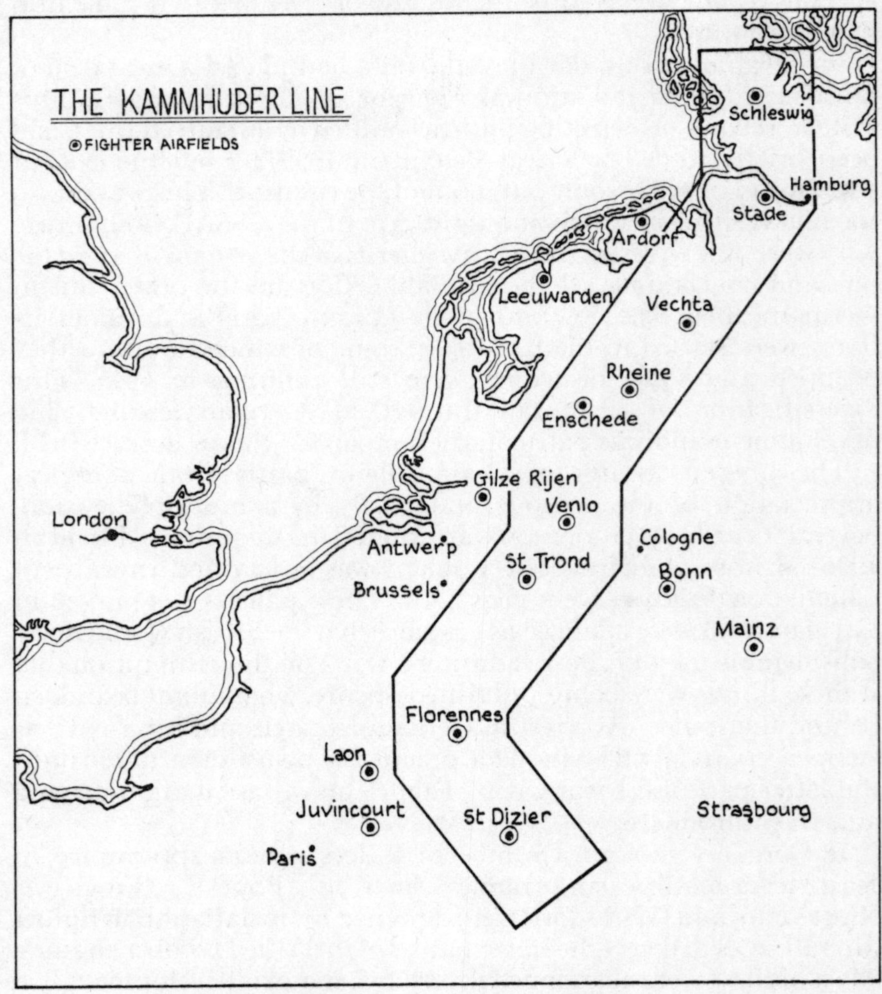

common-sense might expect; cities and towns were ringed with searchlights and guns, while fighter aircraft were dispersed at a number of bases. On being alerted by a radar intercept the fighters would take to the air to fly standing patrols within range of a radio beacon which would give them further instructions. Unfortunately, while patrolling, the fighters frequently came into the searchlight zones and were promptly shot at by their own gunners. Another drawback was that the rings of lights defined the target areas and gave the RAF bombers an excellent form of guidance. To cure these defects Colonel Josef Kammhuber, head of night fighting defences, redeployed the lights and many of the guns into a line stretching from Schleswig Holstein to Liege, thus placing the defensive zone well out from the major industrial areas. Fighters were to be guided to their targets by ground controllers, who based their instructions on indications from the Freya radar, but due to the poor accuracy of this set successful interceptions were few and what damage the RAF sustained was principally from gunfire.

As 1941 came into its final month the Japanese attack on Pearl Harbor (detected by radar but ignored) brought the United States into the war and, as had happened elsewhere, brought the air defences into the limelight. While the prospect of an enemy flying as far as the USA had always been discounted, the Pearl Harbor demonstration of the potential of carrier-borne aircraft put a new complexion on the aerial threat and heightened it by having destroyed much of the naval shield intended to protect the Pacific coast from attack.

During 1939 the first early radar (known then as 'Derax') sets, the SCR270 (mobile) and SCR271 (static) were perfected and production begun, and in 1940 the first operational sets were installed in the Panama Canal Zone. The SCR268 gun control set had also been built and demonstrated but lack of funds and personnel had reduced progress to little more than a token effort. It was not until the Tizard mission went from Britain to the USA in August 1940 to reveal British radar progress and, in particular, the resonant cavity magnetron, the device which enabled high power to be developed on extremely short (centimetric) wave-lengths, that radar research in the USA really gathered speed.

In February 1940 an Air Defense Command had been set up in order to 'explore methods of defense for cities, bases, armies and industrial areas' with control of aircraft, guns and warning service. In August the system was tested in manoeuvres near Watertown, NY, with the aid of two radar sets, and this exercise showed quite conclusively the values of a unified organisation; it was officially concluded that sixteen times the number of aircraft would have been needed had it not been for the presence of the radars and warning system. After this exercise the Air Defense Commander, Brigadier General James E. Chaney, was sent to Britain to study the system in use and see what could be adapted to American conditions.

In pre-war days suggestions had been made from time to time for a civilian-manned reporting system similar to the British Observer Corps; an Army Air Corps study in 1936 reluctantly came to the conclusion that such a system 'was an impossibility, and doubted if public apathy could be sufficiently overcome to render effective any effort to create a landward net in time of peace'. But by early 1941 the events of the war in Europe made sufficient impression to enable over 10,000 volunteers to be enrolled to man 700 observer posts along a sector between Boston and New York, and a four-day exercise proved the system's worth, even while pointing out some of its weak links.

Shortly after this the Air Defense Command was dismantled and a fresh organisation brought into being, four 'Interceptor Commands' covering the entire continental USA. These embodied the lessons of the recent exercises and had charge of all air defence measures in their respective areas except for purely passive measures which were the responsibility of the Office of Civilian Defense. Plans called for the entire system – observers, radar, guns, aircraft and reporting system – to be in readiness by 1 August 1941, a deadline which suggests either incredible optimism or abysmal ignorance of the problems involved. Radar sets had to be built and installed across an immense mileage of coast, Pacific, Atlantic and Gulf; thousands of observers had to be recruited and trained; report centres and communications facilities had to be built and manned, and the whole structure cemented together with guns, balloons and aircraft. The provision of the latter vital items was among the greatest of the problems; in December 1941 I Interceptor Command, responsible for the north-eastern seaboard, could muster only 54 aircraft, while IV Interceptor Command, covering the Pacific coast, had but 16 aircraft to defend California. The Los Angeles area was scheduled to have 120 3in guns, but only 12 were available. 'For San Diego the Army had no mobile AA strength at all to assign. The planners related later that they had done everything they could for San Diego – they had prayed that no attack would come' (*The Army Air Force in World War II*, Vol. VI). Pearl Harbor was a stimulant to all this preparation, but the sudden reinforcement of the Pacific Coast in expectation of Japanese raids and the series of alerts and invasion scares which followed tended to overstrain the infant organisation, resulting, in February 1942, in the 'Battle of Los Angeles', the American equivalent of the 'Battle of Barking Creek' in which misread information led to a delirious and escalating confrontation between nominally friendly forces which fortunately resolved itself before too much damage had been done.

The year 1940 had also seen the standardisation of the 90mm AA Gun M1 and the 4.7in AA Gun M1, both mobile guns, and production began to get under way, albeit slowly; only 171 90mm

The balloon apron barrage across north-east London.

Top: The remains of a Gotha bomber which crashed on Whitsunday 1918 after being hit by gunfire.

Above: On 4 August 1917 an air raid caused this damage to the surround of Cleopatra's Needle; some of the marks can still be seen today.

Top: A 13-pounder in France. Judging by the attitudes of the gunners, this appears to be a genuine 'action' picture and not the usual posed affair.

Above: The American Expeditionary Force in France. Battery B of the 1st AA Battalion at Montrieul on 15 June 1918, with a 75mm auto-cannon. Notice the division of labour: one breech operator, one-loader and four sight-setters.

Top left: A German 8.8cm anti-aircraft gun captured by the Canadian Army in 1918. Though of the same calibre as the more famous Second World War weapon, there was no line of descent between them.

Top right: The 'Modified Improved Anti-Aircraft Gun Carriage' developed by the US Ordnance Department, mounting a French 75mm gun.

Above: The British 3.6in AA gun on tracked trailer.

Right: Another view of the 3.6in illustrating the difficulty of loading the gun when firing at high angles.

Top: The Birch gun ready for anti-aircraft firing.

Above: By the late 1920s the 3in 20cwt had been improved to the extent of adding pneumatic tyres, but the sighting arrangements were still festooned on it like decorations on a Christmas tree.

Top: The Observer Corps. Although taken in wartime this photograph illustrates the usual sort of post – a sandbagged redoubt with the simplest of instruments and the most rudimentary facilities for the crew.

Above: Krupp's 75mm gun of 1928 produced for export and also, by devious means, used to arm the 'Transport *Abteilung*' of the revived German Army.

Top: 'Follow-the-pointer' data receiving dials on a German 88mm Flak 37 gun.
Above: The Bofors L/60 gun, here in its British Mark 1 form.

Top: The famous 'Eighty-Eight', or 8.8cm Flak 18 gun, complete with its semi-tracked towing tractor.

Above: The 88mm gun in firing position.

Top: The British equivalent of the '88' was the 3.7in Mark 1 gun on mobile mounting.

Above: A British three-horn sound detector in use during an exercise in 1936; wearing respirators did not make it any easier to operate.

Top: A Circular Sound Mirror, overlooking Romney Marsh, oriented towards France.

Above: The ex-Naval 4.5in gun adopted by the British Army for use in static locations.

Above: The twin 2-pounder, ready for installation.

Top right: The German 12.8cm Flak 40, heaviest German model to see service.

Below right: Probably the best AA gun available to France was this 90mm Schneider Modele 1926 but there were scarcely enough to protect even one vulnerable point.

Top left: The American 3in on its 'Spider Mount', attended by some incredibly smart soldiers.

Centre left: The American 4.7in gun, later re-christened the 120mm M1.

Below left: In 1938 the Munich affair led to a test mobilisation of British AA defences. London's parks were full of guns.

Top: There was even a 3in on Peerless lorry on Westminster Bridge . . .

Above: . . . and the London County Council had to remove a lamp-post or two in order to give the gun a clear field of fire. (These three photographs by courtesy of Major Julian Pearce, RA Ret'd, who was, at that time, the sergeant in charge of the gun on Westminster Bridge.)

Top: The balloons went up too; a balloon barrage winch truck in Hyde Park.

Above: The India and Millwall Docks: An extract from a German intelligence handbook indicating likely targets along the Thames.

guns were made during 1941 and only half of those had been assembled and tested by the year's end, while only the standardised prototype of the 4.7in had been built. The 90mm gun, complete with its share of the battery's fire control instrumentation, cost about $50,000, and this alone was enough to put a brake on production. But on 3 January 1942 President Roosevelt wrote to the Secretary for War, calling for delivery of 55,000 AA guns within two years. In his State of the Union message on 6 January the President repeated this call, added several tens of thousands of other types of gun for good measure, and rounded off with the stirring exhortation 'Let no man say it cannot be done. It must be done . . .' While the Ordnance Department worked furiously to try to organise a 300 per cent increase in gun production overnight, the regimental officers did some counting on their fingers and made some comments, as a result of which General Somervell, head of Services of Supply, pointed out that the production schedule demanded by the President would outfit 62 heavy AA regiments every month. This was an unrealistic figure and, upon reflection, no-one appeared to know upon what premises the President had based his demands. In less than a month the requirement was halved. Production schedules then looked slightly more feasible, and by the time of the 'Torch' landings in North Africa later in November 1942 some 2,000 90mm guns had been made and issued.

By the autumn of 1942 the American defences were fairly well organised, and on 9 September came the only recorded incursion by an hostile aircraft into US airspace. A ground observer close to the California-Oregon border saw a single-float biplane, a Mitsubishi Pete, cross the coastline from the sea. It flew inland to Mount Emily, an area well known to Japanese timber buyers in pre-war days, and dropped a number of incendiary bombs. Fortunately an unusually heavy rainfall had soaked the forest during the previous days and the fires were soon contained and extinguished. The biplane flew back out to sea without being intercepted. Shortly afterwards a Navy patrol bomber reported attacking a submarine in the general area, and it was assumed that the biplane had been launched from and recovered by this submarine.

After the Battle of Midway in June 1942, in which the Japanese lost four carriers and 253 aircraft, there was no longer any credible threat to the western coast of the USA and, after a decent pause, in February 1943 the degree of readiness on the coast was relaxed. In September the whole air defence apparatus began to be dismantled on both seaboards; in the west the observing posts, filter rooms and reporting centres were to be manned 'at such intervals as might be required to maintain the efficiency of personnel' (*The Army Air Forces in World War II, Vol VI 'Men and Planes'*), while on the east coast the entire system was retained but only manned and operated for four hours every Wednesday afternoon. In April 1944 the Air

Warning Service (the volunteer observing and reporting network) was disbanded, the radar sets reduced in number and the guns and aircraft sent off to other duties. Responsibility for the diminished defence now rested on three 'Fighter Control Centers' on each coast; the east coast retained nine radar stations, the west coast twelve. Yet the only serious threat was still to come.

Germany's attack on the Soviet Union in June 1941 eased the Luftwaffe threat to Britain and gave the defences considerable breathing space. Then the RAF and USAAF bombing offensive on Germany began to gather momentum in 1942 and very soon the aviators found that anti-aircraft guns were more serious than they had thought. American eyes were opened in late 1942 when the submarine depots on the Atlantic coast of France became priority targets. High altitude bombing from well above the flak ceiling proved to be far too inaccurate, so an experiment was tried on St Nazaire to determine the best height for bombing. The leading group of B-17 'Flying Fortress' bombers flew in at 20,000 feet and emerged unscathed; a group of B-24 'Liberators' flew in at 18,000 feet and also were unhurt. Finally a group of B-17s 'barged in at 8000 feet with one squadron at 7000 feet. Every ship in the last group was hit by flak, and three planes went down in flames. What remained limped home with the questionable nom de guerre of the 'Clay Pigeon Squadron'. St Nazaire became known as Flak City to the 8th US Army Air Force.' (*The Army Air Forces in World War II, Vol VI, 'Men and Planes'*.)

In the first year of the war the rather individualistic attitude of bomber crews was their undoing; providing they appeared over the target and bombed it, little heed was paid to how they got there, and bombers took their own routes to targets based on the captain's ideas of how to outwit the opposition. As a result, a scattered flow of bombers would cross the German coast, ideal conditions for the German defences since a fighter or gun battery could select a particular target, deal with it, and then select another from the choice at their disposal.

Early in 1943 a conference of USSAF and RAF intelligence officers and Dr L. E. Bayliss of the Army Operational Research Group met to discuss the flak damage problem, and Dr Bayliss was asked to apply mathematical analysis. This seems to be the first attempt to apply statistical methods to the receiving end of AA fire as opposed to the despatching end, and in February Dr Bayliss produced a 'Curve of Total Probability' which indicated the relative probability of an aircraft being hit when on any particular crossing angle to a gun battery. The curves demonstrated that once outside a range of 2,500 yards from the gun, the probability of being hit was inversely proportional to the cube of the slant range. Meanwhile careful intelligence gathering had enabled most of the flak batteries to be plotted on a map; these were now ringed with 2,500-yard circles to give a visual indication of danger areas and allow navigators to pick a way through the flak. But at the same time the free days came to an end and bombers began to be closely marshalled before hitting the German defensive line in a solid wedge. The reasoning was that if the defence system detected the stream it would be impossible to pick out individual targets and there would only be time to deal with one or two of the leading aircraft before the stream passed on, thus reducing the chance of the flak or fighter controllers being able to pick up second or third targets.

In March 1943 the science of 'Flak Analysis' was beginning. One of the first successes was at Lorient on 6 March when the 306th Bomb Group, US 8th AAF, acting in accordance with an analysis performed with the aid of Bayliss's curve and the map of known guns, flew in and out of the target area on specific bearings and lost only three out of 66 aircraft. On 17 March a similar set of calculations guided an attack on Vogelsack in north-west Germany and again the losses were below average. Careful analysis and plotting showed that there were, in fact, a number of gaps in the German defensive line which allowed bombers to sneak through in relative safety. For a time it was feared that these might be traps, but they were used with success and it was not until the end of the war that the simple solution appeared: the German defences, massive as they were, were stretched to their utmost and the gaps were due to nothing more or less than a shortage of men and material. And considering that in June 1944 the Luftwaffe had 10,919 heavy and 22,246 light guns on the Western Defences, this is an indication of the area they were trying to cover.

These 'gaps' were carefully watched by bomber crews, sensitive to the possibility of AA guns being moved in to fill them. One gap was over the Scheldt estuary, and one day an American pilot reported seeing 42 new AA guns on Nord Beveland Island. War Office intelligence, Air Ministry Intelligence and the Photo Reconnaisance headquarters at Medmenham were questioned, but none had any indication of guns in that location, so a special photographic mission was flown. Next evening a set of damp photographs arrived at the American Squadron which had started the enquiry, accompanied by a note from Medmenham: 'By careful study we have found 42 fisherman's cottages on Nord Beveland, each surrounded by a white picket fence. Please verify.'

There was also the story of the veteran American colonel pilot, being briefed on his flak avoidance run by a new flak analyst who managed to offer two confusing bearings; 'What the hell do you want me to do?' growled the colonel, 'fly in and back out?'

In spite of the analysts' best efforts, though, flak damage continued to rise until eventually guns were doing more damage to Allied bombers than were fighters. The reasons for this were: firstly, the gradually worsening condition of the German fighter force, subjected to attrition on the Eastern Front, with production upset by Allied bombing, less well-trained crews, and shortage of fuel; secondly, the greater numbers of bombers flying over Germany for greater distances which obviously increased the chances of their being hit; and thirdly the introduction of better guns and new tactical ideas.

In September 1939 the Luftwaffe, looking ahead, issued a specification for an improved 8.8cm AA gun, to weigh not more than 8,000 kilogrammes and to fire 25 shells a minute at a muzzle velocity of 3,280 feet per second. Rheinmetall-Borsig were given the contract and produced the first prototype for trial early in 1941, but there were considerable teething troubles with the gun and it was not until early 1943 that the 8.8cm Flak 41 came into service in numbers. The trouble lay in the design of the barrel; like the original 8.8cm Flak 18, the barrel was built up in sections, so that a worn section could be replaced without having to replace the whole barrel. But the joint between two of the sections fell beneath the neck of the cartridge case, and steel cases expanded into this joint and refused to eject cleanly from the gun after firing. A brass case had to be specially developed to overcome the trouble, but the design had to be changed to a two-piece barrel. In all some 556 guns were made, and, once the technical problems were overcome, it was a highly effective weapon, with a practical ceiling of about 35,000 feet.

The tactical change was to the adoption of *Grossbatterien*, 'grand batteries', in order to increase firepower and put more shells into the target area. The *Grossbatterie* comprised three standard six-gun batteries side-by-side, controlled by one radar and three predictors, with a second radar set standing by. Thus one advantage was the saving of one radar set.

Other technical developments included work on a variety of unconventional projectiles intended to reduce the time of flight (by increasing velocity) and thus improve the chance of hitting, force the enemy to fly higher and reduce the accuracy of his bombing, and reduce the barrel-wear which was rapidly becoming an economic and production problem of major proportions. With the quantity of firing called for in dealing with a major raid, an anti-aircraft gun barrel could be worn out in two or three nights. Such solutions as discarding sabot shells, where a shell of smaller calibre was fired in a gun by means of a 'sabot' or sheath; taper-bore guns in which the gradually reducing area of the shell base caused a rise in pressure and thus a rise in velocity; and smooth-bore guns firing finned projectiles were all under development, but none were brought to a successful conclusion before the war ended.

When the development of these unconventional projectiles began, the standard high explosive content was set at 500 grammes, this being the amount considered lethal to a four-engined bomber. Diminution of the explosive content in turn reduced the lethal radius which in turn reduced the chance of a hit. It was left to a Dr Voss, a research scientist in the *Reichsluftfahrtministerium* (RLM), to take this idea to its logical conclusion. In a paper written in 1944 he showed that the chance of putting a shell close enough to the aircraft to damage it was little different to the chance of obtaining a direct hit. From this it followed that fitting the shells with impact fuzes instead of time fuzes would, by removing one source of error (the fuze setting) and another in the actual setting machine, and by speeding up the rate of fire by doing away with the time-lag in fuze setting, would in fact improve the chance of getting direct hits, to such a degree that impact-fuzed shells showed a considerable theoretical superiority over time-fuzed fire.

When one considers that anti-aircraft fire had, since its inception, been built around time-fuzed fire, it is obvious that this proposition was a difficult one to swallow, but Voss's figures were so persuasive that the Luftwaffe asked a number of other scientists to examine the theory, and they also organised a series of firing trials in which the bursts of the shells were filmed. The results showed that Voss had, if anything, understated his case, and a number of flak batteries were forthwith ordered to disconnect their fuze setters and pre-set their time fuzes to maximum time, in effect converting them to percussion fuzes since they now relied on the percussion element in the fuze. The gunners, in their turn, were somewhat sceptical about the idea, but the system appeared to give some remarkably good results. Finally, on 20 March 1945 orders were given for all flak batteries to abandon the use of time fuzes and new percussion fuzes were put into production. But this was so late in the war that no conclusive figures for the effectiveness of the system were ever produced.

One aspect of German air defence which deserves mention is that which might be called the 'lunatic fringe'. The offering of unlikely solutions was not confined to Germany; Britain and the USA had their share of eccentric inventions during the war years; but only in Germany, due to the absence of centralised control of weapon development, did these devices reach the hardware stage. Three which were outstanding were the 'wind cannon', the 'sound cannon' and the 'electric gun'.

The first two were developed at the Zippermeyer Aerodynamic Research Institute at Lofer in the Tyrol. According to Dr Zippermeyer certain types of vortices and air eddies could set up racking stresses in air-frames. Accordingly, a coal-dust and oxygen mixture was discharged from a form of mortar and detonated in the air to give the typical 'heaving' action of a slow-burning explosive and thus create the desired vortex. An alternative form of the cannon system was to detonate a charge in a combustion chamber and direct the blast into the sky through a specially-designed nozzle. Experiments showed that four-inch planks could be pierced at 200 yards range, but since few Allied aviators flew four-inch planks that close to the defences, this was no criterion and as an anti-aircraft weapon it was not a success.

Zippermeyer's sound cannon relied on detonating a methane-air mixture in a combustion chamber; the sound of the detonation was beamed into the sky via a parabolic mirror. The reflected detonating wave triggered off another detonation, and these rapid detonations soon built up into a high-pitched noise which was lethal to animals at short ranges and extremely uncomfortable to humans at longer ranges. But the whole device, with its combustion chamber, amplifying tubes and ten-foot mirror was far from a convenient device to move around in the field, and it too was a non-starter, though there is an unconfirmed report that one was actually set up to protect a railway bridge near Ulm.

The electric gun was slightly more practical. As far back as 1917 a French inventor, Fauchon-Villeplé, had put forward a suggestion for propelling a winged projectile by means of a powerful magnetic field. His invention was produced in model form, but the First World War ended before he could produce a full-sized weapon and the French Army dropped the idea. Today the 'linear motor' is essentially Fauchon-Villeplé's gun in a modified form. In 1944 a German firm called the Gesellschaft fur Geratebau, under Engineer Hänsler, put forward a new form of Fauchon-Villeplé's idea, promising an anti-aircraft weapon with a muzzle velocity of 6,560ft per sec and a rate of fire of 6,000 rounds per minute from a multi-barrel installation. The Luftwaffe were sufficiently impressed with this to give Hänsler a contract to develop a 4cm gun to fire a 500-gramme shell. The full analysis of the Hänsler gun runs to several pages of closely-reasoned and abstruse mathematics, but the final conclusion was that 3,900 kilowatts of power would be needed for the gun, and since this was within the capability of existing generators, work began in February 1945. Needless to say, the war ended before the development could be brought to any useful level of perfection.

From 1941 onwards the Luftwaffe made sporadic raids on Britain which, while not constituting the same level of threat as the Blitz, were sufficient to keep the defences alert. Indeed, the principal enemy during this period seems not to have been German aircraft but forays by other branches of the British service upon the AA defences in search of manpower and artillery for other purposes. Anti-aircraft units were required for armies in the field and for armies preparing to enter the field, and shortages of manpower in other arms led to periodic combing-out exercises which often threatened to reduce the manning levels of the gun batteries to perilously low figures. A partial solution to this was found by the integration of the womens' service, the Auxiliary Territorial Service, into the artillery organisation. In spite of objections by those who thought that the immediate reaction of women to gunfire would be screaming hysterics, girls were slowly brought into the organisation, firstly as radar operators, then to operate height-finders, predictors, trackers and other instruments; everything, in fact, except actually loading and firing the guns, and there were quite a few young ladies who were of the opinion that they could have done that just as well as the men, given the chance.

Even more innovative was the formation of complete searchlight regiments manned by girls, from the commanding officer down to the sentry on the gate. These were greeted by the press as nine-day wonders, but they were not quite the all-female enclaves that they were claimed to be. In the early days of these units, the searchlights, in the more remote locations, were powered by diesel-engined generators which had to be hand-started by a crank, an extremely strenuous pastime, and one which was beyond the physical capability of most girls. On these sites, therefore, tucked away in a remote corner far from prying eyes, dwelt a lone male soldier, carefully selected for his physical strength and also for his moral equanimity; happily-married, mature men who were unlikely to upset the apple-cart by attending upon the young ladies instead of the generator. In view of the field-day which the less-responsible section of the popular press would have had with this revelation, the presence of the generator attendant was kept a close secret; indeed, some Royal Artillery officers were later to claim that it was the best-kept secret of the war.

The ésprit de corps of these girls was tremendous, and they took a fierce pride in their association with the Royal Regiment; unofficially at first, officially later, they took to wearing the Royal Artillery cap-badge on the breast of their uniform jacket and the Royal Artillery's white lanyard around their shoulder. Unfortunately, some of the less-percipient senior officers of the ATS failed to appreciate this loyalty, derided it, and voiced threats against those girls who identified themselves too closely with the Artillery, all of which cut into the morale of the all-girl units and, more particularly, the mixed batteries, but this difficulty was eventually smoothed over. There is no doubt that, but for the timely introduction of the Auxiliary Territorial Service into the defence organisation, the efficiency of the guns and lights would have been severely diminished during 1942–43.

The German raids on Britain during this period fell broadly into two categories: the 'Baedeker Raids', so-called, in which towns of little military value but of greater cultural and historic renown, were systematically attacked; the other, and more difficult to counter, were the 'tip-and-run' raids in which single fighter-bombers flew fast and low across the Channel to evade the radar screen, then soared up and crossed the coast to drop one or two bombs on virtually anything that looked like a target before turning and roaring off home at high speed. These were extremely difficult problems for the defensive system; virtually the only counter-move was to deploy batteries of light guns at the water's edge. The radar watch was improved by the addition of a third layer of 'fence' known as 'Chain, Home, Extra Low'; this was one of the first fruits of the perfection of centimetric wavelength radar. The shorter the wavelength of radar, the more its emissions can be controlled and directed, and centimetre wavelengths permitted the radar energy to be transmitted in a tight beam which could be pointed, as it were, into the gap between the CHL cover and the water-level. Moreover, the short wavelength allowed better separation of the targets from the background 'clutter' due to random reflections from the waves. As a result, the 'tip-and-run' raiders began to be detected, in spite of their low altitude and high speed, and the defences began to take their toll of them.

But if the defences were, by 1943, getting on top of the aeroplane, a new threat was looming ahead, one which was to give the defences some of their greatest headaches but also their greatest successes. As early as 1939 the famous 'Oslo Letter' had warned British intelligence that the Germans were experimenting with long-range rockets, but the first years of the war went by without showing any signs of such devices and the British had several other things to think about. But in 1942 the Germans had two projects in hand: one was the long-range A-4 rocket, developed by the Army as a bombardment weapon, and the other was the shorter-range FZG-76 pilotless aircraft under development for the Luftwaffe. By early 1943 word of these projects had reached the intelligence staffs in Britain but the picture was confused; conflicting reports of 'rocket bombs', 'flying bombs', 'glider bombs' and 'robot bombs' could be construed in innumerable ways. One source said that the weapon was an 'aerial mine with wings' while others averred that it was a pure rocket. Scientists in Britain argued about the possibilities and technical probabilities, while photographic reconnaissance aircraft probed Germany and France for evidence of either sort of device. The German research station at Peenemunde was bombed in August 1943 without really being sure of what was going on there.

The 'Textbook of Anti-Aircraft Gunnery' of 1925 opened with the statement, 'It is impossible to devise suitable methods or to design suitable apparatus unless the problem which it required to solve is clearly appreciated'. This truth was never more clearly shown than in the early days of this debate over the missile threat. The estimates of the likely form of attack were so varied that it was almost impossible to come to any conclusions about how to defend against it. Some sources now said that it was a 60-foot rocket with a 10-ton warhead; others maintained that it was a winged aerial mine launched by catapult. Estimates of its probable speed and altitude, which were fundamental to working out a defence, varied widely.

Some said it would be directed to its target by radio, and suggested extensive counter-measures to jam the controlling transmissions and thus interfere with the guidance. Others claimed it would be compass-guided and advocated laying out vast loops of wire on the ground and pulsing electric current through them to set up huge magnetic fields around London. Eventually, when everyone had had their say, it came back to the same old system of deploying guns, searchlights, balloons and fighter aircraft and waiting to see what happened. At the same time, Percy Scott's early dictum - that defence by aircraft began over the Zeppelin sheds - was borne in mind, and the RAF scoured France and Germany looking for anything which might have a bearing on the problem and destroying it.

In December 1943 the first defensive plan, code-named 'Diver' was drawn up. Five hundred heavy and 800 light guns were allocated for the defence of London, Bristol and the Solent area. To guard the approach to London a thick belt of balloons would be planted between the River Thames and West Wickham; a belt of guns would be placed across the North Downs from Sheppey to Redhill; and the RAF fighters would be free to deal with everything in front of the gun belt. Four hundred heavy and 346 light guns were earmarked for this belt.

No sooner was this plan perfected than it had to be changed. It had originally been drawn up on the assumption that an attack from known areas in Normandy would take place before the forthcoming Allied invasion of Europe in June, Operation Overlord. Now, due to revised intelligence estimates and to damage done to the launch areas by RAF attacks, it seemed unlikely that the flying bomb attack could begin before Overlord was under way, and much of the defensive strength of Diver was made up of gun regiments which were to form part of the invasion force. By the time the attack developed, these units would be either in France or on the way there and unavailable for their Diver roles, and so a fresh plan, known as Overlord/Diver was drawn up in March 1944, reducing the number of guns in the London area to 192 heavy and 246 light, and cutting back the Bristol and Solent defences in a similar proportion. Indeed, the London guns were to be reduced by 54 on D-Day and Bristol's entire defence, 96 heavy and 36 light guns, was to be withdrawn by D-Day. The Solent defences were eventually stripped to nothing, on the assumption that the various units massing in that area ready for shipment to France would be sufficient to take care of the area until D-Day, after which there would be little of military interest left there and thus attacks would be less likely.

Such a reduction in gun strength meant that the main burden of defence would now fall on the fighters of the RAF. In a reversion to the old standing patrol system, it was arranged that when an attack appeared imminent, fighters would patrol over and off the coast between Newhaven and Dover and inland between Haywards Heath and Ashford, at 12,000 feet. Once the attack developed, more fighters would be brought into play, patrolling the same lines at 6000 feet. These patrols would operate by day or night, and at night the usual radar-GCI network would be used to direct the patrols to any likely target.

Much of this planning had been based on certain assumptions about the threat, one of which was that prepared sites, known as 'ski sites' from the shape when seen from the air, were necessary for the launching of the weapons. Most of these sites had been severely damaged by the RAF, and this, it was thought, reduced the threat. But the German Army and Luftwaffe, appreciating that these 'ski sites' had been identified and were prime targets, developed a 'modified site' which was less conspicuous, and it was some time before these sites were identified. When this happened, the intelligence officers and air photograph interpreters rapidly found over 60 modified sites, a figure which made the Overlord/Diver plan much less attractive. But since, by this time, D-Day was only days away, there was no hope of persuading the Chiefs of Staff to agree to any changes.

The invasion duly took place without interference from any form of Diver attack, and everyone breathed rather more easily. The best information now available showed that the modified sites were still several weeks away from a serviceable condition, so the possible scale of attack was thought to be no more than whatever could be mounted from eight undamaged ski sites.

But on 10 June, while anxiously watching the progress of the invasion, the Air Staff received a report from an agent on the continent that a freight train with 33 wagons, each carrying three objects vaguely described as 'rockets', had passed through Ghent en route for the Franco-Belgian border. On the following day an improvement in weather conditions allowed a photo-reconnaissance flight to be made over the area of the modified sites, the first such flight for several days, and this brought back pictures showing that rails had been laid on the launching ramps on these sites and other preparations were in progress which indicated that they might be brought into use very quickly indeed.

In fact on Monday 12 June Colonel Wachtel, commanding the launching regiment, was making hurried preparations to open the attack on that very evening. On 6 June he had been ordered to activate the sites and prepare to open the offensive on the evening of 12th, but the provision of stores and equipment had been disrupted by troop movements after the invasion and he was nowhere near a position of readiness. Launch rails had only been installed at about 55 of his 64 sites, but the dummy missiles, with which the launch arrangements were to be tested and the ground crews exercised, had not arrived, nor had any of the safety equipment which had to be installed before a live missile could be fired. Even so, Wachtel was being pressured to make a start that night, though it was patently obvious that even if he did, the full scale of the attack could not be achieved. But Wachtel was a smart soldier who realised that provided he could loose off one or two missiles at the due time honour would have been satisfied and his immediate superiors could report up the chain of command that orders had been obeyed and the missile campaign had begun.

On that same day the Air Intelligence Branch in England warned the Chiefs of Staff that there was a strong possibility that the mystery weapons would be used within the next few days, and the accuracy of this forecast was borne out when, at 3.30am on 13 June, the first flying bomb was launched. Ten were launched that night, five of which crashed almost immediately and one flew off into the night, never to be seen again. The remaining four crossed the English coast, the first promptly being identified for what it was by an alert Observer Corps spotter who promptly shouted 'Diver!' into his telephone and set the whole machine in progress. These bombs landed at Swanscombe, at Sevenoaks, one in a rural area in Sussex, and one penetrated the London area to reach Bethnal Green. This last bomb crashed on to a railway viaduct and cut all the lines leading to Liverpool Street station; in order not to alarm the public it was announced that 'an enemy aircraft had been shot down' and there may have been more truth in this cover story than has ever been proved, since when the wreckage was cleared away a fuze from an AA shell was found, though no AA battery has ever been identified as having fired at the missile.

Having made his gesture, Wachtel closed down and went back to the basic work of preparing his sites, training his men and building up a stock of missiles ready to resume operations. And to those across the Channel from him, this four-bomb attack seemed to be something of an anti-climax after all the dire threats and forecasts, one which scarcely justified the upheaval which putting Overlord/Diver into effect would bring about. The best answer, it was felt, was to step up the attack on the sites, and over the next few weeks over 70,000 tons of bombs were distributed widely on anything which looked as if it was involved with the missile programme. Unfortunately, the net was spread too wide and much effort was wasted in bombing ski sites and various installations which were either nothing to do with the programme or which had been abandoned. Relatively few of Wachtel's operational modified sites were damaged, and on 15 June, having at last got things organised the way he wanted them, Wachtel opened his offensive in earnest. At about 10.00pm on 15th launching began from 55 sites, and during that night 244 missiles were launched against London and about 50 against Southampton. Of this number, 144 crossed the English coast; 14 were shot down by guns, 7 by fighters, and one credited as being shared between guns and fighters, before they reached London; 73 crossed the boundary of Greater London and 11 were shot down by London defences. Of those which landed in functioning order, the majority fell south of the Thames. One or two managed to get as far as Southampton, and one went wildly astray and finished up in Norfolk.

After this bombardment there was no longer any doubt that it was time to put Overlord/Diver into effect. Orders were issued, and by the following morning the first guns were in place. It had been estimated that 18 days would be needed to relocate the guns but, to everyone's surprise, the whole move was completed in four days, 192 heavy and 192 light guns being lifted from their locations, redistributed, and back into action within that time.

Over the next few days, the average appeared to be about 100 bombs per day coming within reach of the defences; of these, about thirty were falling to the fighters, ten to the guns, and fifty were getting through to London, the rest being wild shots which went astray. Four squadrons of Mosquito aircraft, and eight of Tempest, Spitfire and Typhoon fighters were in action, and this seemed to be as much as the system could stand, so the obvious answer was to increase the number of guns and balloons. Defences of other parts of Britain were reduced, and by 28 June there were 376 heavy guns and 576 light guns manned by the Royal Artillery spread from Maidstone to East Grinstead, plus 560 20mm and 40mm guns manned by the RAF Regiment (which were normally used for airfield defence) on the south coast. The guns of the London area were free from restriction at first, but it was soon decided to prohibit them firing at the bombs; a hit bomb would certainly come down in London, whereas if it was left alone, there was a good chance that it might fly on, pass over the populated area, and fall harmlessly in the countryside beyond. This, of course, was a difficult decision to have to take, but, on balance, it was probably justified. The citizens of London however failed to appreciate the point at first and were somewhat vocal about flying bombs overhead and silent guns beneath.

By mid-July Wachtel had fired over 4,000 flying bombs towards London, of which about 3,000 had come within reach of the defences; fighters had claimed 924, guns 261 and balloons 55. One missile had been fired on by a fighter, ran into a shell burst and then collided with a balloon wire before crashing; it was shared out between the three forces, one-third to each. The principal reason for such a low rate of success against a target which could not dodge was to be found in the complicated rules of the game. When fighters were operating, the guns could not shoot; the fighters could not enter a gun zone unless in active pursuit of a missile, and in that case it was up to the guns to recognise what was happening and stop firing. When the weather was particularly good, and favourable to aircraft operations, the guns could not fire at all and the fighters had a free hand in all areas; when the weather was too bad for the fighters, the guns were free. This sort of division of labour satisfied no-one, since both gunners and RAF were sure that 'How happily could I deal with either, were t'other dear charmer away'.

Another difficulty lay in the technical matter of the peculiar gunnery problem. Since, as we have seen, all anti-aircraft gunnery was based on a target flying on a straight and level course at a constant speed, it might be thought that the flying bomb, which did all three, was a gift; it was not. It flew at 350–400mph and at about 3,500 feet altitude, the worst possible combination for the guns. It was at the limits of height for the light guns, since it was at the limits of visual gun control and beyond the accurate limits of predictors, and it was too low for the heavy guns due to the need for them to make fast angular swings in order to keep up with the target's travel across their front. Power-operated static guns could cope best, because of their faster and smoother rates of tracking, but static guns were meant to be bolted down in concrete emplacements and not dumped about the countryside. Nevertheless, Brigadier Burls, Chief Mechanical Engineer of AA Command, devised what he called the 'Pile Platform', named not for its engineering construction but for General Pile. This was a combination of railway sleepers and rails in the form of a cross, buried in rubble and quick-setting concrete, which could be laid rapidly on any level surface and have a static gun bolted down to it. Rails and sleepers were 'acquired', gangs of gunners, sappers and craftsmen set up a 'platform factory', and 441 static 3.7in guns were uprooted from all over Britain and sent to the North Downs, 365 by road on tank transporters furnished by other units of the British and American armies, and the rest by rail. Royal Engineers appeared and sank wells to provide drinking water for isolated sites, and Pioneers appeared and erected 13,000 ammunition shelters and uncounted millions of sandbags were provided with which to protect the gun emplacements.

But just as all this uproar was getting into its stride, Air Marshal Sir Roderic Hill, in overall charge of the fight against the flying bomb, and General Pile had come to a fresh conclusion. Air Commodore Ambler, one of Hill's staff, had been instructed to prepare a paper to lay down a new policy on excluding aircraft from the gun belt and moving all the guns from the south coast back to join the group on the North Downs. Ambler, however, was not entirely sure that this was the right approach, and, working from first principles, he produced instead a closely-reasoned argument for a completely new arrangement. The correct solution, he suggested, would be to put all the guns on the south coast and give them an unrestricted field of fire, while the fighter aircraft should operate in two separate groups, one over the Channel, well out of range of the guns, and one over Kent and Sussex, behind the guns. What the

Channel fighters missed, the guns were completely free to shoot at, and what was left would be caught by the inland fighters. Finally, the balloon barrage would be thickened up to make a back-stop.

On the morning of 13 July Ambler was about to see Air Marshal Hill when he encountered Robert Watson-Watt, the radar pioneer, and found that Watson-Watt had come to a similar conclusion and had decided to see Hill and suggest it to him. With two high-powered opinions, Hill could scarcely fail to be impressed by the argument, and he asked for the rest of the day to think about it; at the same time he asked General Pile and his staff to see him in the afternoon.

At the afternoon conference General Pile welcomed the idea and revealed that he and his staff had already come to the same conclusion but had refrained from putting it forward because they were sure the RAF would refuse it. Since everyone was in agreement, the only remaining question lay in obtaining the necessary authorisation to perform the switch. Even as they were discussing the matter, the men on the Downs were levelling sites and bolting-down guns; 32 were already in place and more were arriving hourly. If the question were to be referred to the Air Staff, the Chiefs of Staff, the War Cabinet and goodness knew who else, it would be days before a decision was reached, by which time all the extra guns would be emplaced, and moving them would be a monumental task. Hill decided to lay his reputation on the line, and ordered the move to take place forthwith. In fact the Air Staff were extremely angry when they heard of the decision, feeling that somehow Hill had been 'nobbled' to make a decision which favoured (apparently) the guns over the fighters. It was made quite clear to Hill that his head would be first on the block if the idea failed to produce the answer. In fairness, it should be said that when events proved Hill right, the Air Staff were the first to apologise and give him credit.

The great move began before the day was out. 23,000 men, 800 guns and 60,000 tons of ammunition and stores had to be lifted and shifted; despatch riders went out to find transporters with guns aboard and re-route them to new locations; fresh platforms were moved in and new sites prepared; extra weapons were requisitioned. One advantage of the new location was that all the shooting would be over the sea and thus rocket launchers could be added to the guns, since the spent tail units would fall into the water.

By the morning of 19 July the 'Diver Belt' was in action, stretching from Cuckmere Haven in Sussex to St Margaret's Bay in Kent: 412 heavy and 572 light guns, the heavies including 16 American 90mm guns manned by the US Army, plus 584 light guns manned by the RAF Regiment, 28 multiple 20mm cannon on armoured cars manned by gunnery instructors from the Royal Armoured Corps, and 200 rocket launchers. But no sooner was this disposition complete than it became apparent that the Germans were also launching from sites further north, so that the bombs were flying up the Thames Estuary. The defence was extended northwards into the 'Diver Box' covering the estuary area, another 208 heavy and 578 light guns, plus those that were already deployed in the area, forming this additional sector. Arrangements were even made to strengthen the Maunsell forts by sinking barges alongside them and mounting more guns, though this was never actually put into effect. Additional guns continued to flow into the area as they could be made available, until, as an official report later said, 'anyone arriving late would have had a job to find space in which to put his guns'. Eventually there were 800 heavy, 1,800 light guns and 700 rocket launchers deployed, with another 144 heavy guns waiting in reserve.

Two technical advances now made themselves felt. At this time the standard British gunlaying radar was the GL3, which produced a range, a bearing and an angle of elevation to the target, which was manually tracked by the radar operators, the data being transmitted to the predictor which then produced gun data. Improvements in radar were always in the pipeline, and General Pile knew that the US Army were developing a new radar-predictor combination which would produce a smoother flow of data. The SCR 584 radar, when presented with a target, automatically locked on and followed it, more smoothly than could any human operator. The information was then electrically fed to the 'Predictor No. 10' which delivered an output capable of driving a power-operated gun, so that without human intervention the radar would, via the predictor, point the gun at the target and follow it smoothly and accurately; all the gunners had to do was to load and fire the gun as fast as they could. Such a combination gave a vast improvement in accuracy and was tailor-made for dealing with such a target as the flying bomb.

The second technical innovation to appear at the eleventh hour was the electronic proximity fuze. As far back as 1938, when the radar scientists were first confronted with gunnery, the errors inherent in calculating and setting fuzes had drawn their attention. An early suggestion was to make a fuze which carried a simple receiver and thus pick up the radar signals reflected from the target by the early-warning set or gun-laying set, and thus cause the shell to detonate when it got close enough, but the signal strengths involved were far too weak for this idea to be made to work at that period of radar's development. Later came the proposal to put a complete radio transmitter/receiver unit into the fuze so that it would emit its own signal and, when close to the target, would detect the echo of this signal and detonate the shell. This promised better results and much of the theoretical work was done in 1939–40, but the possibility of having such devices made in Britain were practically zero at that time. So in 1940 the proximity fuze was one of the many things taken to the USA by the Tizard Mission. The United States

Navy were attracted by the idea and undertook the development; the Eastman Kodak Company became the prime contractors, with the various components being made by such specialists as Sylvania, Westinghouse, Emerson, Philco, General Electric, Exide and other well-known names in the radio and electrical field. After satisfying the Navy's demands, designs were worked out for Army AA guns and later for ground fire applications, and in mid-1944 the first Fuze, VT, T98 for the 3.7in AA gun were coming from the production line. (The letters 'VT', used to identify this type of fuze for many years, are often said to mean 'variable time', a fiction which was tacitly encouraged. In fact the fuzes were not time fuzes, nor were they variable; the letters came about because the development was begun by Section 'V' of the Navy Bureau of Ordnance and it happened to be that Bureau's 'Project T'.)

With all this in mind, General Pile sent a representative to the USA to see General George C. Marshall, Chief of Staff, taking with him a rebuilt flying bomb to demonstrate the nature of the problem. After seeing the bomb, Marshall asked what aid was required, and was told that 300 SCR 584 radars and 3,000 proximity fuzes would be a good start. Marshall replied, 'The first lot will be on board ship tomorrow, but visit Eisenhower when you get back and see if he agrees'. Eisenhower not only agreed but sent three more regiments of 90mm guns to thicken up the mixture. In fact 165 SCR 584s were shipped immediately, together with the fuzes; they arrived in Britain at the end of June and were immediately sent down to the Diver Belt to be put into use. For a few days chaos reigned as gun positions had two sets of equipment, with the gunners learning all about SCR 584 in between bouts of shooting at bombs with GL3. Once they became familiar with the new material, the old was withdrawn.

More equipment now found its way into the Diver Belt as sundry 'private armies' moved in. The Petroleum Warfare Department appeared with an experimental 9in mortar; the Royal Navy brought along a collection of Parachute-and-Cable 2in rockets, plus some ordinary 2in rockets with high explosive warheads; the 'K' Rocket was brought out and dusted and fired once more. This latter device had appeared earlier in the war and was a 3in rocket designed for defending harbours. It had a double-length warhead into which were packed 1,000 feet of cable, two parachutes and a mine. Fired up to 20,000 feet, the warhead then opened and ejected its contents; the cable unreeled and descended by a main parachute at the upper end. If struck by an aircraft, a special weak link at the top end of the cable snapped, releasing the main parachute, after which a much smaller parachute opened. Due to the drag of this parachute the cable was pulled back across the target's wing, and as the lower end of the cable came up to the target it brought with it the contact mine. This, on striking the wing, promptly blew it off. They were formidable machines but there appears to be no record of one scoring against a flying bomb.

The most spectacular weapons of all, and the ones which deserve their place in history as the heaviest anti-aircraft weapons ever used, were the six 8in coast defence guns of Capel and Hougham Batteries, close to Dover. These massive weapons (the gun's barrel alone weighed 17 tons, almost twice the weight of a pair of 3.7in mobile guns) were actually coast defence guns, emplaced in order to bombard enemy shipping far out in the Straits of Dover, but the mountings were converted Naval mountings and the guns were capable of being elevated to 70 degrees. There was no application for this in coast gunnery but periodically, when an aerial target appeared in the right quarter, the six monsters would elevate and belch a salvo of 256lb shells into the sky to produce a massive curtain of splinters in the path of the approaching bomb. Unfortunately, with so much metal being flung upwards in those days, it was difficult to isolate success and we cannot say with any certainty whether the 8in guns ever scored. They certainly deserved to. As the Duke of Wellington said in another context, 'I don't know what they do to the enemy, but by God they terrify me'.

During five days at the end of June the guns were manned for 108 hours and 12 minutes out of a 120-hour period. The first week of the Diver Belt gave the guns 17 per cent of the missiles launched, the second week 24 per cent, and the figures then gradually improved until by the fifth week the guns were taking 55 per cent. By then the Allied advance into France had overrun the launcher areas and the Germans had moved their operations further north. This, of course, changed the line of approach and the guns had to be redeployed, moving the most southerly guns up towards the Thames estuary and reinforcing the Diver Box. By the end of August the percentage of kills had reached 74 per cent and on one night actually got to 82 per cent.

Although it was not fully appreciated at the time, much of the effort put into sending flying bombs up the Thames was not coming from Colonel Wachtel and his men, but from a Luftwaffe unit who were carrying the bombs into the air underneath specially-modified Heinkel bombers and then releasing them. Not only were they launching them at London, but they could very easily select virtually any target they liked, since they were not restricted by any earthbound launching platform. By the end of August these air-launched bombs included 300 fired at London, 90 at Southampton and about 20 aimed at Gloucester.

On 1 September the 'First Phase' of the flying bomb campaign, as it came to be known, ended as the Pas de Calais area was occupied by the Allied armies and Colonel Wachtel and his unit closed down and evacuated themselves to the Netherlands. The air-launching squadron fired a final instalment and they too withdrew, to north-west Germany. During this period 9,017 missiles had been launched, of which 6,725 were seen by the defences. Of these 6,725, 1,771 (26 per cent) were shot down by fighters, 1,459 (22 per cent) by guns and 231 (4 per cent) collided with balloons. Of those which got through, 2,340 actually penetrated to the Greater London Area.

On 16 September the 'Second Phase' began; the air-launching squadron had been reinforced, was now at a strength of 90 aircraft, and it began air-launching flying bombs in earnest. On the first day nine were launched; the Royal Navy shot two down at sea, fighters got three, two came down in Suffolk and two penetrated as far as London. Guns got none since this new phase outflanked the Diver Belt and Box by launching far to the north of the gun defences. The response to this new threat was to create a 'Diver Strip' running north from the Diver Box to Great Yarmouth, the guns being provided by moving up the Belt guns from Kent and Sussex. This move was ordered on 21 September, but its implementation was much more difficult than had been the setting-up of the Belt. The Strip called for a gun zone as close to the sea as possible, with the guns 2,000 yards apart; 34 heavy batteries and 36 light were moved. But the coast of Essex and Suffolk is not provided with a network of good roads in the same way that Kent and Sussex were, nor was the terrain the same. The guns had to be sited on marshes and desolate dunes, at the end of farm tracks which were never intended to stand up to the passage of gun mountings and ammunition trucks. Two hundred miles of roads had to be built, bridges strengthened or built, the ground at sites reinforced. Accommodation had to be provided for 50,000 men and 10,000 women, on land liable to flooding and frequently below sea level. Four thousand Nissen huts had to be dismantled from sites all over Britain, moved to the seacoast and re-erected; 30,000 tons of hard-core for roads and gunsites had to be provided. General Pile later pointed out that the work involved was the equivalent of building two towns the size of Windsor. And all this work was done by the gunners of AA Command, since there was no other manpower available.

In spite of the appalling difficulties by 13 October the re-deployment was complete, with 300 guns installed, and by the end of the month the 'Box' and 'Strip' between them had 542 heavy and 503 light guns in action. This 'Second Phase' continued until the middle of January 1945, in which time an estimated 1,200 bombs were launched, of which 638 were seen by the defences. Guns got 331½, fighters 71½; 66 reached London, the remainder being distributed around the Home Counties and Norfolk. The guns averaged 156 shells fired for every bomb brought down.

On Christmas Eve 1944 there was an attempt to outflank the guns yet again, when about 50 aircraft launched missiles off the coast near Bridlington. These were all aimed at Manchester, and some 30 bombs actually crossed the coastline. The Humber defences opened fire but it was their first attempt at this type of target and they had no luck with the seven they saw. Only one reached Manchester, however, the remainder being scattered about the countryside en route. As a result of this more guns were removed from Kent and sent to form a last 'Diver Fringe' extending from Skegness to Whitby, but they found very little to do.

During this 'Second Phase' period, however, a new threat appeared. At 6.40pm on 8 September the first of the V-2 rockets landed in England, killing three people in Chiswick. Immediately afterwards, another fell in Epping. During the next ten days, 25 more landed, 16 of them in London. They had all been launched from the Netherlands and the immediate response was to despatch RAF and USAAF bombers to bomb the launching areas. But since the V-2 launching system was small, simple and mobile, the only way to achieve results actually was to catch the rocket as it was being prepared for launch.

There was, though, little else that could be done; the V-2 was travelling at supersonic speed as it descended, and no radar or gun then existing could hope to track it nor, even if that had been possible, could a gun have been manned, loaded, aimed and fired in the time available. General Pile suggested having guns laid on a permanent bearing and firing a barrage of shells into the air to form a screen of fragments, any one of which would be likely to detonate the simple impact fuze on the missile, but the scientists were still arguing about the mathematical probabilities of this idea when the last rocket fell. Radar and optical detection networks were set up on the coast, and a special RAF unit, the 105 Mobile Air Reporting Unit was set up and deployed in the Netherlands to try to detect the upward flight of the rocket as it was launched. 105 MARU used mobile radar stations and was accompanied by flash-spotting and sound-ranging troops from the 10th Survey Regiment RA. A headquarters was set up at Malines, with direct communication to Air Defence HQ at Stanmore, Middlesex, and this 'very early warning' was backed up by sound-ranging and flash-spotting units of 11th Survey Regiment operating throughout Kent and Essex from a headquarters in Canterbury, also in direct contact with Stanmore and also with Malines. These observers managed to pick up the track of the rocket and signalled back to Britain, giving sufficient warning for alarms to be sounded. But the system was from from perfect, producing as many false alarms as failures to spot rockets at all. The RAF performed prodigies, flying in every sort of weather in order to bomb any area suspected of concealing a launcher, but still the rockets came. A total of 1,359 were aimed at London of which 517 arrived in the London area, killing about 2,400 people and injuring about 5,850. The suddenness of the rocket's arrival without warning, and the violence of the detonation of the one-ton warhead, made for some terrible individual incidents.

The last rocket to be fired fell on Orpington on 27 March 1945, the end of the attack being solely due to withdrawal of the German missile regiment in the face of the Allied advance. Only the action of an army in the field of the Continent served to defend Britain from the silent onslaught of the rocket.

Just before the end of the rocket campaign, on 3 March 1945, the 'Third Phase' of the flying bomb attack opened. Peenemunde had managed to improve the range of the weapon, and German troops in the Netherlands had built three launching ramps aligned on London. In the next four weeks they fired 275 bombs; only 125 of these crossed the North Sea, and of these the RAF got four and the guns of the Diver Strip 87, only 13 reaching London. The last flying bomb to be recorded was en route to London at 12.43pm on 28 March when it was blown out of the sky by a Diver Strip gun at Orfordness.

It is appropriate, at this juncture, to quote once again from the *Textbook of Anti-Aircraft Gunnery*: 'The true criterion of the efficiency of the AA defence guns is not the number of aircraft destroyed, but rather what more could the enemy have accomplished in the absence of AA Artillery'. In most cases this becomes a hypothetical question, but in the case of the flying bomb it is possible to do a rough calculation to discover what might have happened without the guns and fighters. The 2,419 bombs which actually reached London caused approximately 5,500 deaths and injured about 16,000 people. Using this as a yardstick, we can assume that had the 3,957 bombs shot down by the defences survived to land in London, they might well have caused another 9,000 deaths and injured another 26,000 people.

During the Second and Third Phases of the flying bomb attack on England, another flying bomb campaign was being waged, one which was not publicly announced until the war was over; this was 'Antwerp X', the German bombardment of the port of Antwerp in Belgium. At this time, Antwerp was probably the most important port installation in the world; through it passed the ammunition and supplies to sustain the Allied advance, and without it the Allies would have had to fall back on hauling all their supplies from the Normandy beachheads. Early in September 1944 Allied intelligence determined that a flying bomb attack on Antwerp was highly likely and the GHQ AA troops of the British 21st Army Group were alerted. These units were equipped with mobile 3.7in guns and GL3 radars; they had no SCR 584s, no Predictors No. 10 and no proximity fuzes, all of which they knew were vital for the task ahead of them. Their commander later confessed that his initial reaction was to persuade the RAF to take on the task, but Air Marshal Coningham would have no part of it. But by some sleight-of-hand which was entirely unofficial, enough SCR 584s for two AA regiments were obtained from England. Since no more could be obtained, 21 Army decided to ask the Americans if they would care to contribute some of their regiments, armed with 90mm guns and SCR 584s; Eisenhower's staff agreed to this and sent a reconnaissance party to look over likely sites, arranging to send regiments when the threat appeared.

On 19 October word was received that the flying bomb offensive was likely to begin within 24 hours; as events turned out this was not to be so, but it gave enough time for the defences to be deployed. Within a week one hundred American guns had arrived in the area, and a whole British field artillery regiment had been rapidly turned into an ad hoc observer corps, spread around in front of Antwerp. Radar sets, plotting equipment, radios and other stores were flown out from England, and all was ready. And at 04.30hr on 27 October 1944 the first flying bomb appeared, winging its way towards Antwerp. It was promptly shot down by a 90mm gun of 'D' Battery, 126th AAA gun Battalion US Army; the second bomb appeared in the wake of the first, three minutes afterwards, and suffered the same fate. From then until 30 March 1945 'Antwerp X' was active.

The first launching sites were known to be in the area of Bocholt and Coblenz and the defence was aligned accordingly. But in November the direction of attack changed, the bombs coming from the direction of Trier, and the batteries were moved around. On 28 November the first major movement of supply ships into the port began, as the Scheldt was finally cleared, and the German attack was stepped up accordingly, reaching 50 bombs a day. The guns were now deployed in three belts, two of heavy guns and a backstop of light, spaced sufficiently far apart to allow all guns a chance at any one target. In the first days of December the attack stopped; no explanation was offered for this, but it was later realised that the launching troops were building up a stock to be able to support the Ardennes offensive. When the attack was resumed on 11 December the direction of attack had radically changed, most of the missiles now coming in from the north-east. The Ardennes offensive had its effect on the defence forces, as seven American gun battalions were hurriedly removed in order to counter the German advance.

More British units were now brought into Antwerp, and as the Ardennes affair quietened down, so the American units were brought back. Eventually there were 22,000 AA troops involved; 5 US Groups and 16 AA Battalions, 12 British AA regiments, 2 Polish AA Batteries and several small service detachments. In January attacks began coming in from due north of Antwerp, some from air-launched bombs and some from ground-launched, and the defences had to be re-aligned once more; this move caused problems, since there was an Allied airfield right where the guns wanted to be; they could not deploy behind it, since it would be impossible to fire over it, and so, in spite of the fact that the airfield was home to no less than four wings of Spitfires, it was moved, and heavy guns were emplaced across the runways.

Aircraft caused considerable problems in this battle, since thousands of Allied bombers passed over the area during the period of the attack, and there was a constant coming and going of fighter aircraft to and from the airfields in the area as they went out to support the ground battle. Every aircraft coming towards the defences looked like a flying bomb at first, but it is to the credit of the gunners that they never shot down a manned aircraft by mistake; though there were some close calls.

February and March saw the worst period of the attack; in the 24 hours ending at 6.00am on 16 February, 160 bombs were launched; on several nights the ammunition expended was over 15,000 rounds; some gun batteries were into their fourth replacement gun barrel by the end of the battle, and such items as breech blocks, which were popularly supposed to be everlasting, were beginning to give up under the strain.

When the battle finally ended and the arithmetic was done, the results were a triumph for the artillery: 4,883 flying bombs were known to have been launched against Antwerp; of these, only 211 landed within an eight-mile radius of the centre of Antwerp docks, the defined area which had to be protected. Of those 211, 55 got through because at the crucial moment the guns were unable to fire because of the proximity of Allied aircraft; the other 156 were fired on but escaped. From a kill rate of 67 per cent at the beginning, it was improved to a rate of 97 per cent at the end; and it must be stressed that the defence of Antwerp was entirely by guns; there were no fighter aircraft involved and no balloons.

As the defences of Diver and Antwerp X were deploying against the German's final throw, a similar, if less formidable, final fling came to the United States from the Japanese Army. In early December 1944, following the recovery of a rubberised-silk balloon from the sea off the California coast, the recovery of a paper balloon from the sea near Hawaii, a report of a mysterious bomb explosion in Wyoming, and the finding of a paper balloon in Montana, the US Army and Navy and the Federal Bureau of Investigation began investigating the source and purpose of these mysterious free balloons. It was eventually discovered that the Japanese Army, after two years of research and experiment, had launched about 9,000 free balloons from Honshu, beginning on 1 November 1944. These rose to a height of 35,000 feet into the stratospheric air stream which then carried them across the Pacific in three to five days. The balloons carried a height-regulating mechanism which released hydrogen when the balloon rose above 35,000 feet and ballast if it fell below 30,000 feet. When the last packet of ballast had been released, the mechanism dropped the bomb load, one or two incendiary or high explosive bombs of about 10lb weight each, and then a self-destruction charge would destroy the balloon. Some balloons carried, instead of bombs, a radio sonde transmitter which could be monitored by position-finding stations and thus track the balloon stream across the ocean and confirm the general direction of their drift.

It had been estimated that about 10 per cent of the balloons would have reached the American continent; about 150 were actually reported as having landed, from the Aleutian Islands to Mexico and from the Californian coast to as far inland as Michigan, but there is room to suppose that several more met their programmed end in the forests and mountains, far from human view, so the 10 per cent figure may well be right. The only casualties caused were on 5 May 1945 when a picnic party near Bly, Oregon, discovered a bomb and, disturbing it, detonated it killing six members of the group. These bombs could, however, have been a serious threat, and only the caprices of the wind kept them away from populous centres.

By this period the defences of the west coast had been reduced to an extremely patchy form, and there were numerous gaps in the radar cover and few AA guns. In order to avert the need to activate the whole system again an attempt was made to intercept the balloons with fighter aircraft, but due to bad weather, inaccurate reports, and the very great altitude of the balloons, only two were ever intercepted and shot down. Eventually it was decided to set up mobile radars to cover the gap areas, but before this could be done the sightings died away and the ballons ceased to arrive. Due to a rigid news black-out throughout the USA and Canada on the subject, no reports of balloon bombs were ever made public and the Japanese, who had been relying on public announcements to give them some indication of the success of the campaign, came to the conclusion that no balloons were reaching the USA, no results were being achieved, and abandoned the whole idea.

6 HIGHER AND FASTER

In 1941 a Professor Wagner of the Bayerische Motoren Werke (BMW) put together an experimental model of a winged rocket which could be controlled in flight by radio signals and which he considered might be worth developing as an anti-aircraft device. On suggesting this to the Luftwaffe he was bluntly informed that Germany did not require defensive weapons. But in 1943 the Luftwaffe sought out the Professor and the Henschel Company were given a contract to develop the device under the designation 'Hs-117', code-name *Schmetterling* (Butterfly). Orders for experimental production followed, with a view to putting *Schmetterling* into service in February 1945, but due to bomb damage to factories which were producing components the project was never completed.

Schmetterling appears to qualify as the first guided missile to be accepted for service. It consisted of a cylindrical body with stubby wings and a cruciform tail, inside which was a bi-fuel rocket using 'Tonka' – a hydrocarbon – and 'Salbei' – nitric acid – the reaction between which produced thrust. Ahead of the motor unit was a 55lb warhead fitted with a *Fuchs* (Fox) radio proximity fuze. Mounted on booms alongside the body were two solid-fuel rocket units to give additional thrust during launch, which were jettisoned after they had burned out and the sustainer motor was running. After launch the sustained speed was supposed to be governed to 850km/hr (460mph) and the missile was visually tracked from the ground, the observer sending signals by radio to operate control spoilers in the wings and tail unit to steer the missile to interception. The effective range was about 10 miles and the ceiling 35,000 feet, with an accuracy radius of 8 metres.

All this was a very inspiring specification for 1944, but the actual performance fell rather short of that promised; of 59 experimental launchings, 34 failed for one reason or another. But by late 1944 the missile idea had gained momentum in Germany. In 1942 Rheinmetall-Borsig began work on *Rheintochter*, a solid-fuel rocket with a 330lb warhead and *Kranich* acoustic fuze which reacted to the sound of the target's engines. Fired from a rail launcher fitted to an 88mm gun mounting, it could reach to about 20,000 feet, and test firings began in August 1943. Before much more could be done the Luftwaffe demanded a ceiling of 30,000 feet, so an improved version, *Rheintochter III* (there does not seem to have been a II) was begun in May 1944. This was designed to use either liquid or solid fuel sustainer motors, rocket-assisted launch, and had a command firing system added so that the controller could detonate the missile when he wished, overriding the proximity fuze; this was so that a rocket could be fired into the middle of a flight of bombers and their detonated, to do as much damage as possible. Flares on the tail delineated the missile's flight path, and guidance was by visual observation and radio control. As before, several test shots were made, but the *Rheintochter* was nowhere near service acceptance when the war ended.

Other weapons under development in 1945 included *Wasserfall* – 65,000 feet ceiling at 30 miles from launch, with a 660lb warhead; *Mowe* – 2,000 metres range with a 25lb warhead; and *Enzian*, designed by Messerschmitt – 52,000 feet and a 1,000lb warhead. In addition to these, which were fairly well forward in their development, there was a handful of others of which little beyond a project name were ever discovered – *Hamburg-B, Hecht, Kampf* and *Fliegerschreck*. Although none of these came to fruition, examination of the records suggests that had there been a more receptive atmosphere in 1941–42, a ruthless pruning of the more visionary ideas, and a more single-minded pursuit of more limited goals, the Luftwaffe could well have had serviceable AA missiles in use by late 1944.

Development of guided missiles was also begun by the Allies, but these were mainly with a view to use in attack – the British Stooge, and the American Bug and Weary Willie projects were for controlled, power-driven bombs resembling pilotless aircraft; indeed, Weary Willie was just that, a 'war-weary' B17 or B24 bomber which had outlived its usefulness and was loaded with ten tons of explosives and a radio control unit. After being flown off the ground by a live pilot, the radio controls were set on a course calculated to bring it over a target in Germany and the pilot took to his parachute just as the aircraft cross the English coast. They were tried in limited numbers, and at least one case is recorded of a premature explosion just as the pilot was about to jump. They can hardly be called successful.

But as far as air defence went, the Allies were well content with the conventional gun. Britain had revitalised the 3.7in by putting a 3.7in calibre liner into a 4.5in gun, allowing the 28lb 3.7in shell to be shot out by a much larger than normal cartridge. This gave the '3.7in Gun Mark 6' a muzzle velocity of 3,470 feet per second and an effective ceiling of 45,000 feet, quite sufficient for most applications. For the rare event requiring more effort, and looking to the next generation of aircraft, the 4.5in gun was retired in favour of a 5.25in naval design which fired an 80lb shell to over 50,000 feet. This weapon was proposed in 1941, and General Sir Frederick Pile later told how, when at dinner with A. V. Alexander, then First Lord of the Admiralty, the subject was broached; Alexander promptly drove a hard bargain – six twin 5.25in equipments for 300 Bofors guns. And after the 300 Bofors had been delivered, the Navy reneged on their side of the bargain and supplied only three guns. These, though, were sufficient to convince the Army that they were what was needed, and a suitable single-gun mounting with full power assistance was designed. By the end of the war 5.25in guns were being installed in the more important areas – Plymouth, Portsmouth, London, the Humber and the Tyne.

The American 90mm gun had been given a much improved mounting, with power operation and power ramming, a mounting which, like the British 5.25in, could be emplaced so as to serve the dual roles of anti-aircraft and anti-motor-torpedo-boat gun. This obsession with making one gun fo two jobs never seems to die completely; after a period of hibernation after the demise of the Birch Gun in 1931 it reappeared in Britain during the war, allied with a proposed 'intermediate' gun. This was to fill the same gap in the sky as the German 5cm weapon, that above the reach of the 40mm and below that of the 3.7in. The new gun was a 57mm six-pounder which began as a twin-barrel equipment for anti-aircraft work and was then modified to become a potential AA/Coast Defence gun. Then an existing twin six-pounder anti-motor-torpedo-boat gun was modified to give greater elevation and thus become a dual role CD/AA gun. The whole affair, as might be imagined, became inextricably confused, neither weapon was a success in its auxiliary role, and the whole project was quietly interred soon after the war ended.

With the arrival of peace the victorious anti-aircraft gunners took stock and considered the future. The hasty dismantling of defences which had followed the Armistice in 1918 was avoided: the defences were, naturally, run down from their massive wartime strengths, but the basic requirements for a systematic defence system were kept in being. The greatest challenge facing ground defences was the arrival of the jet-propelled aircraft, which could travel at 600mph. The nature of this challenge is easily expressed: consider a 600mph bomber attacking at 25,000 feet altitude with a 500lb bomb, which is a good average case. The trajectory of the bomb's fall demanded that it be released when the aircraft was 7,200 yards (4 miles) from the target. Since the bomb-aimer needed a steady run-up of some sixty seconds flight to ensure an efficient job, the run would begin 25,200 yards (14.4 miles) away. This meant either many guns set well out from the objective, or fewer guns with longer range, short times of flight and high rates of fire. Allowing ten seconds to load, aim and fire the gun and thirty seconds for the shell's flight, the aircraft would have flown 12,000 yards (6.8 miles) before the shell got up to its altitude.

Arithmetic of this sort, plus the fact that the 600mph would soon become 700mph, and then 800mph and more, lent some urgency to the thought of developing guided missiles, but the usual post-war relaxation meant that two or three years were to pass before serious work began, urged on by the worsening political situation. And even then, missiles were obviously going to take some time to perfect; the wartime standard, well exemplified by Sir Robert Watson-Watt's much-quoted maxim 'Give them third best; second best takes too long, and best never comes', was no longer acceptable to the government-run research establishments. They had all gone back to basic research, tying up all the loose ends which had been left flapping in the haste of war. For example, while the wartime proximity fuze worked, there was a divergence of scientific opinion as to how and why it worked. Some very elegant theories were being argued, and before any more work could be done in this field the whole matter had to be thoroughly investigated and a solid foundation of scientific fact well and truly laid.

While the scientists chased their electrons, the mechanical engineers were less in need of basic science and they carried on with programmes of development aimed at improving the rate of fire of the conventional gun. One great advantage of the proximity fuze was that it did away with the mechanically awkward business of setting a time fuze before loading; all that now needed to be done was to get the shell and cartridge into the gun's breech as quickly as possible. The first move in this direction came in August 1944 in the USA when work began on the 75mm Gun T22 which was 'to be compatible with proximity fuzes and have on-carriage fire control'. By January 1945 a gun had been built and was awaiting its carriage which, being more mechanically involved, took longer to produce. It incorporated its own radar and optical tracker on the mounting and used two revolver-type magazines to feed ammunition to an automatic rammer, giving a rate of fire of 45 rounds per minute. By June 1945 a complete equipment had been tested and found to work well; the only snag was that the gun's muzzle velocity was only 2,300 feet per second, which was poor by modern standards, and a fresh design, with the gun lengthened, was begun in the hope of raising the velocity to 3,000 feet per second. Before this was reached the war ended, whereupon the high priority evaporated and the design was completely overhauled. Eventually the 75mm Gun M51 entered service in the early 1950s with the nickname 'Skysweeper'.

British development into high rates of fire began in 1946 as 'Project Ratefixer', a trials project aimed at stepping up the rate of the 3.7in Mark 6 gun. Mechanical loading had always sought simply to duplicate the operations of hand loading – present the round to the breech, ram, close the breech, fire, open the breech, eject the spent case, and present the next round. It was now suggested that this might not necessarily be the right solution; that it might be possible to begin presenting the fresh round while the gun was being fired, and so arrange the paths of the incoming round and the ejecting case that they passed each other in mid-flight. Four different designs were built: 'Ratefixer K', designed by Captain Kulikowski of the Polish Resettlement Corps, used two drums at 90 degrees to the mounting, feeding alternating arms which swung the cartridges across to a central rammer; 'Ratefixer C', by Colonel Carmichael, REME, used a 30-round hopper feeding a cross-table and then through a five-foot-diameter trunnion; 'Ratefixer CR', by Mr Russell Robinson, a noted machine gun designer, was the 'C' model modified to belt feed; and 'Ratefixer CN', by Frazer-Nash, was belt-fed and powered by an hydraulic motor.

These experimental weapons all worked well, and 'CN' eventually reached a rate of fire of 75 rounds per minute which, considering the complete 3.7in Mark 6 cartridge weighed some 62½lb, meant shifting some 2¾ tons of ammunition a minute, no mean feat. But by 1949, when the project was completed, it was obvious that while the exercise had been of great value in solving the loading problem, the gun was now becoming obsolescent and an improved weapon would have to be developed.

The chosen solution was two-fold. Firstly a taper-bore gun, with the calibre reducing from 4.26in to 3.2in would be developed by Vickers, while a 5in gun using a fin-stabilised 'dart' shell would be developed by the Royal Armaments Research and Development Establishment. But by 1951 progress on the 4.26/3.2 model was slow – it was, after all, a difficult problem to solve – and a conventional 101mm gun was put in hand, to fit the same mounting, as a form of insurance. This became the 'Gun 102mm X1' but it too was dogged by delays in development; it was not ready until 1956 and it was abandoned in 1957. The 4.26/3.2 idea was also scrapped. The 5in, known as 'Green Mace' fired its trials in 1956 and, on completion, it too was abandoned, one defect being that it weighed a matter of 28 tons.

Meanwhile another weapon had appeared; the 'Gun X4' or 'Longhand', which was a 3.7in Mark 6 resurrected and fitted with a 12-round rapid-loading conveyor. This got as far as being approved for service introduction on 15 February 1957, but nothing further was done, and in 1958 a policy statement was promulgated: there would be 'no further attempts at a cannon solution for medium or heavy anti-aircraft defence'. The guided missile was now waiting in the wings.

However, the policy statement said nothing about light guns, and there had been some progress in that field. Naturally the weapons and research uncovered in Germany after the surrender were examined very closely in the hope of unearthing something useful, but there was very little of value which was not already under investigation in either Britain or the USA. One idea which looked attractive was the Hänsler electric gun, since a similar idea had been put forward in Britain. But after close examination of the proposals and some laboratory experiments, it was discovered that Hänsler's calculations had been too optimistic and that a single electric gun would require a power station capable of providing illumination for a medium-sized city all to itself.

On reflection, there seemed to be nothing better than the faithful Bofors gun in sight, provided its rates of traverse and elevation could be speeded up to cope with faster aircraft. A power-operated Bofors had been perfected by the end of the war, to be used in conjunction with a predictor. But experience in the war showed that the Bofors more often found itself distributed about the countryside in ones and twos, bereft of predictor and generator and thus unable to use power control. The answer to this was to put a suitable power supply and fire control system on the mounting itself; this was less of a drawback than might be thought, since the predictor was less vital in the light role than in the medium and heavy applications. The flying-bomb campaign had shown that power-operated medium guns when allied with auto-following radar sets were capable of dealing with targets much lower than previously thought possible. This left the light guns to deal with the lower part of the sky where, with hedge-hopping targets, eye-shooting was the only feasible method. There was also the inescapable fact that light AA gunners during the war had to be dragooned into using predictors; as General Pile related: 'gunners who fired over open sights swore blind that they had been using the predictor all the time'.

Development was done by the Bristol Aircraft Company and, in the late 1940s, the result was issued as the 'Bristol-Bofors'. It was the same old Bofors gun but on a somewhat heavier carriage which had a small petrol-engined generator unit to provide the necessary power. The operating mechanisms had been strengthened and improved to give extremely fast tracking rates, the laying was now done by one man using a joystick instead of handwheels, and a gyroscopically stabilised computing sight of advanced design gave the weapon a high degree of accuracy. The platform was enlarged to carry two loaders who were held securely by padded rails to prevent them being dislodged during rapid changes of traversing direction.

But while this had been under development, AB Bofors in Sweden themselves had also been working quietly away on the same sort of idea. Their first move had been to improve the ballistics by lengthening the gun barrel and developing a better-shaped shell and more powerful cartridge. Then the breech mechanism was redesigned slightly to improve the rate of fire from 120 to 240 rounds per minute. Finally the carriage was overhauled and fitted with a generator, electro-hydraulic power operation and joystick control. The prototype was tested in 1947 and approved for service with the Swedish Army as the M48 in the following year. In 1951 the 'Bofors

L/70' (it took this name from the barrel being 70 calibres long – the old gun was 60 calibres) was placed on the market and among the first in the queue was the British Army, who adopted it in 1953 as the new standard light gun, phasing out the Bristol-Bofors. Provision was made in the Bofors design for application of remote-control signals, and several countries developed radar/predictor systems to suit the weapon; Britain has the 'Fire Control Equipment No. 7' or 'Yellow Fever'; the Netherlands use 'Super Fledermaus', and the French have 'Eldorado'.

The interrogation of German weapons' technicians after the war brought to light the secrets of the numerous missile projects, and the Allied scramble to secure more information led to some undignified body-snatching in which the Americans and Soviets gained most of the plums by their application of carrot or stick respectively. Work on missiles thus began almost as soon as the war ended, on a relatively leisurely basis, which accelerated when the Cold War began. America was probably the first to produce a missile for service when it introduced the Nike Ajax system in December 1953 (note that we refer here only to surface-to-air – the new 'in' term for anti-aircraft – missiles; other types of missiles reached service at earlier dates). Nike was a two-stage solid-fuel rocket which owed a good deal to German wartime work; it carried a high explosive warhead with proximity fuze and was guided by radio command from a controller on the ground. Emplaced in permanent sites in the United States, each battery had an acquisition radar to detect the target, a tracking radar to follow it, a missile radar to follow the missile, and a computer-controller to compare the two tracks, generate the necessary commands to the missile and transmit them. The range was in the order of 50 miles, which gave each battery considerable coverage, but the system was limited by the fact that once the battery radars and computer were dealing with a target, another target could not be engaged until the first mission was completed.

The Ajax model was replaced by the Nike Hercules version in 1958. This had a better flight performance, giving a range of 75 miles, and also had a nuclear warhead as an alternative, so that the system would perform as an anti-ballistic missile weapon. It was known that the Soviets were working on missiles with inter-continental capability and carrying nuclear warheads, and the only possible way to combat these seemed to be to use a faster and more powerful missile and intercept the trajectory. As well as re-equipping the permanent batteries, a mobile Nike Hercules battery was developed, but this was more mobile in intent than in practice; the radar sets alone required some 26 trucks to move them, let alone the rest of the equipment.

In 1959 the Bomarc missile appeared, a winged missile launched by a solid-fuel rocket and sustained in flight by two ramjet engines.

These missiles were designed as 'strategic' AA weapons, having sufficient range – almost 400 miles – to be able to intercept a target long before it closed with any target area in the continental United States. Bomarc was kept in a state of readiness which allowed it to be launched with no more than 30 seconds warning and after launch it was radio-commanded to interception by the computers of the SAGE defence system. Once delivered into the general area of the target the missile command system was switched off and the missile's own radar system went into action, seeking the target, locking to it, and then homing the missile on an intercepting course. With a cruising speed of almost 1,800mph Bomarc was an extremely effective device; the warhead could be either nuclear or conventional, and during a variety of trials and demonstrations it frequently exhibited the ability to destroy targets at great ranges and at altitudes well in excess of anything that a manned aircraft could do at that time.

In Britain, in spite of various projects and programmes in government establishments, the first generation of practical missiles came from private manufacturers. This system worked so well – and there was ample precedent for it in the history of gun development – that henceforth the development of missiles was left entirely in private hands, only the warheads and propellants coming from government facilities. The first British surface-to-air missile to appear was Bloodhound, the development of which, by the Bristol Aircraft Company and Ferranti, had begun in 1949. In 1958 it entered service with the Royal Air Force, thus putting a primary ground weapon under complete RAF control for the first time. Its operation was tied to the existing reporting and control system, the RAF controllers deciding whether a target was to be engaged by fighters or by missiles. Bloodhound was a winged ramjet with four solid-fuel launch booster rockets; the warhead was high explosive, with a proximity fuze, and interception was achieved by radar reflections from the target, which was 'illuminated' by a ground radar, being detected by a radar receiver in the missile which then operated the missile's flight surfaces to steer a course for interception. The first Bloodhound units were deployed in permanent locations on the east coast of England, but later a mobile version was developed which really *was* mobile and could either accompany an RAF expeditionary force or be deployed in Britain to thicken up the defences in a particular area. This mobile battery could either operate independently or could easily be tied in with the permanent air defence scheme.

In 1960 the Army adopted the Thunderbird missile to replace the medium and heavy anti-aircraft guns. Development was done by the English Electric Company (later to become the British Aircraft Corporation) and Thunderbird's similarity in appearance to Bloodhound has led to some ill-informed observations to the effect that they had to be given different names so that the soldiers could tell theirs apart, or that the development of two identical missiles for the different services was evidence that ancient inter-service rivalries with their concomitant waste of time and money were still alive. The fact is, though, that Bloodhound and Thunderbird, while superficially alike, are completely different in one vital technical respect; Thunderbird is all rocket, and not a rocket-ramjet hybrid like Bloodhound. It uses four similar solid rockets for launch boost but is then sustained in flight by a large solid-fuel rocket motor; as a result it is somewhat faster but has a slightly shorter range. The second major difference is tactical. Thunderbird is wholly a mobile system, designed to accompany a field army. There have never been any permanent Thunderbird emplacements.

Both Bloodhound and Thunderbird were improved to 'Mark Two' systems in the middle 1960s. The improvements lay in the electronic and technical fields but the general employment is the same, with performance, accuracy and response time showing improvements over the original. In addition to equipping British forces the Bloodhound system was sold abroad to Australia, Singapore, Sweden and Switzerland and Thunderbird to Saudi Arabia and Libya.

While much work went into making missiles fly and go where they were told, a great amount of effort went into the design of more lethal warheads. In the first missiles these were simply canisters of high explosive which produced fragments and blast when they detonated; in other words, the same sort of effect as the high explosive shell fired from a gun, but bigger. But as designers realised they were no longer contrained by questions of high acceleration, as in guns, or spin or the relatively small dimensions dictated by calibre and stability considerations, they began to look at ways of making the warhead more effective. By controlling the size of the fragments, for example, it would be possible to break the warhead casing into pieces certain to inflict lethal damage on an aircraft; hitherto the uncontrolled shattering of a steel casing had produced a high proportion of tiny fragments incapable of doing serious damage to a modern aircraft. One solution was to fabricate the warhead casing of pre-formed 'fragments', rods or blocks of steel held together by a plastic casing, which became high velocity fragments once the explosive detonated.

A more exotic approach was to link rods together in a zig-zag fashion so that the detonation would fling them outward in an expanding circle of steel strong enough to chop off an aircraft wing or tail. This 'continuous rod' warhead is believed to have been employed by the Soviets to bring down the American U-2 high altitude 'spy plane' in May 1960.

An alternative to relying on fragments is to use a lightweight container, pack it with as much high explosive as possible, and rely

Top: Illustrating that the Germans' attentions were not confined to London; the Hams Hall Power Station near Birmingham.

Above: A Heinkel bomber with a cable-deflecting device to divert balloon cables. It may have worked but there were other ways of bringing them down.

Opposite top left: The Anderson shelter in which Mr G. Mollett, his father, mother, sister and dog survived a near miss in 1940.

Opposite top right: A Naval Maunsell Fort in position in the Thames Estuary.

Left: The British GL3 gun-directing radar set and its carpet of chicken-wire.

Top: The Army version of the Maunsell Fort used a design which reproduced the layout of a normal ground-sited battery.

Above: 3in rockets laid out ready for loading.

Top: A 3in multiple projector. The operator stood inside the steel box between the banks of launch rails.

Above: Setting time fuzes (foreground) and loading the 88mm gun.

Top right: The American SCR-268 radar, their first gun-directing radar.

Below right: An American 40mm Bofors gun firing at night.

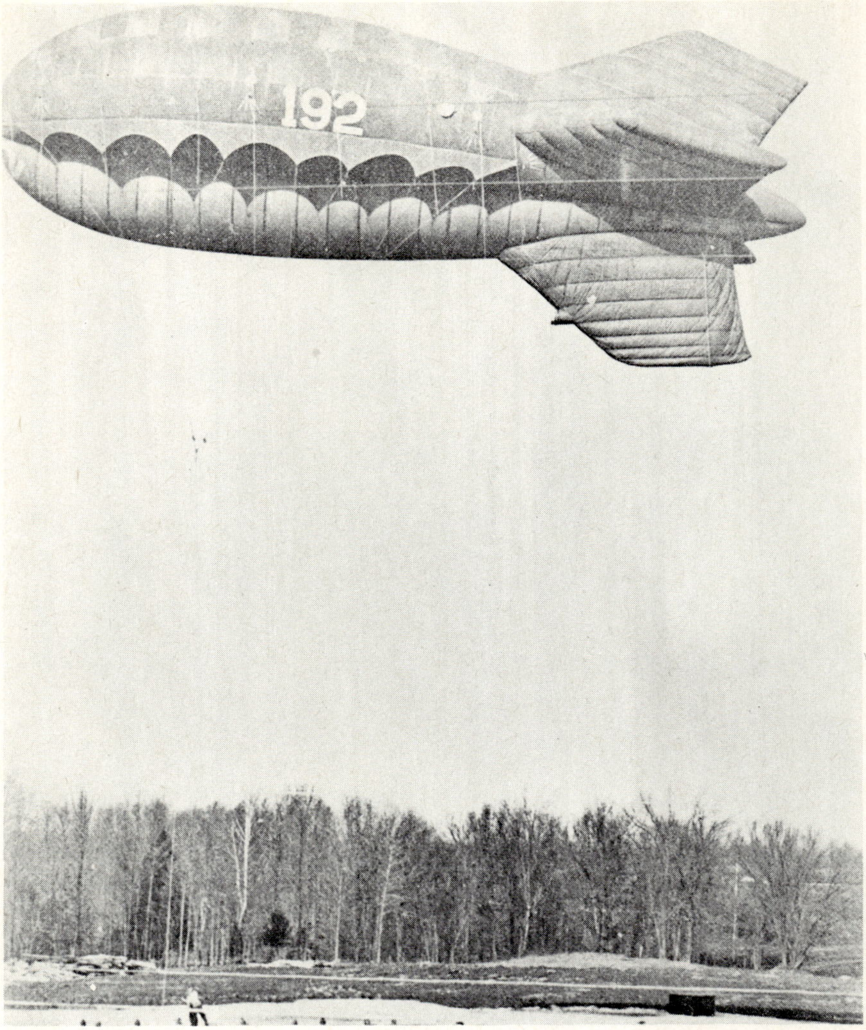

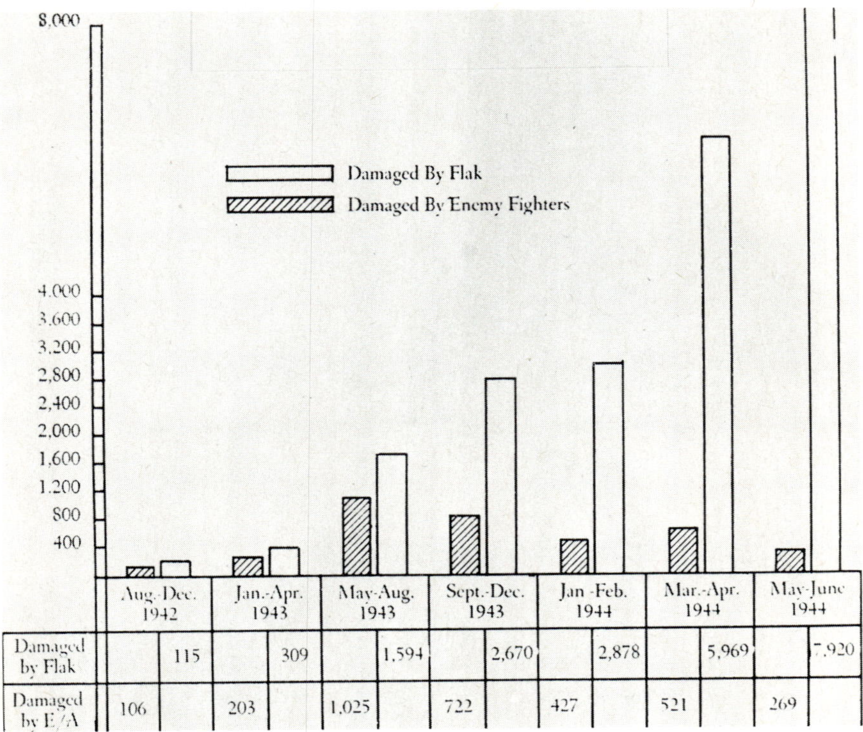

	Aug.-Dec. 1942		Jan.-Apr. 1943		May-Aug. 1943		Sept.-Dec. 1943		Jan -Feb. 1944		Mar.-Apr. 1944		May-June 1944	
Damaged by Flak		115		309		1,594		2,670		2,878		5,969		7,920
Damaged by E/A	106		203		1,025		722		427		521		269	

Top left: The first barrage balloon to be put up at Camp Tyson, Tennessee, the US Balloon Training School, in February 1942.

Below left: The 90mm Gun M1 in travelling order.

Top: The 90mm Gun M2 had an improved mounting with power control and with the ability to function as an anti-motor-torpedo-boat gun for harbour defence if required.

Above: A US 8th Air Force chart showing the ratio of bombers damaged by fighter attack and by flak gunfire.

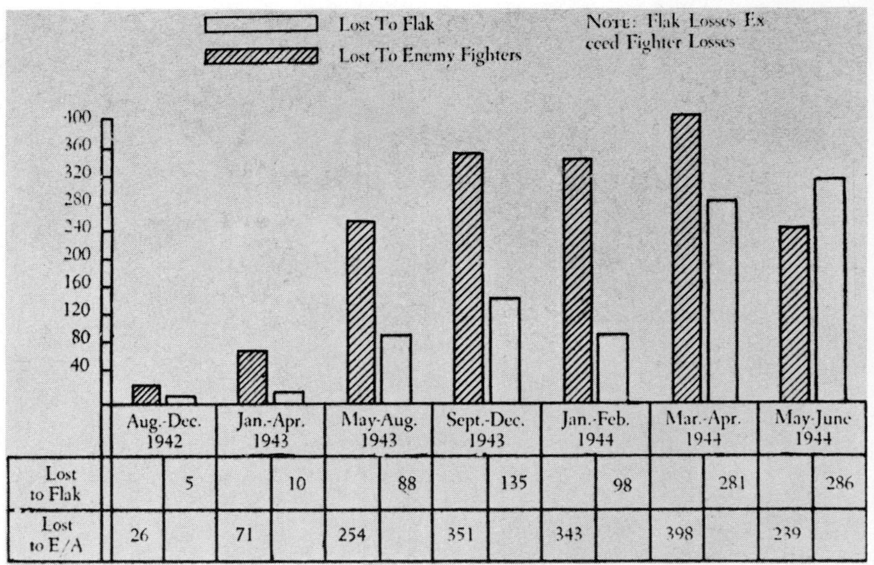

	Aug.-Dec. 1942	Jan.-Apr. 1943	May-Aug. 1943	Sept.-Dec. 1943	Jan.-Feb. 1944	Mar.-Apr. 1944	May-June 1944
Lost to Flak	5	10	88	135	98	281	286
Lost to E/A	26	71	254	351	343	398	239

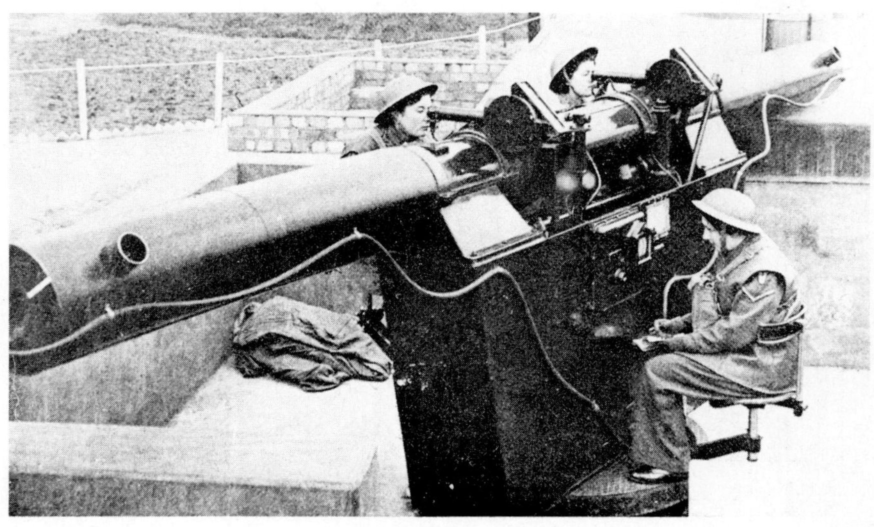

Top left: A second 8th USAAF chart showing bomber losses. This sort of comparison led to a growth in the technique of Flak analysis.

Centre left: A German experimental shell for a 105mm Flak gun, with the barrel tapering to 88mm calibre at the muzzle. The centering cones and the rear skirt were squeezed down during the passage up the bore and this reduction in surface area allied to the propellant gas pressure behind the shell led to higher velocity and a shorter time of flight.

Below left: Women found increasing employment in British 'Mixed' AA Batteries, doing everything except actually firing the guns. These girls are operating a height-finder.

Above: The Observer Corps were an invaluable part of the 'Diver' plan and, in fact, correctly identified the first V-1 flying bomb to cross the English coast.

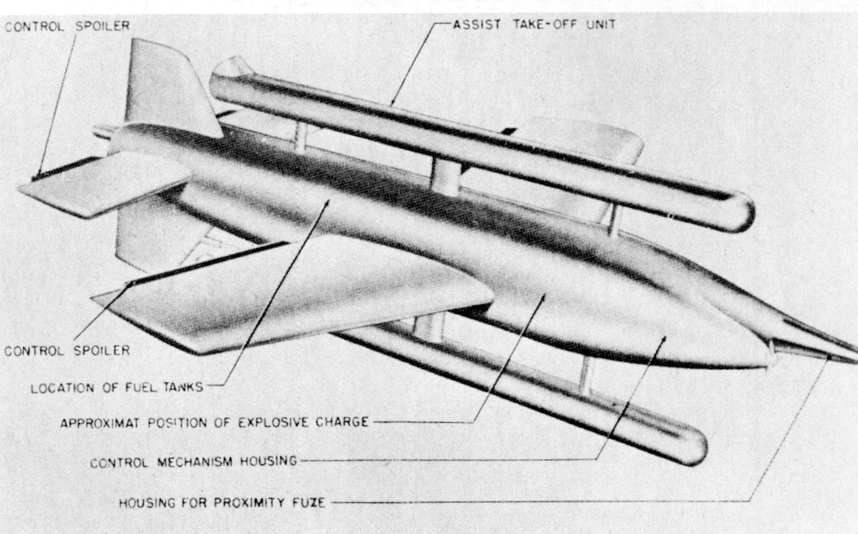
CONTROL SPOILER
ASSIST TAKE-OFF UNIT
CONTROL SPOILER
LOCATION OF FUEL TANKS
APPROXIMAT POSITION OF EXPLOSIVE CHARGE
CONTROL MECHANISM HOUSING
HOUSING FOR PROXIMITY FUZE

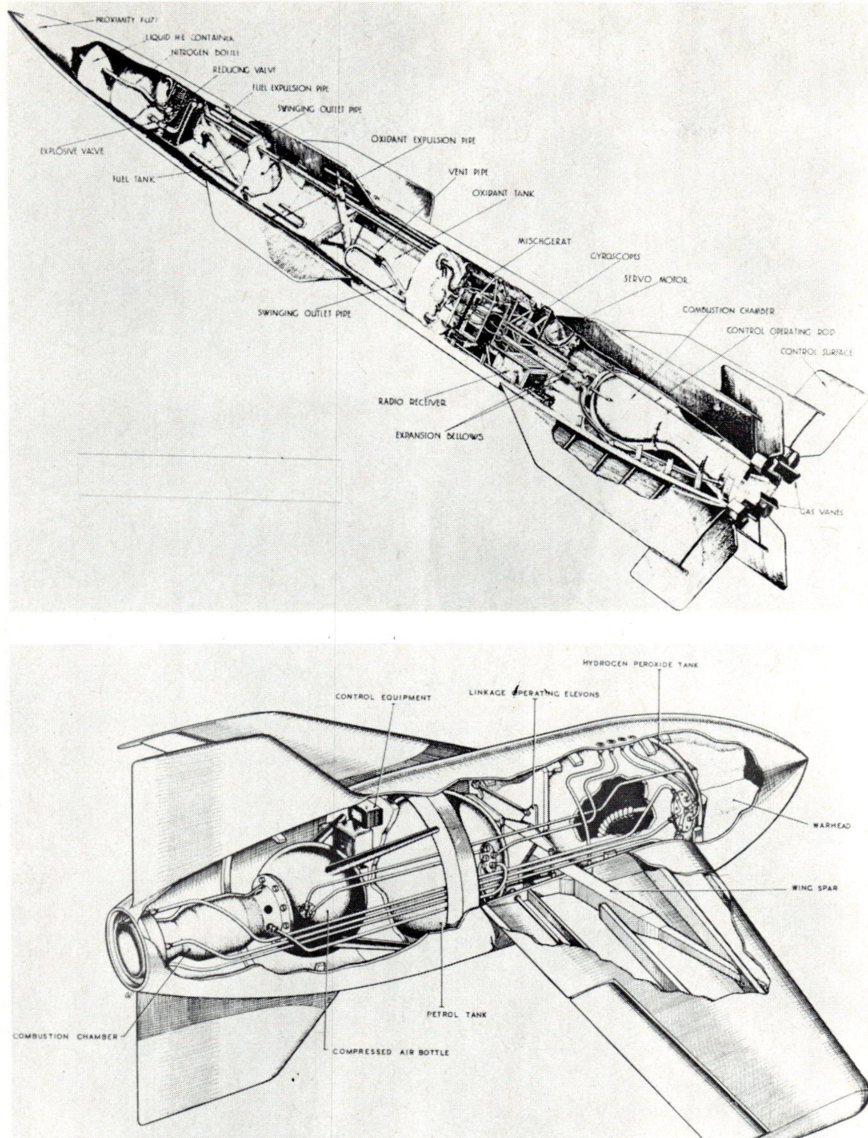

Top left: The fully power controlled 3.7in Mark 2C gun, which proved to be the best solution to the flying bomb.

Centre left: Another view of the 2C. The man on the platform has dropped the cartridge into the loading tray, from which it will have the fuze set, be aligned with the bore and rammed, and the gun fired without further human intervention. He will now be given another cartridge by the man on the ground, who will go off for another, while everyone else moves up one.

Below left: Schmetterling, the first AA guided missile.

Top: Wasserfall, a sectioned drawing showing the principal features.

Above: The Messerschmitt *Enzian* missile, which could have been a serviceable weapon if more attention had been devoted to it.

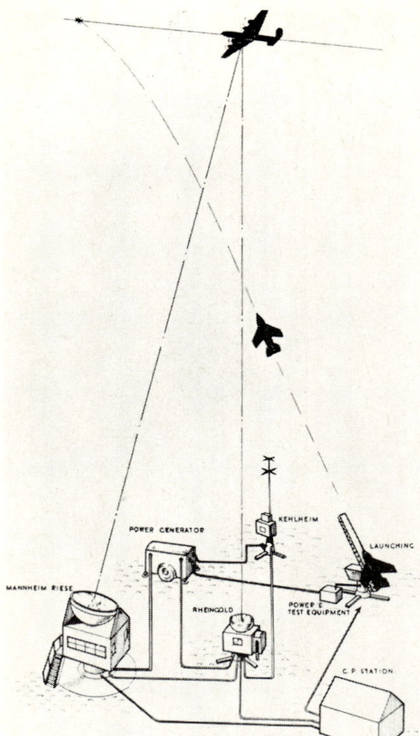

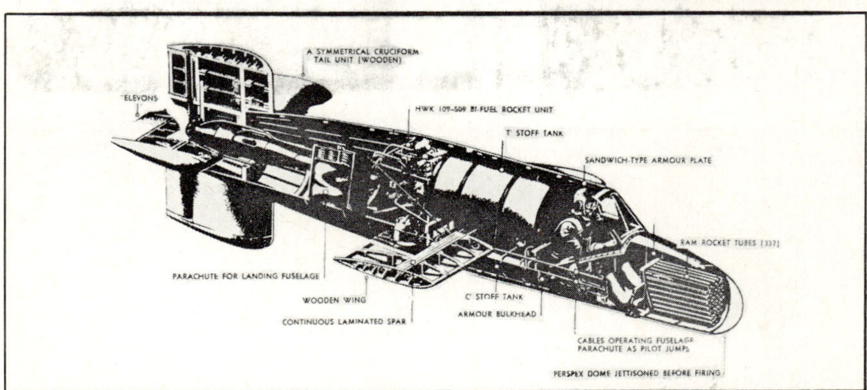

Top left: The *Elsass* guidance system for the *Enzian* missile. The *Mannheim Reise* radar tracked the target; *Rheingold* tracked the missile; and *Kehlheim* issued the guidance orders to the missile.

Top right: 'Longhand', the last heavy AA gun to be approved for service with the British Army. It was never put into supply, since the guided missile arrived in time to supplant it.

Above: Natter, a last-ditch German idea. It was a manned rocket-propelled fighter which took off vertically, flew at high speed into a formation of bombers, loosed off the battery of R4M rockets in its nose, and was then abandoned, the pilot gliding to near his base and baling out. Its flight duration was four minutes. Only one manned flight was ever made, in which the pilot fell out and was killed.

Top: The British 3.7in Mark 6 gun, a 3.7in barrel in a 4.5in gun.

Above: The Bristol-Bofors 40mm gun at practise in 1953.

Top: A Soviet 37mm M1939 gun in action in Königsberg, 1945.
Above: A Soviet 76.2mm gun on lorry mount, camouflaged for winter operations.

Top: The Soviet ZU-23-2 twin 23mm gun, here shown in use by the Polish Army.

Above: The Vulcan Air Defense System, towed and self-propelled versions.

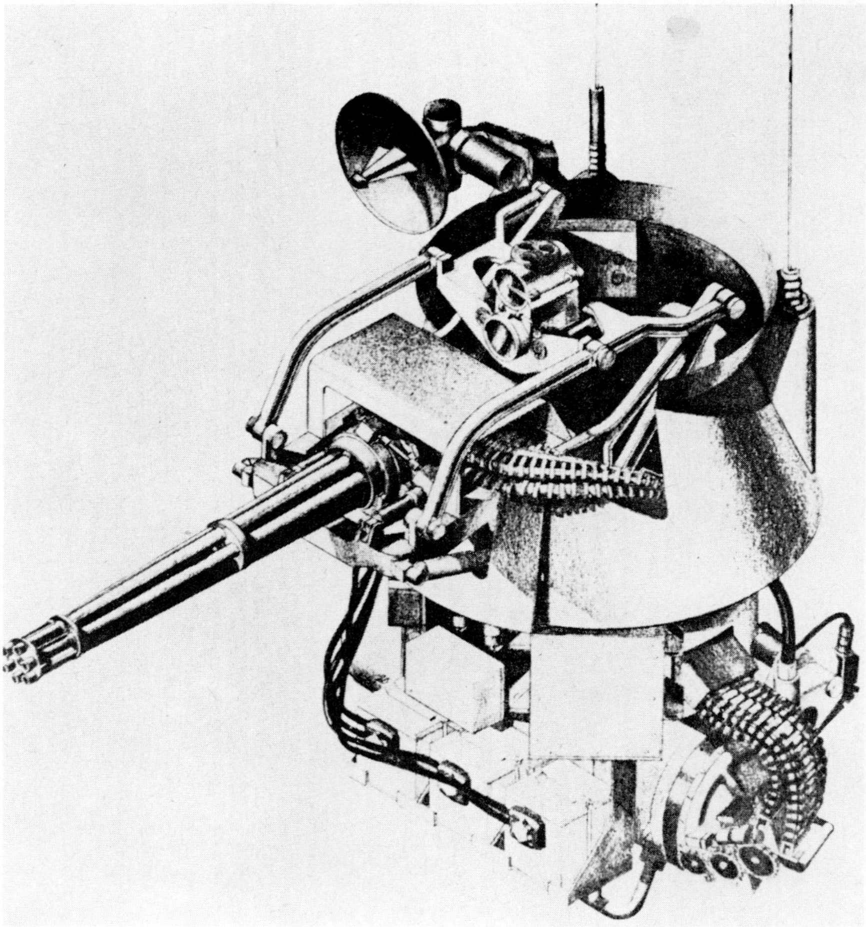

Top: The Vulcan M163 turret complex.

Above: Rapier missile launcher; the surveillance radar is concealed by the dome above and between the missiles.

on blast over-pressure to damage the aircraft. But blast transmission relies on the air through which it passes, and as operational altitudes increased, so the atmosphere became rarified and the thinner air attenuated the blast wave. At 60,000 feet it needs almost twice as much explosive to produce the same amount of damage as could be done at sea level. Moreover, there was the ever-present physical law which says that blast damage diminishes as the cube of the distance to the target. If 10lb of explosive could do a specific amount of damage at ten feet distance, it would require almost 300lb to do the same damage at thirty feet. So in effect blast warheads were only for low-level weapons with a high degree of accuracy.

A third line of approach is to use the warhead simply as a vehicle and eject the lethal effect from it. One way to do this was to fill the warhead with small explosive bombs with impact fuzes and then scatter them around the point of burst. Another was to mount a number of hollow-charge units pointing in all directions from the warhead, and detonate them simultaneously thus emitting piercing jets of high explosive vapour.

Finally, of course, if the target is worth it, a small nuclear warhead can be carried, a warhead which allows a considerable degree of inaccuracy before the target can hope to escape, but one which demands interception at great altitude so that the effect of the nuclear explosion is not felt on the earth beneath.

All these types, and several more which are shrouded in confidential mystery, have been proposed and several have been used, but the precise form of warhead employed in any particular missile is rarely divulged in public.

Fuzing today is almost entirely by proximity methods; there is relatively little restriction on space, ample electric power is available, and some very complex devices have been built. For small missiles there has been a move back to impact fuzing, relying on extreme accuracy and homing devices to ensure a direct hit, while one or two older missiles – for example, the American Nike series – were provided with a facility which allowed the ground controller to detonate the missile at his discretion, a useful feature when dealing with a formation of targets.

One effect of the move to guidance of missiles, proximity fuzes, command destruction and similar systems, is that the air becomes full of electronic signals of one sort and another, and as early as the middle of the Second World War a new dimension had been introduced into the air defence battle, that of electronic warfare or electronic counter-measures (ECM). Even before the war Watson-Watt had pointed out that a small piece of wire, half the wavelength of the signal transmitted by an RDF set, could generate a return echo indistinguishable from that of an aircraft, and such wires, attached to small balloons, were used as early as 1937 for testing RDF sets. As wave-lengths shortened, so these 'half-wave dipoles' became smaller, until eventually they could be produced as short lengths of metallised paper. Dropped from aircraft by their thousand, these strips took as long as two or three hours to fall to the ground, during which time they could produce multitudes of confusing signals on radar screens. This device, code-named 'Window' by the Royal Air Force and 'Chaff' by the Americans, was first used on 24 July 1943 to blind the German defences to a massive raid on Hamburg and was overwhelmingly successful.

Other methods were perfected; Mandrel, Carpet, and Airborne Cigar (ABC) were all types of transmitter designed to emit confusing signals on radar frequencies and produce false echoes or, more simply, blot out the cathode-ray tube with a ragged mess of 'noise' which obscured everything. The early response to this was to develop radar sets with widely differing frequencies so that if one group of sets was blinded, another could be brought into action which used a different portion of the electro-magnetic spectrum in which the jammers and 'Window' were ineffective.

Since then, though, electronic warfare has become a major, if little-advertised, business. 'Ferret' aircraft fly constantly, listening for radar emissions and measuring frequency, pulse length, pulse interval and similar parameters. Having thus 'finger-printed' a radar set, highly sophisticated devices can be developed to counter them. More complex radars are then built in order to defeat the jammers, and so the battle goes on. Today it is no longer merely a matter of producing 'noise' on a specific frequency to smother the receiving tube. Radars have been developed which change their frequency constantly during operation, so that 'sweep' jammers have had to be developed to cover a wide frequency range. Other devices on an aircraft can pick up the emitted radar pulse sent to detect, delay it, amplify it, and then return it to appear in the receiver as if the target were at a greater range, since the false signal will be slightly stronger than the true one and will cause the automatic following circuits to reject the true signal and lock on to the false. Another technique is to emit a powerful signal on the radar frequency, vastly more powerful than the expected echo and so powerful as to overload the receiving circuitry and burn it out. There seems to be no end to human ingenuity in this field.

Electronic warfare has become a major factor because in addition to missile guidance and command, electronics forms the basic building blocks of every system of defence which presently exists. In the immediate postwar years the systems which had been built up during the war continued to function, with some slight improvements in equipment. Britain's Chain Home remained the primary warning system for many years simply because there was nothing available which could give a better detection range. The principal change in Britain's air defence system was to reduce the number of sectors covering the country, since the speed of modern aircraft would have meant passing information from small sector to small sector and clogging the communications net. Changing to larger sectors gave the sector controllers more opportunity to keep an engagement under their own control, from detection to interception. Moreover the radar sets controlling fighter interception could be repositioned in the best tactical and technical locations, rather than being hurriedly assembled in order to fill a gap and sited in any convenient piece of ground that was handy.

By 1951 the nuclear threat was a factor in all defence planning, leading to the general policy of placing vital command functions deep underground, and in the following years the RAF Sector Operations Centre and Ground Controlled Interception Rooms were all buried, a task involving some intricate engineering to deliver the radar signals from the antennae on the surface to the displays deep underground.

The last step came in the late 1950s with the adoption of a new radar which had a range of over 200 miles with extremely good definition, so that the vulnerable CH stations could be finally retired and, since one radar could now provide both early warning and interception facilities, the sequence of radar–filter room–operations room–intercept controller could be radically compressed. The radar display, in the form of an animated map, was optically enlarged to take the place of the old-time map table, so that the controller, instead of working from third-hand information, now had the actual radar-generated picture in front of him and could make immediate assessments.

As this system was being built up in Britain, across the Atlantic the American and Canadian authorities began showing concern over a new threat, the possibility of Soviet bombers flying across the wastes of the North Pole to deliver an attack. In 1957 the NORAD (North American Air Defense) system was inaugurated to provide a unified defence throughout the USA and Canada. Primary warning came from a string of 78 radar sets stretching from the Aleutian Islands across north Canada to Greenland and Iceland – the DEW (Distant Early Warning) Line. This was backed up by 98 sets on the Mid-Canada Line, 256 sets in the Pinetree Line along the US–Canadian border and inside the USA, US naval picket ships on standing patrols in the Atlantic and Pacific Oceans, 'Texas Tower' maritime radar platforms and early warning aircraft patrols. All these poured information into a communications and control network called SAGE (Semi-Automatic Ground Environment) which could assess a threat and, by means of computers, instantly issue orders to the teeth of the NORAD system, 100 squadrons of fighters, Bomarc missiles, and 180 Nike batteries.

No sooner had several hundreds of millions of dollars been sunk into this system than news arrived of the existence of Soviet intercontinental ballistic missiles with nuclear warheads which could be launched across the Pole while a fighter pilot was still getting into his aircraft. To detect the flight of these devices the BMEWS (Ballistic Missile Early Warning System) was devised. Three exceptionally powerful radar stations were built; one at Thule, Greenland, one at Clear, Alaska, and one on Fylingdales Moor in Yorkshire. These three cover the entire western hemisphere and are able to detect any missile while still on its upward path. This, in the best estimates, allowed a 'four-minute warning' of attack by missile. No time to do much in the defensive line, but sufficient time to push the button to launch the West's retaliatory missiles before the Soviet strike landed. That, at least, was the theory; long experience suggests that the four minutes would probably have passed to the sounds of voices demanding confirmation in writing.

It will be apparent by now that one of the most difficult tasks in designing a modern defence control system is concocting a suitable title which will result in a pronounceable set of initials. The newest in this line originated in December 1966 when nine NATO countries agreed to set up an early warning and control system called NADGE for NATO Air Defence Ground Environment. At an estimated cost of $330 million, the system consists of some 80 radar stations spread from North Norway to Turkey. In addition, those countries having air defence networks which are compatible with the NADGE equipment will be able to feed information in and draw it out of the system – examples of this being Britain and France. The ultimate objective was that any controller in the system, irrespective of nationality, could deploy any available weapon from any convenient base. Thus, for example, a West German controller could call on an American fighter squadron flying from an airfield in Britain if that happened to offer the best solution to a particular target threat. By and large this has been achieved, though the French have insisted on retaining over-riding control of their own aircraft.

The NADGE radar stations are connected by data transmission links to a smaller number of sector stations, which in turn are linked to a central control, to fighter stations and to missile launch sites. Computers are kept informed of all civil and military air activity within NATO airspace, and when a radar sighting is made the details are fed into the computer system which, in a matter of seconds, compares it with the notified flight patterns and indicates either that it is in accordance with known data or that it is unidentified. The sector controller then decides on what action to take; in peacetime, of course, this can only mean sending up a fighter to inspect the intruder and report back, but in wartime the controller would have the option of sending a fighter or launching a missile. When Nadge was first planned it was intended to automate the entire response; the computer would calculate the target course, calculate the fighter's interception course, compare the two and then send a stream of data to a display in front of the pilot who would then act on this to arrive at his intercept point. This, though, threatened to be prohibitively expensive and was abandoned; the computer still does the arithmetic but passes the result to the controller who then directs the aircraft by voice radio. Automation has been achieved only in the missile system; if the controller elects to use a missile he simply switches the computer output to the missile control computer and from then on the interception is entirely automatic, though the controller does have an over-riding control available to him should the target belatedly identify itself as being friendly.

As evidenced by the BMEWS system with its four-minute

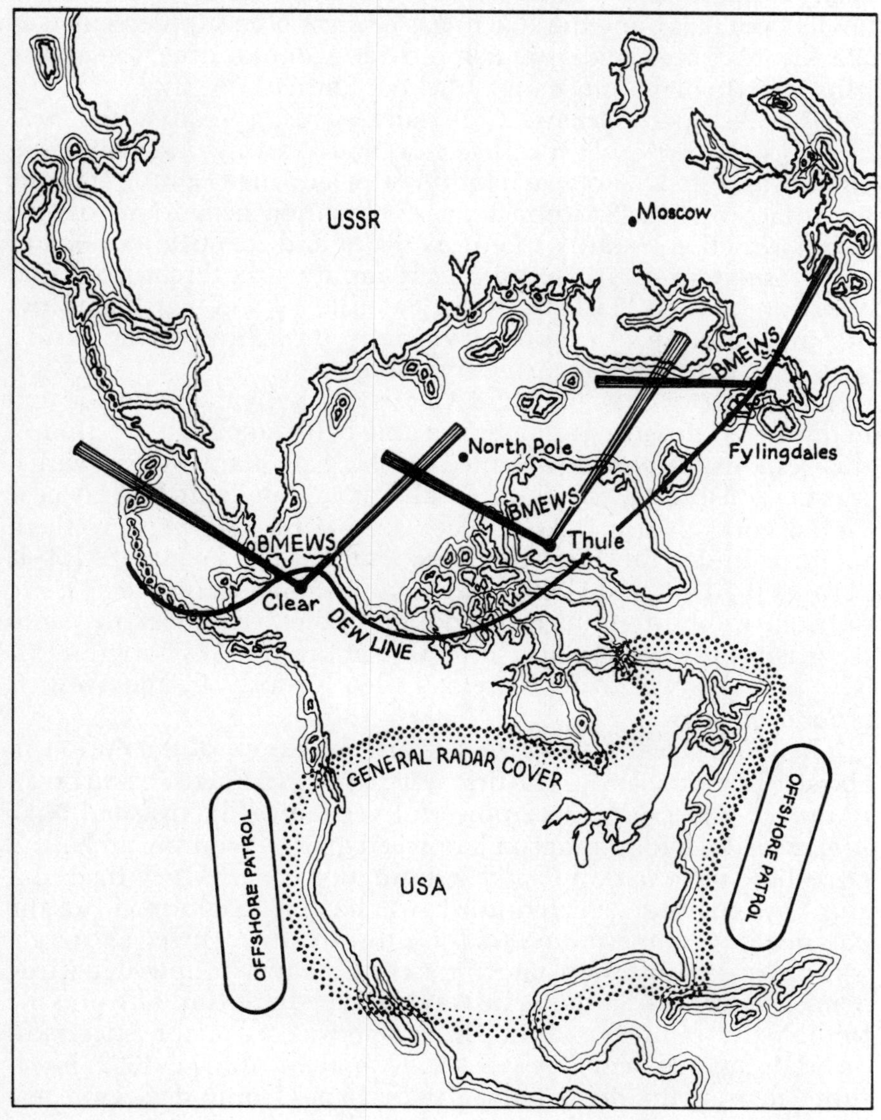

warning, the principal target of today's defence systems is slowly turning from the manned aircraft to the ballistic missile, and the effort which has gone into this field is the most technically advanced and the least publicised. The US Aerospace Command is the US Air Force component of NORAD, and while concerned with 'conventional' targets it has also developed facilities for ballistic missile detection, such as the 'Over-the-Horizon Forward Scatter' (OHFS) radar which emits a continuous high-frequency signal to reflect off the ionosphere. Launching a missile through the ionosphere disturbs this reflectance, indicating the passage of a missile even though the actual missile may not be detected. Nine such equipments are in operation, keeping watch over the entire Soviet land mass, and the system has recently been supplemented by 'Backward Scatter' radars which provide a similar detection ability plus an extremely long range tracking ability.

Other Aeropace Defense Command elements include the 'Sea-launched Ballistic Missile Detection and Warning System' using eight coastal radars to watch for missiles launched from submarine or surface vessels; 'Spacetrack', a seven-station network across the world which constantly monitors space and identifies any man-made object in orbit so as to detect rapidly any threat from that direction; and an 'Early Warning Satellite' system which employs orbiting satelllites to monitor virtually the whole of the earth's surface to detect any missile being launched.

The US Army's part in NORAD is principally the provision and manning of missile sites, and the anti-ballistic-missile portion of this responsibility is represented by the 'Safeguard' system which was designed to protect the US ballistic missile launch areas near Grand Forks, North Dakota. The Anti-ballistic Missile agreement in force under the Strategic Arms Limitation Treaty (SALT-1) permits the USA and USSR to maintain two ABM complexes each; only one was built in the USA, though studies have taken place into the feasibility of setting up a second system around Washington DC. The only known Soviet system, called 'Galosh' by the West, is around Moscow.

The ABM defence problem set forth in search of a solution in about 1956 in the USA. The first system was Nike Zeus, based on an improved and much more powerful version of the original Nike Ajax missile. A long-range radar picked up the incoming target and passed the information to a 'discrimination radar' which tracked it and, by computer, determined whether it conformed to the parameters of a missile and was on a threatening course. The target was then taken over by a 'target track radar' which followed it, while a 'missile track radar' launched and guided the anti-missile-missile to the point of interception. The system was reasonably successful on trials against actual missiles at Kwajalien Atoll in 1962, but it suffered from the disadvantage that it could only deal with one missile at a time and it was highly susceptible to electonic countermeasures.

While the Zeus system was under development, several advances in electronics techniques were perfected, notably the 'phased array radar' which used electrical phase-shifting in the antenna to deflect the beam instead of having physically to move the aerial array. (In some respects this was the perfection of the idea devised by Watson-Watt in 1935 for determining bearings from CH stations.) This made it possible to sweep a large area of sky very rapidly and thus keep an eye on several targets at once. In addition, a new generation of missiles was under development and so, in 1961, before the Zeus system had actually been proved, it was dropped in favour of a new one, called 'Nike X'.

The basic idea was similar to that of Zeus, but simplified. A phased array radar could detect at long range, discriminate and track the target, while a missile site radar guided the interception. Two missiles were to be used, the Nike Zeus for long-range interception and a new high-acceleration missile called 'Sprint' which could move fast enough to cope with any target which evaded Zeus or which was not identified as hostile until close to its target. Nike X was a practical system and plans were made for a number of installations around major cities in the USA, though due to cost limitations only a few cities were actually provided with the system.

Once again things came to a halt while those in charge took a step back and contemplated the situation. Apparently providing 100 per cent cover to the entire continental United States was out of the question, and so a careful analysis of defensive systems, possible threats and cost-effectiveness was carried out in the middle 1960s. The result was a decision to develop a long-range missile with a nuclear warhead which could intercept incoming missiles well above the earth's atmosphere where the nuclear detonation would have little or no measureable effect on the ground beneath. Such a weapon would be able to cover an immense area and, by careful placement and dispersal, a relatively small number would be able to provide a defensive screen for the whole of the United States. The new missile was 'Spartan', with a range of 'several hundred miles'. Except for the fact that it works, very little else has ever been publicly released about Spartan. The new system, using Spartan and retaining Sprint for short range back-up, was provisionally called 'Sentinel' and then, following modifications, 'Safeguard'; in 1970 Congress approved $1,351 million and work began. In subsequent years the People's Elected Representatives proved to be a lot less open-handed, and instead of becoming operational in early 1974 as intended, it was not until late 1975 that it was ready for operation. It was then, for reasons not made public, de-activated in the following year, and as far as anyone can tell there does not appear to be a functioning ABM system in the United States at the present time.

During the Second World War the self-propelled field gun became a standard weapon, to provide field artillery support which had the same degree of mobility as the armoured forces it was supporting. In a similar manner, self-propelled anti-aircraft guns were developed to afford protection to armoured columns whilst on the move and encamped and also to permit rapid deployment in support of forward troops until such times as towed equipments could be brought up and emplaced. For simplicity's sake these were usually the standard light gun mounted on to any convenient chassis which could be butchered to fit; thus, the US Army placed an open-topped turret with twin 40mm Bofors guns on to a converted M24 light tank chassis to make the 'Gun, Motor Carriage, M19', the British put a single Bofors into a modified Crusader tank and the Germans placed a variety of 20mm and 37mm guns, single, twin and quadruple, on to all sorts of chassis from half-track tractors to captured French tanks.

Reception of this device was mixed. For reasons not readily apparent the British Army never enthused over the AA Tank, and scrapped the Crusader as soon as the war was over. The only self-propelled equipment they retained was a somewhat odd contraption consisting of a single Bofors 40mm on the back of a Morris-Commercial 30cwt truck. Even this appears to have been under-valued, or at least under-employed; the last one I saw was acting as a special despatch vehicle, carrying official mail around in the Commonwealth Division area in Korea in 1952. The American M19 saw rather more use and the design was perpetuated in postwar years with the M42, a similar twin 40mm but on an improved chassis. The relative importance, in the war years, which was placed on the AA tank by the Americans and British on the one hand and the Germans on the other, undoubtedly reflects the balance of air superiority in 1944–45; Allied aircraft were giving the German army a harder time than German aircraft were giving the Allied.

In postwar years there was little development of the SPAA gun, except for the American M42 which appeared as a result of the Korean War. (In my own experience the M19 showed its greatest value in that war as a short-range assault gun for helping infantry on to an objective and 'taking out' small obstacles.) This may well have been due to the problems associated with fire control; with modern aircraft speeds an anti-aircraft gun was only viable if it was tied-in to an early warning network, capable of giving even minimal warning of a target's approach. The relatively slow approach of aircraft during the 1939–45 war had meant that a visually-controlled gun could still pick up targets in time to take action against them, and so a lone gun, unconnected with any form of warning system, was quite a practical weapon. But once it became necessary to tie the gun down to a radar set and a warning network, its free-ranging abilities counted for little.

By the late 1950s, though, advances in ground-attack aircraft had begun to make military staffs think again about the AA tank, and advances in electronics had reached the point where it was feasible, both from the economic point of view and the physical one, to think of putting a small radar on to the chassis along with the gun to produce a self-sufficient module which embraced warning, tracking, computing and shooting. In order to keep things as simple as possible the first attempts at this idea were based on the assumption that aircraft attacking ground troops would only be likely to do so in clear weather so that they could see their targets; by the same token, the guns were then able to see the aircraft and could use optical sighting systems allied with electronic fire-control computers. From this premise the idea of the 'fair-weather' equipment was born. Early examples of this type of weapon were the French AMX-13DCA, an AMX 13-tonne tank chassis mounting two 30mm guns, and the Swiss Oerlikon equipment which also used the AMX chassis but mounted a large turret with four 20mm cannon.

These designs were useful in providing designers with some basic experience but they were limited in their uses and they were soon supplanted by more sophisticated apparatus. The AMX-DCA was soon redesigned on the heavier and larger AMX-30 chassis and provided with an integral fire-control and acquisition radar, while the Oerlikon design was similarly improved. In 1965 the Oerlikon company, in association with Contraves AG, experts in radar and fire control devices, and Albiswerk AG, also radar experts, set to work on a fresh design based on the chassis of the German Leopard I main battle tank. The turret contained the fire control computer and carried an early warning radar with a range of 15km, a fire control radar, and two 35mm automatic guns. The Federal German Bundeswehr received the first models for test in 1969 and, after some modifications and further testing, adopted it as the Gepard Flakpanzer in 1975, ordering over 400 for a total cost reputed to be DM3,000 million. More orders followed from the Belgian and Netherlands armies, and several other countries have since shown interest in the design.

In spite of the British Army's known reluctance to adopt this type of weapon, the Vickers company have developed the 'Falcon AA Tank' as a private venture. This used the chassis of their successful 'Abbot' self-propelled field gun, with a special turret mounting two 30mm Hispano-Suiza cannons. Sighting is optical, aided by a laser rangefinder and an electronic computer, so that 'Falcon' comes under the heading of 'fair-weather' equipments. But it has the virtues of cheapness and simplicity, which the makers hope will enable them to sell the weapon overseas, while people in search of more complex facilities at least have a sound basis on which to work and can doubtless tailor the necessary additions to suit.

The logical successor to the self-propelled AA gun is the self-propelled AA missile but, as already mentioned, some of the first attempts at this, such as the US Army's 'Mauler', ended disastrously. This was principally due to trying to run before walking had been mastered; the project goals were unrealistic and the degree of complexity demanded led to systems which required more repairmen than operators. At one stage of the 'Mauler' development it was hoped to produce a system which, once switched on, would require no further human intervention other than to chalk up the score; the radar would acquire, identify, track, fire and control the missile automatically. By modifying the demands, the goals have now come down to a point where improvements in electronic technique have come up to meet them, and recent European developments suggest that a practical solution is now attainable.

Probably the most outstanding SP missile equipment in existence at the moment is Roland, which was first devised as the answer to a French General Staff specification demanding a simple and cheap system capable of destroying aircraft flying at speeds up to 0.9 Mach. As with the gun developments, the first solution was a 'fair weather' system, work being concentrated on the missile and vehicle aspects rather than trying to get too involved in complicated fire control problems. Shortly after work had begun on this in about 1968, the Bundeswehr showed interest; it became a joint Franco-German development and, at German insistence, studies of an 'all-weather' system were put in hand.

The 'fair-weather' system, Roland I was ready in 1969, and the test firings scored four hits out of five shots with live missiles against target aircraft. This equipment consisted of the chassis of the AMX-30 tank carrying a turret on which are two missile launch tubes, an optical sighting system, and the command guidance transmitter. Inside the built-up superstructure of the hull are two magazines with more missiles, from which the launcher tubes can be rapidly re-loaded. The missile has a multiple hollow-charge warhead, is proximity fuzed, and comes packed in a sealed cylinder so that no maintenance is required and a shelf life of five years is guaranteed. This cylinder is loaded, just like a round of gun ammunition, into the launcher, and the missile ejects itself on launch. leaving the empty tube to be ejected, again, like a gun cartridge case. The operator lays an optical sight on the target and this generates radio commands to the missile, bring it on to the optical axis, after which it is guided to the target.

The 'all-weather' version is Roland II, which, since it was primarily German-developed, mounts everything on a German Marder armoured personnel carrier chassis. Everything is the same except that in this version a tracking radar takes over the functions of the optical sight and follows the target; the missile is also tracked and the two tracks compared, after which correctional signals to the missile bring it into line with the tracking radar's beam and guide it to the target. Provision of Roland II for the Bundeswehr was scheduled to begin in 1978, and a total of 180 are to be issued. It has also been adopted by the US Army for use, in the first instance, by their forces in Europe.

For all the good intentions of the French General Staff, Roland ended up heavy, complex and expensive, though for all that it has to be admitted that it works well. But smaller armies require less involved designs, and companies hoping to interest the commercial market have to aim somewhat lower in the scale of sophistication. A good example of how to go about this is seen in Crotale, a system developed privately by the French Thomson-CSF/Engins Matra consortium. Their first simplification was in the mounting itself; instead of an expensive and heavy tracked vehicle, they adopted the chassis of a Hotchkiss armoured car. On to this was mounted a simple turret structure carrying four launcher tubes and a tracking radar, and inside the turret is the fire control computer. Simplicity is achieved by splitting the whole unit into two parts; the other part is another Hotchkiss chassis which mounts the search radar, IFF equipment, another computer, and a digital Data Transmission System which passes information to the tracking radar and points it in the right direction to acquire the target. Crotale has been adopted by the South African Army (who call it Cactus) and by the armies of Libya and Saudi Arabia, and several other countries have shown interest.

Until now the Soviet Union has figured little in these pages, for the simple reason that practically nothing has ever been made public about their air defences up to and including the war. Their range of anti-aircraft guns was similar to that of other nations – 25mm, 37mm and 45mm of their own design, some 40mm Bofors, 76mm and 85mm mobile guns, and a static 105mm gun. So far as is known no comprehensive warning system existed and fire control was based on optical rangefinding, searchlights and mechanical predictors. During the war a few British GL radars were sent to the Soviet Union but no report of their efficiency in Soviet hands was ever received. At the end of the war large numbers of German technicians and research facilities were taken away to the Soviet Union and, as in so many other fields, once pointed in the right direction by Western fingers, the Soviet progress was rapid, if only because of the enormous reserves of manpower and resources which could be devoted to the field.

During the period in which their missiles were being developed, the Soviets continued to work on guns and they produced two excellent designs during the post-war period. In 1949 a 100mm gun firing a 35lb shell to 50,000 feet appeared, followed, in 1955, by a 130mm gun firing a 74lb shell to 72,000 feet. The 100mm gun replaced the older 85mm models and was little more than an enlargement of them; the 130mm appears to have been influenced by the American 4.7in (120mm) design, there being notable similarities in the mounting and in the fuze-setter/rammer for use with separated ammunition. Both guns were later replaced by missiles in

A connected narrative of Soviet missile development is unlikely ever to be written for Western consumption, and the best that can be done is to identify those missiles known to the outside world. Since their official names were never discovered until long after their existence was known, NATO and the western world in general have adopted a practise begun in the Second World War by the Americans; arbitrary naming. Faced with various Japanese aircraft of unknown naming. Faced with various Japanese aircraft of unknown nomenclature, the American Technical Air Intelligence Unit in 1942 decided to give all Japanese types an easily-remembered name, so that for example the Kawanishi N1K2-J fighter became 'George' and the Mitsubishi Ki-67 bomber became 'Peggy'. In similar fashion all Soviet missiles (and military aircraft) are given names, the initial letter of which indicates their basic role; thus, all surface-to-air missiles have names beginning with 'G'. In addition, they have been given a numerical identification to indicate the order of their appearance. The only thing not made public is the paper which lays down the principles to be followed in selecting the names which is a pity since, judging by some of them, it would be the most hilarious document to have been seen in print since Mark Twain died.

SA-1 or 'Guild' was the first Soviet air defence missile to be revealed to the West; this was done in the usual manner by including it in the annual October Revolution parade in Moscow in 1960. Little was ever discovered about it since it appears never to have been taken into service in large numbers. It was a relatively simple weapon, a single-stage rocket with command guidance. The same year saw the unveiling of the SA-2, 'Guideline', a much better weapon which was, by all appearances, the second-generation version of Guild. It was similar in appearance, with cruciform wing and tail surfaces, and used a two-stage rocket – one to boost it from the ground and one to sustain it in flight – the first stage of which was a solid-fuel motor and the second a liquid-fuel type. It carried a 290lb warhead, reliably reported to be of the continuous-rod type, and was radio-controlled. As well as becoming standard in the Soviet air defence system, Guideline was later to be widely exported, though it is believed that the most advanced versions were retained for use in Soviet hands. A number of variant models have been identified at various times, representing advances in motor power and guidance, and one version, seen in Moscow in 1967, is believed to have a nuclear warhead.

The SA-3 or 'Goa' also appeared in 1960. This was a much smaller weapon, carried in pairs on a six-wheeled truck. It comprised a two-stage rocket with a 150lb warhead and the usual radio guidance. The range is estimated as being 12 miles, and it appears to be used as a medium-to-low level weapon for field armies. As with Guideline, it has been exported to Communist-inclined countries in some quantity.

It was not until 1964 that the next weapon appeared, the SA-4 or 'Ganef'. More powerful than Goa, it was carried in pairs on a tracked launcher and was employed to give medium-to-high level protection to field armies. Propulsion is by ramjet, with four solid-fuel launch boost rockets arranged around the body in the same fashion as those of the British Thunderbird. The Ganef uses radio command guidance, the warhead is high explosive, and the operational range is said to be about 40 miles.

SA-5 was a training rocket and never received a NATO name. SA-6, which appeared in 1967, is called 'Gainful' and, due to numbers being captured in the Arab–Israeli war of 1973, more is probably known about this one than about any other Soviet weapon. Gainful is ramjet propelled, with a single solid-fuel launch booster. It is guided through the major part of its flight by radio command, but on reaching the target area it transfers to a self-contained homing system which relies on the target's reflecting the signals from a 'target illuminating radar' on the launch site. The HE/Fragmentation warhead weighs about 175lb and is activated by proximity or impact fuzes. The maximum operating range is about 35 miles and the maximum ceiling about 60,000 feet. Three missiles are carried on a tracked launcher which is built on the chassis of the PT-76 amphibious tank, and a missile battery consists of eight launcher vehicles accompanied by a long-range surveillance radar, a tracking radar, and the target illuminating radar.

The first generation missiles, of whatever country, whilst being notable technical achievements, suffered from much the same sort of defects as had the medium and heavy guns which they replaced; they were too heavy and cumbersome to be quickly aligned on a close, fast target, and their guidance systems were such that the missile was not under control until it had flown for some considerable distance and steered itself into the command beam. As a result these missiles were of little or no use against low-flying ground strafers. The designers and manufacturers were well aware of this and worked diligently to develop fast-reacting missiles which could take on targets at short range, but this demanded a degree of miniaturisation which took some years to perfect. In the meanwhile, the only answer was the 'cannon solution'.

There were two points of view among the gun advocates; one maintained that the only hope was to produce a weapon with the highest possible rate of fire so as to fill the sky with metal, while the other party insisted that the only proper solution was to produce a gun capable of firing a shell which would be lethal with one shot and then back the gun with a fire control system of superlative accuracy so that only one shot would be necessary. The first theory was well represented by the many 20mm and 30mm automatic guns which had appeared over the years, while the second school had arisen as the result of a wartime German development programme, the *Gerat 58*. This was a 55mm 'intermediate' (the Germans preferred to call it 'medium') gun intended not only to replace the disappointing 50mm Flak 41 but also to meet a new specification drawn up as a result of looking at the defence problem with a fresh eye. By 1943 the RAF and USAAF had made sufficient forays into Germany to allow some new parameters to be drawn up relative to what a gun ought to be expected to do, and a 'medium AA tactical theory' was expounded. This was later paraphrased in a post-war interrogation report as follows:

> 'The employment of a medium gun can only be justified where it is vital to *destroy* every attacking aircraft. These conditions will occur relatively infrequently, but they are likely to occur both in the furthest rear areas (eg the defence of the Möhne Dam) and in the forefront of battle (eg the defence of the Remagen Bridge). In either case one single enemy aircraft escaping destruction can cause a catastrophe. An expensive equipment can therefore be justified, provided it is 100 per cent successful.
>
> The solution to this problem is the employment of extremely accurate massed fire from several guns. This can be achieved by controlling four to six guns from one predictor, the guns being provided with displacement correctors and power traverse and elevation remotely controlled from the predictor. The whole equipment, despite its complications, must be highly mobile.'

As a result of this theory a 5.5cm gun was developed, together with a carefully integrated system of radar, predictor, displacement corrector and power control, but the work was not completed by the time the war ended. In the post-war 'gold rush', neither the British, who were still fiddling with their abortive twin six-pounder, nor the Americans, who were putting their money on the 75mm Skysweeper design, were particularly interested in *Gerat 58*, but the Soviets were. They saw it as a useful intermediate-sized weapon and they were attracted by the tactical theory behind it; so the development was removed to the Soviet Union and continued until it became the Soviet Army's 57mm Model 1950 AA gun. There were one or two changes in general design in order to conform with Soviet standard practice, but the essentials – high velocity, high rate of fire, and an integrated fire control system – were all there.

With the 57mm in production, Soviet attention now turned to lighter guns based on the other school of thought, the stream of smaller shells school. The earlier 37mm and 45mm guns were mechanically similar to the Bofors 40mm and could not produce a sufficient volume of fire, so a totally new design in 23mm calibre was begun. It is probable that the starting point was an existing weapon, the 23mm NS23 aircraft cannon, but as finally evolved it was a totally new gun which first appeared on the ZSU-23-4, a self-propelled mounting carrying four guns in a power-operated turret. Each gun was capable of firing at a rate of 1,000 rounds per minute, and fire control is either by a radar built in the vehicle turret or by a computing optical sight. The self-propelled version was later supplemented by a twin-barrel model, the ZU-32-2, carried on a light two-wheeled trailer.

In the United States the 37mm gun was long obsolete and the 40mm, being a foreign design, was unlikely to be perpetuated in American service. At the end of the war there was a project underway to perfect a .60in heavy machine gun for aircraft use, and the Army was following this development in the hope that it might turn out to be a useful light AA weapon. But the development reached an impasse when the mechanism achieved such a point of rapidity that the gun had several bullets in the barrel at the same time, which usually resulted in a ruptured or bulged barrel. Moreover there appeared to be little advantage in a .60in weapon, since it was operationally little more effective than the existing .50in machine gun and was too small to use any form of exploding projectile, so the development was abandoned. In order to achieve the desired rate of fire a multiple-barrel solution was suggested, and from this somebody had the inspiration to obtain an 1883 model Gatling-gun from a museum, connect an electric motor to it and see what happened. To most people's surprise the idea worked, delivering short bursts of fire at rates of up to 5,000 rounds per minutes. So the project was handed to the Armaments Division of the General Electric Company under the name 'Vulcan', and in 1949 a .60in calibre Vulcan gun was demonstrated.

The Vulcan, like the Gatling, uses six barrels in a rotating frame; the lock and breech mechanism are arranged so that the various functions of feeding, chambering, firing and extracting are performed on each barrel at one specific point during the rotation cycle; thus, firing always takes place at the bottom, while ejection is done as it begins its rise and feed begins as it starts the downward movement. As a result, each barrel has time to cool between shots and when the gun is firing at 6,000 rounds per minute, the individual barrels are only firing at 1,000 rounds per minute each.

The Vulcan, in 20mm calibre, was adopted in 1956 as an aircraft cannon, but the Army had followed its development very closely and saw that it offered a highly attractive solution to the low-level gun problem. Work began on an integrated gun-radar unit to be mounted in a modified tracked armoured personnel carrier, and in 1966 it entered service as the 'Vulcan Air Defense System M163', to be soon followed by a towed model on a wheeled trailer, the VADS M167. In an effort to reduce the logistical strain the rate of fire was reduced to 3,000 rounds per minute, still quite enough for the task at hand, and a pre-set selector mechanism allowed the gunner to select 10, 30, 60 or 100-round bursts of fire. A built-in radar provides range and speed of the target, which is fed to a computing optical sight which automatically sets the graticules to give the correct lead, after which the gunner tracks the target optically.

It is probably fair to say that at the time of their inception such weapons as the ZU-23 and Vulcan were regarded, by most people, as expensive stopgaps and a form of insurance in case the next stage in close defence failed to come up to expectations. This next stage was, of course, the development of smaller missiles with more agile control systems, so that they could track, lock on to, out-accelerate, out-manoeuvre and destroy fast low aircraft targets, and some large sums of money were being expended in the hunt. One of the earliest and most expensive exercises was the US Army's 'Mauler' project, a self-propelled mounting carrying four small missiles, together with a radar, computer and guidance system. This was projected in the early 1960s, an extremely sophisticated and attractive package, and in 1962 the British government decided to 'buy in' to the project to save themselves the expense of developing a comparable system of their own. But the cost of Mauler went up as rapidly as its missiles should have done, while the missiles stayed as low as the cost ought to have done. The whole project was dogged with development setbacks, the cost went out of sight, and in 1965 the whole of the Mauler project was abandoned, which left the British and American armies short of a great deal of cash and of an effective low-level AA system.

While the Mauler project was still under way the British had come to the conclusion that even if it did do everything promised it would still be prohibitively expensive and they would not be able to afford enough of them to counter any serious threat. The answer seemed to be to buy sufficient Maulers to provide protection for more important installations and develop a simpler and cheaper missile which would be optically controlled and thus capable of acting in good weather and clear visibility, conditions when the scale of attack might be expected to be most dangerous. Studies of a suitable system began in 1963, and since the basic features were similar to a project called 'Sightline' which the British Aircraft Corporation had been working on as a private venture for some years, BAC were given the project. Once Mauler collapsed, there was a greater need than ever, and a preliminary study showed that it would be possible to add radar guidance to the missile to give day and night capability, so bringing the system up to the standard of performance promised by Mauler.

The new system became known as 'Rapier', and the first equipments for service tests appeared in 1967. A highly mobile assembly, the basic units are a surveillance radar which also carries the launchers for four missiles, an optical tracker, and a generator. In action the three units are dispersed on the ground, easily concealed, and the radar performs an all-round scan until it detects a target. On detection, the radar automatically 'challenges' the target; if, by the use of the standard IFF (Identification, Friend or Foe) responders, the target announces itself as friendly, then the radar goes back to searching. If the target does not identify itself, then the radar sounds an alarm to alert the operator on the optical tracker and slews both the tracker and the missile launchers to face the threat.

The tracker operator begins following the target in his optical sight, using a joystick which controls both tracker and launcher. As soon as the target is within range the radar informs the operator by a lamp signal in his optical field, whereupon he presses a button and a missile is fired. While the operator tracks the target, a separate television camera tracks the missile; a computing system constantly compares the two tracks and correctional signals are sent to the missile to bring its flight line on to the axis of the optical sight, so that eventually the missile is flying along the operator's line of sight to the target. Provided, therefore, that the operator keeps his sight aligned, the missile cannot fail to intercept the target, and indeed, the accuracy of the system is so high that the users soon began to call Rapier a 'hittile' instead of a 'missile'. In darkness an additional unit, the Blindfire tracking radar, replaces the optical tracker; this locks on to the target and then tracks both target and missile, generating correctional signals to bring missile and target into collision.

The American response to Mauler's collapse was to begin development of a similar self-propelled equipment called 'Chaparral' but to economise by adopting an existing missile to the new role. The missile was Sidewinder, an air-to-air rocket which used an infra-red detector to home on to its target; the particular version selected was Sidewinder 1C, a US Navy variant with a more powerful rocket motor than the Air Force original model, and with minimal alteration it became a useful ground-to-air weapon. Guidance is minimal; the Chaparral is locked on by optical sighting, the missile is fired, and its subsequent course is determined by its heat-seeking head which, sensing the target, generates signals to steer the missile towards it.

This is obviously a less versatile system than Rapier but it is backed up by a second, more sophisticated, system called 'Hawk', being an acronym from 'Homing All-the-Way-Killer'. This began development in 1955 but it was not envisaged as a self-contained unit like Mauler or Chaparral. Hawk was planned more on the lines of a conventional gun battery, with a number of launchers dispersed and connected to acquisition and target illuminating radars. Two acquisition radars are used, of different types to give the most thorough possible cover from ground level upwards. Once a target is acquired it is passed to the illuminating radar which tracks it; in addition the signal illuminates the target for the missile, since the reflected radar signal is detected by a receiver in the nose of the missile. Before the missile is launched this receiver is switched on to detect and lock on the reflected signal. Launch then takes place and the missile simply follows the reflected signal until it intercepts the target.

One might reasonably think that with this sort of missile armoury covering everything from the ground to the outer layers of the earth's atmosphere, the armies might be content. But there is always a reluctance to leave everything to the specialists and there is always a demand for weapons, in any field of application, capable of one-man operation by the ordinary foot-soldier. In the earliest days of air defence the foot-soldier, with his magazine rifle, stood as good a chance as anyone else of scoring against a flying target, but as the years went by his chances became more slender until they approached the vanishing point. A well-placed rifle bullet can still bring down the most sophisticated and up-to-date aircraft, but the placing of the bullet becomes less feasible with each new generation of aircraft, and with supersonic aircraft the pilot is a good deal more likely, statistically speaking, to be hit twice in succession by lightning than once by a rifle bullet.

The soldiers never gave up hope, though, and as late as the 1960s the official British Army 'All Arms AA Weapon' was the .50in Browning machine gun, and even today every major army provides an AA machine gun for its tanks and other vehicles. But obviously, something better than this is needed, and with the small missiles out of the drawing office and into service, the designers began looking at the possibility of one-man-portable missile systems.

The first to appear was the American Redeye, development of which began in 1959. This is a 29lb infra-red homing missile packed in a sealed launcher tube which can be aimed and fired from a man's shoulder. On seeing an aircraft the operator points the optical sight at it and presses a switch to activate the missile homing head. As soon as the missile detects the heat from the target it locks on and sounds a buzzer to tell the operator. He then presses the trigger and a small expelling charge shoots the missile from the tube at low speed; once it is some 20 feet away the rocket motor ignites and the missile departs on its course. This delayed launch is for protecting the operator from the back-blast of the rocket. The maximum effective range is about 3,000 yards.

The next of this type to be seen was of Soviet origin. It first appeared in small numbers in Vietnam and was then employed in quantity in the 1973 Arab-Israeli War. There was, at first, some confusion over its title, but it is now known to the Western powers as SA-7 or 'Grail'. Its development history is not known, but by accident or design it is practically the same as Redeye, a heat-seeking missile which is pre-locked to the target and fired when the operator has been informed that lock has been achieved. Its performance is about the same as that of Redeye, though the whole equipment is smaller, the missile weighing about 20lb.

Both Redeye and Grail have one basic defect: since they use heat-seeking homing units of spartan simplicity (due to size limitations) they home on to the hottest part of the target, which is generally the tail pipe of the jet engine. As a result they tend to damage rather than kill; the Israeli Air Force dismissed Grail somewhat slightingly by observing that 'they bent a lot of tail pipes' but did nothing worse. As a consequence of this 'tail-chasing' propensity, they are of little use against an aircraft until it has completed its attack and is presenting its tail to the missile, which generally refuses to lock on to any other aspect of the target. So the second generation of missiles had to be more complex.

The only second-generation missile in this class to have achieved service status at the moment is the British Army's Blowpipe. This launches an impact-and-proximity fuzed missile which is released as soon as the operator has the target in his optical sight. A flare at the tail of the missile is tracked by an independent sensor in the sight unit of the launcher and its position compared with the optical line of sight. Signals are then sent to steer the missile into the optical field of view, whereupon the operator takes over control and, by using a thumb-switch, keeps the missile aligned with the target until it hits. At present no details of weights or performance have been released, but obviously a target can now be attacked from any angle, and tail-chasing is a thing of the past.

Since 1945 there have been few occasions when modern air defence systems have been used in anger. The first item of significance, and one which revealed the potentials of missile systems, was when the American U2 'spy plane' was shot down over Sverdlovsk in the Soviet Union in 1960 at an altitude hitherto considered safe. Then came the American involvement in Vietnam, where batteries of Soviet 130mm guns and SA-2 Guideline missiles were deployed. Published American reports tended to discount the missiles; pilots reported they were able to see them coming and out-manoeuvre them and that they considered the guns to be a greater danger. There was some degree of truth in this, but in later years it was admitted that some of the tales were embroidered slightly to conceal the fact that the Americans had developed an effective electronic countermeasure against the SA-2 missile guidance system.

The 1967 'Six-Day' Arab–Israeli War was far from a success from the standpoint of Egyptian Air Defence systems, because the Israeli Air Force achieved tactical surprise. Instead of attacking at dawn, the traditional time, the attack was delayed for some three hours until the Egyptian air defence units had 'stood down' from their habitual dawn readiness and were engaging in such matters as maintenance, breakfast and driving to work. The result was catastrophic, the Egyptian Air Force virtually ceasing to exist within minutes of the outbreak of war.

After this salutary lesson the Egyptian Army obtained large numbers of SA-2 and SA-3 missiles from the Soviet Union and emplaced them in fixed batteries to defend the Suez Canal. Electronic warfare 'ferret' techniques soon provided the Israelis with information on the control and guidance systems and, in view of American successes in dealing with the SA-2 in Vietnam, they were confident that when the day arrived these missiles would be no obstacle. Later, though, batteries of SA-6 and quantities of SA-7 missiles were brought into the Egyptian system, as well as large numbers of ZU-23 light AA guns. These, too, were underestimated by the Israelis, with the result that when the 'Yom Kippur' war was launched in October 1973 the Israeli Air Force lost about 100 aircraft in the first two days, while the Egyptians, who had built hard shelters for their machines, escaped damage. Shaken by their losses the Israelis appealed to the Americans and received a number of the latest electronic counter-measure devices which allowed them some protection from the SA-6 missiles. Fortified by these they essayed once more to repeat their 1967 tactics of fast, low approaches but then found themselves at hazard from the SA-7 and ZU-23 light weapons which were accompanying the Egyptian field forces. Precise figures have still not been released, but indications are that the ZU-23-4 quadruple gun equipment was probably the most successful weapon of all.

Apart from the defences of Hanoi, which one can safely assume were a well-integrated network of observers, radar, control centres, interceptor airfields, guns and missile batteries, and of which nothing is publicly known, this means that the only air defences which have operated in war conditions since 1945 have been those with field armies. Korea in 1950–53, the Indonesian confrontation, the India–Pakistan wars and such affairs have all been point-and-shoot engagements. Lessons have been learned even so; it is doubtful if any projectile has ever been fired skyward without somebody learning something from it. But the massive and complex networks which form an invisible screen above the major nations of the earth will remain, to be manned, exercised, maintained and tuned to a fine pitch, replaced by something even more miraculous, and again maintained in operational readiness in perpetuity, or so it seems. It is unfortunate that such brilliant technical achievements, representing the acme of human ingenuity and brilliance, should at the same time be the most enormous and costly monument to human folly.

APPENDICES

In order to expand upon some of the themes mentioned in the body of the book, but so as to avoid interrupting the flow of the narrative with tables of figures or long extracts from documents, the following Appendices have been inserted. The first four tabulate the two sides of the air defence problem – the aircraft making the attacks and the guns defending the targets – during both World Wars, and comparison of these figures will illustrate the problem of matching gun performance to aircraft performance.

The remainder are extracts from wartime intelligence, interrogation and technical reports dealing with various aspects of the air defence problem as seen by various people, and taken together they tend to show both sides of the question. It should be borne in mind that, apart from Appendix 7, which is the result of interrogation of a German officer after the war had ended, these reports and estimates were based on the best available knowledge at the time, and in some cases their estimates of future events were not borne out in practice.

APPENDIX 1

Performance of Anti-Aircraft Guns/First World War

Gun	Shell weight lb	Muzzle velocity ft/s	Rate of fire rpm	Effective ceiling ft
Britain				
1pr Pom Pom	1.00	1,310	250	3,000
12pr	12.0	2,200	15	19,500
13pr 9cwt	13.0	2,150	20	18,000
13pr Mk 4	12.5	1,600	20	16,000
3in 5cwt	12.5	1,650	20	16,000
3in 20cwt	12.5	2,500	15	20,500
18pr	18.5	1,615	15	18,000
3.6in	25.0	2,000	20	26,000
4in Mk 5	31.000	2,350	10	28,750
5.5in Mk 1	82	2,600	5	35,000
France				
75mm M1897	13.8	1,880	25	21,000
Germany				
76.2mm Russland	20.5	1,935	15	18,000
77mm Ballon K	17.3	1,675	20	16,000
77mm Franz	17.5	1,600	15	17,000
80mm Flak	27.0	2,575	10	22,000
88mm M1918	33.7	2,575	12	27,000

APPENDIX 2

Performance of Bomber Aircraft/First World War

Type	Speed mph	Operational ceiling ft	Bomb load lb	Range miles
Britain				
De Havilland 4	135	20,000	460	420
De Havilland 10	125	17,000	900	600
Handley-Page 0/400	97	8,500	2,000	650
France				
Breguet 14	112	18,000	560	435
Germany				
AEG G IV	90	13,000	750	400
Gotha G IV	87	21,000	1,100	525
Staaken R	80	12,500	4,400	500
Zeppelin	65	21,000	2,200	3,000

APPENDIX 3

Performance of Anti-Aircraft Guns/Second World War

Gun	Shell weight lb	Muzzle velocity ft/s	Rate of fire rpm	Effective ceiling ft
Britain				
40mm Bofors	2.0	2,700	120	5,000
2pr	2.0	2,275	120	6,000
3in 20cwt	16.5	2,000	25	25,200
3.7in Mk 3	28.0	2,600	25	32,000
3.7in Mk 6	28.0	3,425	19	45,000
4.5in	54.0	2,400	8	34,500
5.25in	80.0	2,800	10	43,000
France				
37mm M1925	1.2	2,870	120	12,000
75mm M1897	13.8	1,890	25	21,000
75mm M17/34	13.5	2,300	25	25,000
75mm M1933	19.9	2,300	20	22,000
75mm M1936	14.2	2,300	20	25,000
90mm M1926	21.2	2,650	15	32,000
USA				
37mm M1	1.4	2,600	120	10,500
3in M3 (Mobile)	12.9	2,800	25	28,000

Appendix 3 continued

3in M4 (Static)	12.9	2,800	25	29,000
90mm M2	23.4	2,700	27	33,800
105mm M3	32.8	2,800	15	37,000
120mm M1	50.0	3,100	12	47,400
USSR				
37mm M39	1.6	2,700	160	12,000
40mm M1933	2.2	2,950	120	10,000
76mm M31	14.3	2,700	15	24,000
76mm M38	14.5	2,700	20	26,000
85mm M39	20.2	2,650	20	25,000
85mm M44	20.2	2,950	20	31,000
105mm M34	33.0	3,050	12	38,000
Germany				
75mm Flak	14.3	2,780	20	25,000
37mm Fl.37	1.4	2,690	80	6,500
37mm Fl.43	1.4	2,690	180	13,000
50mm Fl.41	4.9	2,760	130	18,000
88mm Fl.36	20.7	2,690	15	26,000
88mm Fl.41	20.7	3,280	20	35,000
105mm Fl.39	32.6	2,890	15	31,000
128mm Fl.40	57.3	2,890	12	35,000
Italy				
75/46 Mod 34	14.5	2,350	20	22,000
75/49 Skoda	14.0	2,690	20	24,000
75/50 Ansaldo	14.0	3,200	15	24,000
75/53 Schneider	14.0	2,280	15	22,000
76/40 Ansaldo	14.5	2,265	15	14,000
76/45 Mod 11	14.3	2,460	15	18,000
90/53 Ansaldo	22.2	2,755	20	32,000
102/47 Mod 29	33.0	2,950	8	29,000

Note: First figure indicates calibre in mm, second indicates length of barrel in calibres; eg. 75/53 is 75mm calibre, 53 x 75mm in length of barrel.

Japan				
75mm Type 88	14.5	2,360	25	21,250
80mm Type 10	13.0	2,230	15	17,000
88mm Type 99	18..0	2,650	20	26,000
100mm Type 98	29.0	3,050	15	28,000
105mm Type 14	35.2	2,300	10	23,500
120mm Type 10	43.0	2,700	15	27,000
127mm Type 89	51.0	2,360	8	26,000

Note: In Japanese nomenclature, the 'Type' number indicates the year of introduction on an involved system; in the above table, Types 10 and 14 refer to 1921 and 1925, while Types 88, 89, 98 and 99 refer to 1928, 29, 38 and 39 respectively.

APPENDIX 4

Performance of Bomber Aircraft/Second World War

Type	Speed mph	Operational ceiling ft	Bomb load lb	Range miles
Britain				
Blenheim	285	31,000	1,000	1,950
Halifax	310	24,000	8,000	1,250
Hampden	255	19,000	4,000	1,100
Lancaster	285	24,500	14,000	1,650
Mosquito	380	35,000	2,000	1,800
Stirling	280	17,000	14,000	600
Wellington	250	22,000	1,500	2,000
Whitley	220	20,000	3,000	1,600
France				
Amiot 143	190	25,000	1,750	750
Bloch 174	330	36,000	880	800
Potez 63	275	33,000	1,300	
USA				
B-17 Fortress	317	35,000	12,800	1,100
B-29 Super-Fort	355	36,000	10,000	3,250
B-24 Liberator	290	28,000	5,000	2,200
Mitchell	275	24,000	4,000	1,500
USSR				
Ilyushin Il-4	255	32,000	2,200	1,600
Petlyakov Pe-8	275	23,000	8,800	3,000
Tupolev TB-3	180	25,000	4,850	1,500
Tupolev SB-2	280	35,000	1,350	750
Germany				
Dornier Do 17	265	27,000	2,200	720
Heinkel He111	260	25,500	4,400	745
Junkers Ju 88	270	27,000	6,610	1,100
Italy				
Cant Z-1007	280	26,500	4,400	800
Fiat BR-20	265	22,000	3,520	1,250
Japan				
Mitsubishi Ki21 (Sally)	297	32,000	2,200	1,350
Mitsubishi G4 (Betty)	270	30,000	2,200	2,900
Nakajima Ki-49 (Helen)	300	26,000	2,200	1,500

APPENDIX 5

Deployment of Luftwaffe Flak Guns etc
(Abstracted from Luftwaffe Equipment returns of irregular date)

Date	Area	Heavy guns	Light & medium guns	Search-lights	Balloons
Sept 1939	Western front	2,450	6,500	2,060	220
Sept 1940	Western Front	2,870	7,970	2,540	380
Dec 1940	Western Front	3,100	8,750	2,710	500
	Other Fronts	60	250	—	—
Dec 1941	Western Front	3,650	9,900	3,420	940
	Other Fronts	1,600	4,100	40	—
Dec 1942	Western Front	5,522	15,171	4,200	1,625
	Other Fronts	2,052	5,759	328	250
Dec 1943	Western Front	8,030	19,996	5,776	2,552
	Other Fronts	3,693	7,789	796	484
June 1944	Western Front	10,919	22,426	7,624	2,088
	Other Fronts	4,168	8,037	1,193	293
Sept 1944	Western Front	10,225	18,508	6,260	1,550
	Other Fronts	4,625	7,842	1,110	380

APPENDIX 6

Effect of German Anti-Aircraft Fire on US Eighth Air Force Bombers

(Extracts from *Air defense Review No. 6,* Supreme Headquarters Allied Expeditionary Force, January 1945)

During the three months ending August 1944, German Flak accounted for no less than 66 per cent of the 700 bombers lost and 98 per cent of the 13,000 bombers damaged.

No less significant is the presentation of comparative trends: in 1943, 33 per cent of the bombers lost and 66 per cent of the bombers damaged were attributed to Flak. The greatly increased percentages of total loss and damage attributed to Flak in 1944 is due to a sharp decrease in the percentage lost to enemy fighters, this decrease being chiefly due to saturation techniques and employment of long range escorts.

Factors affecting these trends are a greater concentration of enemy flak defenses and a large increase in 'bomber exposure hours' which is the product of the size of the force employed and the depth of penetration into enemy flak-defended territory. Too much importance must not, however, be attributed to penetration because statistics reveal that 70 per cent to 90 per cent of all flak damage has occurred in the target areas. In comparing experience in 1943 with experience in 1944, the impression is gained that the Germans were nearly as successful (relatively) in concentrating guns on the ground as were the 8th Air Force in concentrating bombers in the sky.

Defensive Tactics against Flak

Avoidance of Flak defenses and flying at higher altitudes are standard and call for no comment. Investigation of Radar Counter-Measures places equal emphasis on the quantity of 'Window' used and on the proper positioning of

Appendix 6 continued

bomber units relative to the course of this protection. It is, however, in regard to the optimum number of bombers flying together as one unit and the formation to be adopted that the recommended tactics are of greatest interest to AA gunners. To counter the threat of enemy fighters, the tactic preferred by the bombers is to fly in close formations of, say, 18 aircraft. Such tight formations, in which all elements are concentrated in trail within 1,500 feet, are, however, very vulnerable to AA fire, as one aircraft is liable to be hit by fire aimed at another. Saturation of the defenses is, therefore, not achieved by increasing the number of aircraft in a single bombing unit, nor by flying in very tight formation. Reduction in risk is best achieved by diminishing the interval between successive bombing units crossing the target. To counter the threat of AA fire to the individual bombing units, the desirable tactic is to spread the formation to a limited extent. For example, if the 12-aircraft bombing unit is spread out from 1,500 feet to 5,000 feet in trail, the risk from accurate Flak is halved. A suitable formation for this purpose is the 'Javelin' type, which has the formation split into six 3-aircraft elements, each separated by 1,000 feet in trail. This type of tactic is, however, prejudicial to fighter defense and to the accuracy of 'follow-my-leader' bombing. The requirements of fighter defense and Flak defense are therefore somewhat incompatible, and a compromise has to be accepted.

The only Flak defensive tactic which gives no corresponding advantage to other elements of enemy counter-measures is reduction in the interval between successive bombing units (eg. squadrons or wings). It has been calculated that two wings flying 11 miles apart instead of four miles apart are exposed to twice as many shells. Flak saturation will be the more easily achieved if the interval between the successive formations is so short that the ground defences have not sufficient time to break off engagement against the preceding and engage the succeeding formation. This tactic may also be applied, if the target is suitable, by formations bombing abreast. Admittedly certain disadvantages of a technical and internal nature arise, such as propeller-wash, danger of collision and, if formations are staggered in height, air-to-air bombing. These disadvantages can, however, mostly be overcome by training. The final Flak defense tactic is evasive action. Since this militates against achievement of briefed bombing altitude and course, this tactic is generally applied after 'bombs away'.

Conclusions

If any degree of similarity between German Flak against 8th Air Force targets and Allied AA against the German Air Force is admissible, the results of investigations of Flak and Flak defensive tactics are greatly encouraging to the AA gunner, who only too frequently sees the result of his efforts badly under-estimated. It is also understandable that the fighter component of the Air Force, with which AA Artillery is operationally associated in defense, does not always show the same profound appreciation of the potentialities of Flak which bomber forces derive from battle experience.

APPENDIX 7

The Effect of Allied Bombing upon German Flak Layouts

(Extracted from a Flak Intelligence Report based on interrogation of a major of Luftgau XI after the war had ended)

The deployment of Heavy Flak at the beginning of the war was in accordance with peacetime principles which assumed that only daylight raids would take place. The majority of authorities concerned over-estimated the chances of success of Heavy Flak considerably, and a minimum of two *Abteilungen* was considered sufficient even for the protection of large towns. The *mobility* of Flak was considered to be a decisive technical factor in deceiving the enemy.

A special type of defensive layout employed at this time was the so-called 'Air Defence Area West' (*Luftverteidigungszone* West). This was formed shortly before the war in connection with the general Westwall plan and consisted of heavy, medium and light flak positions, deployed in a belt some 20 to 30 kilometres deep. The zone originally stretched from the Black Forest to the Saar, but it was later extended to Aachen, the Heligoland Bight, and ultimately up into Schleswig-Holstein. The defences of the original sector were of permanent construction; the later extensions were of an improvised nature.

The tasks of LVZ-West were threefold: (1) Deep artillery support of the Westwall; (2) anti-tank defence in conjunction with the Westwall fortifications; and (3) a Flak zone to neutralise enemy air activity. In the construction of the later sectors, emphasis was placed on the Flak committment. It was generally considered that such a Flak zone could weaken, if not entirely prevent, the enemy air attacks in strength in that area.

The LVZ-West was never in full operation, as there were never enough personnel available to man all the gun positions. The first heavy night attacks on Germany, moreover, proved that this type of Flak deployment was relatively ineffective.

In the layout of a Gun Defended Area at this time, the following were the guiding principles:

1. An assumed average aircraft speed of 155mph and height of attack of 12000 feet, giving a line of bomb release (LBR) approximately 2500m from the target.
2. A 30-second zone of engagement for the guns before the aircraft reached his LBR.
3. A three-battery minimum gun density, both within the zone of engagement and within the LBR.

These principles proved correct at the beginning of the war, particularly in the case of forward air protection during the Polish and French campaigns and in opposition to the few air attacks carried out on Germany during that period. With the beginning of the first night raids, however, it became evident that the defences were insufficiently concentrated and that, under existing arrangements, air attacks could neither be prevented nor appreciably obstructed. The first result of this appreciation was a considerable reinforcement of Flak in the Ruhr and Berlin.

Introduction of the Grossbatterie

The complete ineffectiveness of the Flak defences in repelling the large-scale RAF night raids which began in the spring of 1943 led to the compulsory introduction, in May 1943, of the *Grossbatterie* system throughout the Reich. The orders issued by the GAF Central Command (*Luftwaffe Befehlshaber Mitte*) laid down the following principles:

(a) The concentration into *Grossbatterien* of approximately two-thirds of all batteries in Gun Defended Areas.
(b) the deployment of *Grossbatterien* in

Appendix 7 continued

the ring formation in sufficient numbers to provide overlapping fire.
(c) The siting of the *Grossbatterien* ring on an LBR calculated for an aircraft speed of 265mph and a height of attack of 25000 feet, ie. at a distance of approximately 6km from the edge of the target area.
(d) The retention of a number of batteries within this LBR to ensure a three-battery density over the target and so prevent the unobstructed flight of any aircraft which succeeded in penetrating the outer defences.
(e) The concentration of fire of batteries with high performance – 88mm Flak 41 and 12.8cm Flak 40 – immediately over the target area as a defence against high-altitude Mosquito attacks.

Practical experience soon showed that the deployment of *Grossbatterien* together with the use of 'Lane of Approach Batteries' (*Vorfeldbatterien*) produced an all-over increase in the concentration of fire before the LBR, and an increased toll of Allied aircraft resulted.

Introduction of USAAF daylight attacks

The necessity of further concentration of Flak fire arose with the introduction of high altitude bombing by the USAAF. These attacks, carried out by tight formations, entailed the precision bombing of pin-point targets from great height and only the strongest concentration of fire was likely to break up the formations or affect the accuracy of bombing. As a result the deployment of single batteries was, with few exceptions, discontinued and the ring of *Grossbatterien* was in many cases redeployed to protect specific important objectives rather than the GDA as a whole. The number of guns surrounding important VAs (vulnerable areas) was steadily increased from 100 to 200, 400 and 600, and the defences of minor GDAs (less than ten batteries) was scrapped entirely in order to achieve the maximum concentration around priority targets.

Light Flak

At the beginning of the war, light flak was usually deployed by 'zugs', with a distance of 100-120m between guns. Special emphasis was placed on defence against dive-bomber attacks, and for this purpose several guns or, in the case of large target areas, several Zugs, were to be deployed inside the target area. In most cases light weapons were on roofs or on Flak Towers so as to have as large a field of fire as possible.

In the first year of the war hardly any experience in light Flak defence was gained in Reich territory as there were no attacks by low-flying planes. Field experience, however, showed that light flak fire could only be effective where the fire was concentrated, and on the basis of this a concentration of gun sites within Reich territory was ordered, bringing guns in to an interval of 50-60m.

With the onset of heavy attacks by the RAF in 1943 it became evident that light Flak deployed on roofs and towers suffered heavy losses without themselves being able to offer any effective opposition. The low level attacks against the Mohne, Eder and Sorpe dams in May 1943 also showed that the defence of these targets by light Flak was insufficient.

Luftwaffe Befehlshaber Mitte therefore ordered a modification of deployment principles. Light Flak was now to be used to defend targets where high altitude attacks were not to be expected but which were particularly vulnerable to low level attack. The use of Light Flak on roof sites was forbidden and deployment on Flak Towers to be avoided wherever possible. And deployment within the target area was to be discontinued, deployment on the perimiter of the target area being adopted instead.

As a result of these orders, the big industrial areas were now left almost completely without light guns. Most of

Appendix 7 continued

the light Flak was now concentrated around the most important dams, which had become a Number One priority, and near the locks and aqueducts of the canal system.

This situation changed radically when, during the high altitude daylight attacks of the USAAF in spring 1944, the fighter escort at first and then special fighter formations carried out low-flying attacks deep into Reich territory. Their targets were at first fighter airfields, then communications (rail and waterways), and later any promising target in the west of the Reich. As a result of these attacks the dams and the industrial plants, including the synthetic oil industry which has been, up to now, protected by Light Flak, were largely stripped of their protection. The first priorities now became the defence of airfields and the most important bridges, especially those over the Rhine. The number of guns was continually increased, and at the end of the war there were 40-60 Light Flak guns and 120-180 auxiliary weapons (machine guns and 20mm aircraft cannon on ground mounts) available for the protection of a fighter airfield.

After D-Day, in summer 1944, protection of supply routes against low-flying attacks became a problem on which the outcome of the war depended. By deploying whole Flak *Abteilungen* along a road, it was sometimes possible to ensure, during daytime at least, the passage of individual vehicles. The number of Flak units available was, however, not nearly sufficient to ensure the flow of supplies, and a great number of so-called 'Road Protection Regiments' were therefore formed. These were equipped with machine guns and light cannon and were mostly horse-drawn. But the plans calling for their formation were carried out very slowly due to the general difficulty of the supply and manpower situation. The deployment of these units could not reduce the overwhelming air superiority of the Allies in the combat areas.

For the protection of railway traffic, railway transport protection battalions (*Eisenbahntransport schutzflakbatterien*) were founded as early as the beginning of 1943. Each troop consisted of two gun trucks, which were equipped with a 20mm weapon (single barrel at first, quadruple later) and later with a quadruple mounting at each end. At the beginning of 1945 there were three ETR regiments, with 20 *Abteilungen* and 100 batteries in action in Germany. Each battery was composed of 48 gun trucks. They were very successful; air attacks on protected trains were very rare.

Searchlights

The main principles of Flak deployment before the war were concerned almost exclusively with defence against daylight raids. Night raids were considered to be unlikely, despite the experience of World War One. The equipment and training of searchlight units had therefore been neglected. At the beginning of the war S/L Units with 150cm lights were deployed in conjunction with the heavy Flak artillery for the protection of the big towns. Deployment was on a chess-board pattern with intervals of 4 to 6km. These sites were well in front of the gun sites in order to allow the lights to pick up targets on the extreme outer edge of the protective belt.

During the first British attacks in the winter of 1940-41, searchlights proved a failure; only very few targets were picked up, operational drill was poor, and the targets, once picked up, could only be kept in the beam for a short time. On the basis of this, the spacing was reduced to 3km, a maximum number were linked with radar, the illuminated zone was extended to some 10km in front of the outermost flak batteries, and much greater emphasis was placed on training. This led to improved results in 1942. In that year

Appendix 7 continued

also a remote-controlled 200cm searchlight was introduced, and during the intensive night attacks of winter 1942-43 great numbers of planes were picked up and kept in the beam for long periods of time. For example, during the first night attacks on Berlin in March 1943, 20 searchlight batteries were in action, and an average of 60 planes were picked up and kept in the beam for approximately four minutes.

The decrease in operational efficiency of the searchlights during the last months of the war (from November 1944) can be ascribed to the sudden change-over to female personnel. This measure, necessitated by the manpower shortage, was carried out in too great haste and without the requisite care in training.

APPENDIX 8

Japanese Anti-Aircraft Organisation

(From an American Intelligence Summary dated January 1945)

The bulk of Japanese AA Artillery is made up of independent units which are normally Army troops assigned to lower formations as required. The Japanese also rely on these units for anti-tank firepower.
The principal AA units are as follows:

1. **AA Regiment** Employed in a static role. Consists of Headquarters, two gun battalions each of HQ and three companies, and a searchlight battalion. *Total strength:* 1276 officers and men. *Armament:* 24 x 75mm guns (4 per company).

2. **Independent AA Battalion, Static** Consists of headquarters and three companies. *Total strength:* 448. *Armament:* 12 x 75mm guns and 6 AA machine guns.

3. **Field AA Battalion, Mobile** Consists of HQ, three companies, and a battalion ammunition train. *Total strength:* 643. *Armament:* 12 x 75mm guns, and six AA machine guns. *Transport:* 18 half-track tractors, 10 light cars, 60 trucks.

4. **Independent AA Company, Static** *Total strength:* 120 men. *Armament:* 4 x 75mm guns.

5. **Independent Field AA Company, Mobile** *Total strength:* 180 men. *Armament:* 4 x 75mm guns. *Transport:* 6 half-track tractors, 2 cars and 6 trucks.

6. **Field Machine Cannon Company** This is a highly mobile unit, with either mule-pack or motor transport. *Total strength:* 115 men. *Armament:* 6 x 20mm machine cannon. *Transport:* 17 trucks or 134 mules.

For the AA defence of a specific area, a 'Field AA Unit' can be made up from any combination of the above-mentioned units and placed under command of a headquarters commanded by a colonel. For example, '15 Field AA Unit' in the New Georgia area had three Field AA Battalions, three machine cannon companies, and a field searchlight battalion.

APPENDIX 9

Japanese Anti-Aircraft Methods

(A summary, based on all available flak intelligence, published after a conference on Japanese AA Defences held in Washington, January 1945)

For all theaters of war the ratio of anti-aircraft losses to fighter losses in US Army Air Forces increased sharply during 1944 until, beginning with the third quarter of 1944, enemy AA Artillery caused more Army Air Force losses than fighters. Broadly it can be seen that the effectiveness of Japanese AA is now approximately equal to Japanese fighters as a cause of loss in AAF combat aircraft. This has been due primarily to the effectiveness of automatic weapons and small arms fire against low-flying airplanes. The US Navy has incurred very much heavier losses to Japanese AA fire than to fighters, the ratio for the first eight months of 1944 being approximately three AA losses to one fighter loss; for Navy bomber types the ratio was almost 13 to one.

The growing importance of enemy AA Artillery is further emphasised by a study of Army Air Force battle damage, which study has revealed that more than 80 per cent of AAF battle damage in 1944 was caused by AA fire. The ratio of AA damage to fighter damage has been highest in the European Theatre of Operations because of the tremendous concentration of Flak around Germany's vital targets. However, the 1944 AA/Fighter ratio in the Pacific Theatre is large; Japanese AA has caused approximately 70 per cent of all Army battle damage in the Pacific and about 88 per cent of the battle damage to US Navy aircraft.

Capabilities of Japanese AA Weapons

The Japanese Navy has been more progressive than the Army in the early development and production of modern AA guns and fire control equipment. As a result the Navy has been able to furnish effective AA weapons for use in land emplacements on important inner perimeter islands and vital installations. In considering Japanese AA defences, therefore, it is necessary to regard land-emplaced naval weapons as a very potent threat to Allied aircraft.

At the beginning of the present war the Japanese Army had only two types of heavy AA gun in service; the standard Model 88 (1928) 75mm gun and the reportedly ineffective Model 14 (1925) 105mm gun. These two guns have a relatively low muzzle velocity, limiting their effective ceiling to about 22,000 feet. Land emplaced naval dual-purpose guns manufactured in 1943–44 have, however, increased the general capabilities of Japanese AA artillery.

In the beginning of the war the Navy also excelled the Army in AA Automatic weapons. The largest-caliber Army automatic was the 20mm Model 98 cannon, while the Navy had the 25mm Model 96, a highly efficient weapon. In the Malayan campaign the Japanese captured about 200 Bofors 40mm guns from the British, and these are still apparently being used by the Army.

Fire Control: At the beginning of the war the Japanese Army AA fire control equipment was limited, for all practical purposes, to a crude system developed about 1928. A Model 97 (1937) director was apparently in process of development, but events to date have indicated that it was not made in any quantity.

On the other hand, the Navy Model 2 (1942) AA director, which has been found on important islands in the inner perimeter, is an effective fire control instrument. Originally designed for use with Naval dual-purpose guns, by relatively simple insertion of appropriate drums this instrument can be used to control the fire of any other AA gun. One naval director of this type

Appendix 9 continued

was captured on Leyte, emplaced for use with a battery of Army 75mm guns. The fact that this director was equipped with selsyns, for receipt of basic fire control data from an exterior source, indicates preparation for the use of gun-laying radar. It is certain that the Japanese Army now has one or more types of gun-laying radar, but location and use thus far have been confined principally to Japan proper and certain important outlying areas.

Searchlights: The Japanese Army possess standard 160cm AA searchlights. B-29s operating on night raids over Japan have reported their use throughout Japan, with a heavy concentration in the Tokyo area. They are reported to have operated effectively at 33,000 feet. The operational reports check roughly with aerial photographs of the Tokyo area, indicating the presence of about 150 searchlights, about 25 per cent of which appear to be equipped with radar.

Barrage Balloons: Ballons have been employed by the Japanese at altitudes up to 5,000 feet over a few key objectives. Their principal function appears to be the protection of harbour facilities and shipping against low-level attack. As many as 30 have been reported over a single area, but the greatest number so far seen on aerial photographs is ten. Although balloons flying at these altitudes constitute a hazard to aircraft attacking at low levels, it is not believed that the Japanese will be able to employ such balloons in sufficient number to have more than a negligible effect upon our air operations.

AA Rockets: There have been several air-crew reports and one aerial photograph indicating the possible use of ground-to-air rockets by the Japanese. These reported rockets have, to date, been inaccurate and are not known to have cause any damage to our aircraft.

Barrage mortars: Two types of AA Barrage Mortars are employed by Japan for use against low-flying aircraft. The older 70mm size fires a projectile to a height of about 1,700 feet. At that point, the projectile scatters seven small parachute-supported explosive charges which remain airborne for about 2½ minutes; explosion will occur when a pull is exerted against the parachute.

The second type, which has only recently come into use, is 81mm in size and is considered more dangerous than the 70mm. Approximately 12 seconds after firing, a four-ounce explosive charge, supported by one parachute, is ejected from the shell and floats down. A second parachute is attached to a cord 33 feet in length and this cord in turn is attached to an igniter within the explosive charge. An aircraft striking the 33-foot cord will cause it to explode the charge. The Japanese claim that the projectile will reach a height of 1,000 meters and that the bursting radius of the lethal device is approximately 10 meters, but these claims have not yet been confirmed.

Current Trends

Development of Fire control: There are indications that the Japanese Army has given high priority to production of AA weapons and modern fire-control equipment, including gun-laying radar. Existence in Japan of a new 88mm Army gun, which is a modification or copy of the German 88mm gun, is now quite definitely confirmed.

Another new Army weapon thought to be in production is a 120mm AA gun. Certainly a pilot model of this gun, with a new 'locator' was demonstrated near Tokyo in May 1944. This new gun may have contributed to the accurate AA fire up to 33,000 feet altitude which has been encountered by our B-29s over the Japanese mainland. If the maximum vertical range was correctly reported, the 120mm gun is a very definite improvement over the naval 120mm dual-purpose gun, which has a muzzle velocity of 2,700 ft/sec.

Appendix 9 continued

Trends in Tactical Employment: The most significant trend lies in the appearance of concentrated groups of two, three and even four six-gun batteries in the vicinity of vital areas on the mainland of Japan. This conforms to the German *Grossbatterien* system, and is a fairly recent development. Deployment of AA guns in the Tokyo area, where recent photo coverage indicates the presence of about 400 AA guns, is typical of this tendency. As an example, one AA gun site in the Tokyo area apparently consists of a group of four six-gun batteries concentrated in a small area, all apparently receiving data from one gun-laying radar in the vicinity. Concentrated fire from guns in a group of this size can be a serious hazard to aircraft flying in formation.

Conclusions

Experience to 1944 indicates that Japanese AA weapons have become a potential threat to Allied aircraft operating over important Japanese installations. It may be expected that accuracy and effectiveness of Japanese AA Artillery will continue to improve during 1945. However, it is unlikely that they will be able to attain anything like the concentration or effectiveness of German AA fire at high altitude.

APPENDIX 10

First US Army: Resume of AAA Action 6 June 1944 to 8 May 1945

Every artillery unit, of any nation, prepared daily ammunition states showing what had been expended, and most anti-aircraft units correlated this with their record of aircraft shot down or damaged. But very rarely did the ammunition statistics ever get beyond the Divisional or equivalent headquarter, and even more rarely was it published. The U.S. First Army was an exception to this; after the war their Ammunition Section prepared a meticulous record of every round fired, from their landing in Normandy on 6 June 1944 to the cease-fire on 8 May 1945, a record which covered field, anti-tank and anti-aircraft guns. The full record is in the form of a weekly return by natures of gun, and discloses some interesting details; for example, that the 1st US Army actually employed 36 British 25pr guns due to a shortage of 105mm howitzers; that during late 1944 ammunition was rationed; and even that in the second week of the invasion some unknown gunner was incautious enough to fire a 25pr high explosive shell with a smoke shell fuze, an error which was solemnly carried through the accounts as '25pr HE Shell with Fuze 221 – 1' to the end of the war.

The anti-aircraft statistics lent themselves to correlation with the claims for aircraft shot down and damaged, whereas, of course, the figures for field and anti-tank artillery were not capable of being neatly tied to results in the same fashion. A brief extract of the anti-aircraft figures is given here and are of some interest. It is frequently asserted that the Allied troops enjoyed air superiority in Northwest Europe and thus had little to fear from air attack: the figure of 5,372 aircraft reported over 1st Army tend to argue against this conclusion. The acute shortage of proximity fuzes (by far the greater part of the supply had been siphoned off to the batteries dealing with the V-1 Flying Bomb) also shows,

Appendix 10 continued

as does the considerable improvement in results when proximity fuzes were used, the 'rounds-per-bird' figure coming down from 364 to 233. Note also the vast amount of machine gun ammunition expended; much of this must be counted as 'morale shooting' rather than effective fire.

It might be added that the returns also show that 90mm AA guns, when used in the ground role for anti-personnel or anti-tank shooting, accounted for a further 34,229 rounds of high explosive and armour-piercing shell.

1.

Raids (daylight hours)	925
Number of enemy aircraft	3,000
Raids (night)	1,435
Number of enemy aircraft	2,372
Total raids, day and night	2,360
Total enemy over US 1st Army	5,372
Average sorties per day	16

2.

Enemy aircraft destroyed (Category I) by:

90mm time fuze fire	167
90mm proximity fuze fire	25½
40mm	382
37mm	104
.50 machine gun	118
Barrage balloon	1
Total Category I	797½

3.

Enemy aircraft probably destroyed (Category II) by:

90mm time fuze fire	100
90mm proximity fuze fire	17
40mm	177
37mm	81
.50 machine gun	74
Total Category II	449

4.

Ammunition Expenditure (AA firing):

90mm time fuze	60,720
90mm proximity fuze	5,935
40mm	191,525
37mm	64,736
.50 machine gun	5,915,737

5.

Effectiveness of weapons: rounds fired per enemy aircraft destroyed (Category I):

90mm time fuze	364
90mm proximity fuze	233
40mm	501
37mm	622
.50 machine gun	50,133

APPENDIX 11

Summary of German Air Raids on Britain, 1914–18

	Raids	Bombs	Killed	Injured
Great Britain				
by Airship	51	5,806	557	1,358
by Aircraft	52	2,772	857	2,058
Total	103	8,578	1,414	3,416
Greater London				
by Airship	12	746	183	516
by Aircraft	19	1,078	487	1,444
Total	31	1,824	670	1,960
London figures as a percentage of British totals	28%	21%	48%	57%

Note: Although the percentage of raids and bombs on London is about one quarter of the total for the country, that of casualties is about one-half, reflecting the greater population density.

APPENDIX 12

Anti-aircraft Defences of Great Britain as at 10 June 1918

(1) Guns and Searchlights

Area	Search lights	13pdr (9cwt)	4in	18pdr	3in (20cwt)	75mm	12pdr	Total	Planned strength
Cromarty & Inverness	3			2			4	6	100
Aberdeen & Firth of Tay	5			5	9	8		25	100
Firth of Forth	33			8	9	8		25	100
Tyne	36			5	19			24	100
Tees	29				14			14	100
Leeds	45				25	5		30	100
Humber	34				18			18	100
Manchester	24			2			20	22	100
Nottingham	36				5		10	15	100
Birmingham	14					14		14	70
London, Central	40				22			22	100
London, West	30				16			16	100
London, East	94				43			43	100
London, North	18			21	3			24	68
London, South-west	9			19				19	85
Redhill	11			13				13	50
Harwich	50			2	12			14	100
Thames & Medway	28				38			38	100
Dover	39				20			20	100
Portsmouth	17			11	4			15	75
Mobile Brigades, LADA	19	54						54	100
Reserves, School, etc.	8	7	1	2	7	1		18	95
Totals	622	61	1	90	255	28	34	469	92.5

Appendix 12 continued

(2) Aircraft

Northern Defence Area	*Establishment:*	192 Bristol Fighters
London Air Defence Area	*Establishment:*	94 Bristol Fighters
		98 SE5 'Viper'
		72 Sopwith Camel
Totals		376 aircraft
	Effective:	13 Bristol fighters
	Effective:	43 Bristol fighters
		42 SE5A
		66 Sopwith Camel
		2 Martinsyde
Total		166 aircraft – 44% of planned strength

(3) Personnel

RAF Flying Squadrons	4,614 all ranks – 102.5% of establishment (surplus in male other ranks)
RAF Balloon Squadrons	2,655 all ranks – 74% of establishment
RGA AA Gun detachments	3,491 all ranks – 38% of establishment
RE Searchlight detachments	2,645 all ranks – 56% of establishment

Note: Figures for manpower had been considerably higher on 1 January 1918 but had been severely pruned in order to provide troops for France, as the German Spring Offensive in 1918 threatened to be a greater danger than the possibility of air raids on Britain.

APPENDIX 13

Distribution of AA Guns in Great Britain, as at 11 September 1940

(1) Medium and Heavy (3.7in and 4.5in) Guns

London Area	235	
Thames & Medway	120	
Dover	14	
Harwich	8	
Leighton Buzzard	4	
Norwich	4	
Nottingham	16	
Derby	32	
Sheffield	27	
Humber	26	
Barrow	8	(Vickers Shipyard)
Liverpool	58	
Manchester	20	

Appendix 13 continued

Crewe	8	(Rolls-Royce aero-engines)
Birmingham	64	
Coventry	24	
Pembroke Dock	4	
Swansea	24	
Cardiff	26	
Newport	20	
Brockworth	24	(Gloster Aircraft Co.)
Bristol	32	
Falmouth	6	
Plymouth	26	
Yeovil	4	(Westland Aircraft Co.)
Portland	14	
Holton Heath	8	(Royal Naval Propellant Factory)
Southampton	31	
Portsmouth	40	
Bramley	8	(Central Ammunition Depot)
Leeds	20	
Tyne	50	
Tees	30	
Belfast	7	
Londonderry	4	
Clyde	34	
Ardeer	8	(ICI Explosives factory)
Kyle of Lochalsh	4	(Convoy assembly area)
Aberdeen	4	
Scapa Flow	88	
Shetlands	12	

Aerodromes, vital points, throughout the entire country – 115

(2) Light (2pdr, 40mm and 3in) Guns

London area 44

Aerodromes, vital points, factories, etc, throughout the entire country 684

Total heavy guns	1,311
Total light guns	684
Total machine guns	2,987

Note: In one or two cases above I have indicated a reason for locating guns in an otherwise obscure place; I have not yet discovered any good reason for the four guns at Leighton Buzzard.

INDEX